AF687168

Immigration Act 2016

CHAPTER 19

Explanatory Notes are available separately

GRAN*GIS* UK Publishing

Adapted and published by GRANGIS (Grand Register Library).
Online: www.grangis.com
E-mail: contact@grangis.com

© Crown Copyright
Contains public sector information licensed under the Open Government Licence v3.0.
You may re-use this publication free of charge in any format or medium. You must re-use it accurately and not in a misleading context.

© GRANGIS 2022.
In this version:
ISBN: 979-8-88559-057-0
Where we have identified any copyrighted material, you will need to obtain written permission for re-use.
Note: This is the original version (as it was originally enacted). Title, sub-title and the generated date is as marked on the pages.

Immigration Act 2016

CHAPTER 19

IMMIGRATION ACT 2016

PART 1

LABOUR MARKET AND ILLEGAL WORKING

CHAPTER 1

LABOUR MARKET

Director of Labour Market Enforcement

Gangmasters and Labour Abuse Authority

Support

Transfer of responsibility for relevant children

PART 6

BORDER SECURITY

PART 7

LANGUAGE REQUIREMENTS FOR PUBLIC SECTOR WORKERS

PART 8

FEES AND CHARGES

Immigration

Passports and civil registration

PART 9

MISCELLANEOUS AND GENERAL

Welfare of children

Immigration Act 2016

2016 CHAPTER 19

An Act to make provision about the law on immigration and asylum; to make provision about access to services, facilities, licences and work by reference to immigration status; to make provision about the enforcement of certain legislation relating to the labour market; to make provision about language requirements for public sector workers; to make provision about fees for passports and civil registration; and for connected purposes. [12th May 2016]

BE IT ENACTED by the Queen's most Excellent Majesty, by and with the advice and consent of the Lords Spiritual and Temporal, and Commons, in this present Parliament assembled, and by the authority of the same, as follows:—

PART 1

LABOUR MARKET AND ILLEGAL WORKING

CHAPTER 1

LABOUR MARKET

Director of Labour Market Enforcement

1 Director of Labour Market Enforcement

(1) The Secretary of State must appoint a person as the Director of Labour Market Enforcement (referred to in this Chapter as "the Director").

(2) The Director is to hold office in accordance with the terms of his or her appointment.

(3) The functions of the Director are exercisable on behalf of the Crown.

(4) The Secretary of State must provide the Director with such staff, goods, services, accommodation and other resources as the Secretary of State considers the Director needs for the exercise of his or her functions.

(5) The Secretary of State must—

(a) pay the Director such expenses, remuneration and allowances, and

(b) pay or make provision for the payment of such pension to or in respect of the Director,

as may be provided for by or under the terms of the Director's appointment.

2 Labour market enforcement strategy

(1) The Director must before the beginning of each financial year prepare a labour market enforcement strategy for that year and submit it to the Secretary of State for approval.

(2) A labour market enforcement strategy (referred to in this Chapter as a "strategy") is a document which—

(a) sets out the Director's assessment of—

(i) the scale and nature of non-compliance in the labour market during the year before the one to which the strategy relates, and

(ii) the likely scale and nature of such non-compliance during the year to which the strategy relates and the following two years,

(b) contains a proposal for the year to which the strategy relates setting out—

(i) how labour market enforcement functions should be exercised,

(ii) the education, training and research activities the Secretary of State, and any other person by whom, or by whose officers, labour market enforcement functions are exercisable, should undertake or facilitate in connection with those functions,

(iii) the information, or descriptions of information, that should be provided to the Director for the purposes of his or her functions by any person by whom, or by whose officers, labour market enforcement functions are exercisable, and

(iv) the form and manner in which, and frequency with which, that information should be provided,

(c) sets out the activities the Director proposes to undertake during the year to which the strategy relates in the exercise of his or her functions under section 8, and

(d) deals with such other matters as the Director considers appropriate.

(3) The proposal mentioned in paragraph (b) of subsection (2) must, in particular, set out how the funding available for the purposes of the functions and activities mentioned in sub-paragraphs (i) and (ii) of that paragraph should be allocated.

(4) The Director may at any time prepare a revised strategy and submit it to the Secretary of State for approval.

(5) The Secretary of State may approve a strategy either with or without modifications (but a modification may not relate to the assessment described in paragraph (a) of subsection (2)).

(6) Any person by whom labour market enforcement functions are exercisable during a year to which a strategy approved under this section relates must, in exercising those functions, have regard to the strategy.

3 Non-compliance in the labour market etc: interpretation

(1) For the purposes of this Chapter each of the following constitutes "non-compliance in the labour market"—

- (a) the commission of a labour market offence;
- (b) failure to comply with the requirement under section 1 of the National Minimum Wage Act 1998 (workers to be paid at least national minimum wage);
- (c) failure to pay any financial penalty required to be paid by a notice of underpayment served under section 19 of that Act (see section 19A of that Act);
- (d) breach of a condition of a licence granted under section 7 of the Gangmasters (Licensing) Act 2004;
- (e) failure to comply with any other requirement imposed by or under any enactment and which is prescribed by regulations made by the Secretary of State.

(2) In this Chapter "labour market enforcement functions" means—

- (a) any function of the Secretary of State in connection with prohibition orders made under section 3A of the Employment Agencies Act 1973,
- (b) any function of an officer acting for the purposes of that Act (see section 8A of that Act),
- (c) any function of an officer acting for the purposes of the National Minimum Wage Act 1998 (see section 13 of that Act),
- (d) any function of the Gangmasters and Labour Abuse Authority conferred by section 1(2)(a) to (c) of the Gangmasters (Licensing) Act 2004,
- (e) any function of an enforcement officer or a compliance officer acting for the purposes of that Act (see section 15 of that Act),
- (f) any function of the Gangmasters and Labour Abuse Authority under Part 2 of the Modern Slavery Act 2015 (slavery and trafficking prevention orders etc),
- (g) any function of an officer of that Authority acting for the purposes of Part 1 or 2 of that Act (see sections 11A and 30A of that Act),
- (h) any function of an enforcing authority under this Chapter,
- (i) any function an officer has by virtue of section 26, and
- (j) any other function prescribed by regulations made by the Secretary of State.

(3) In this section "labour market offence" means—

- (a) an offence under the Employment Agencies Act 1973 other than one under section 9(4)(b) of that Act;
- (b) an offence under the National Minimum Wage Act 1998;
- (c) an offence under the Gangmasters (Licensing) Act 2004;
- (d) an offence under section 1 of the Modern Slavery Act 2015;
- (e) an offence under section 2 or 4 of that Act—
    - (i) which is committed in relation to a worker or a person seeking work, or

(ii) which is otherwise committed in circumstances where subsection (2) of section 3 of that Act applies;

(f) an offence under section 30(1) or (2) of that Act which is committed in relation to—

(i) an order which was made on the application of the Gangmasters and Labour Abuse Authority, or

(ii) an order which was made under section 14 of that Act and which falls within subsection (4) below;

(g) an offence under section 27;

(h) any other offence prescribed by regulations made by the Secretary of State;

(i) an offence of attempting or conspiring to commit an offence mentioned in paragraphs (a) to (h);

(j) an offence under Part 2 of the Serious Crime Act 2007 in relation to an offence so mentioned;

(k) an offence of inciting a person to commit an offence so mentioned;

(l) an offence of aiding, abetting, counselling or procuring the commission of an offence so mentioned.

(4) An order made under section 14 of the Modern Slavery Act 2015 falls within this subsection if—

(a) the order was made following—

(i) the conviction of the defendant of an offence mentioned in subsection (3)(d), (e) or (i) to (l), or

(ii) a finding of a kind mentioned in section 14(1)(b) or (c) of that Act in connection with any such offence, and

(b) the prosecution resulted from an investigation conducted by a labour abuse prevention officer (within the meaning of section 114B of the Police and Criminal Evidence Act 1984).

(5) In this section "worker" has the same meaning as in the Employment Rights Act 1996 (see section 230 of that Act) and the reference to a person seeking work is to be read accordingly.

(6) In this section references to the Gangmasters (Licensing) Act 2004 are references to that Act only so far as it applies in relation to England and Wales and Scotland.

4 Annual and other reports

(1) As soon as reasonably practicable after the end of each financial year in respect of which the Secretary of State has approved a strategy under section 2, the Director must submit to the Secretary of State an annual report for that year.

(2) An annual report must include—

(a) an assessment of the extent to which labour market enforcement functions were exercised, and activities of the kind mentioned in section 2(2)(b)(ii) were carried out, in accordance with the strategy during the year to which the report relates,

(b) an assessment of the extent to which the strategy had an effect on the scale and nature of non-compliance in the labour market during that year, and

(c) a statement of the activities the Director undertook during that year in the exercise of his or her functions under section 8.

(3) The Director must submit to the Secretary of State a report dealing with any matter—
 (a) which the Secretary of State has requested the Director to report on, or
 (b) which a strategy approved by the Secretary of State under section 2 states is a matter the Director proposes to report on,

and must do so as soon as reasonably practicable after the request is made or the strategy is approved.

5 Publication of strategy and reports

(1) The Secretary of State must lay before Parliament—
 (a) any strategy the Secretary of State approves under section 2, and
 (b) any annual or other report the Secretary of State receives under section 4,

and must do so as soon as reasonably practicable after approving the strategy or receiving the report.

(2) A document laid under subsection (1) must not contain material removed under subsection (3).

(3) The Secretary of State may remove from a document to be laid under subsection (1) any material the publication of which the Secretary of State considers—
 (a) would be against the interests of national security,
 (b) might jeopardise the safety of any person in the United Kingdom, or
 (c) might prejudice the investigation or prosecution of an offence under the law of England and Wales, Scotland or Northern Ireland.

6 Information gateways

(1) A person may disclose information to the Director or a relevant staff member if the disclosure is made for the purposes of the exercise of any function of the Director.

(2) Information obtained by the Director or a relevant staff member in connection with the exercise of any function of the Director may be used by the Director or a relevant staff member in connection with the exercise of any other function of the Director.

(3) The Director or a relevant staff member may disclose information obtained in connection with the exercise of any function of the Director to a specified person if the disclosure is made for the purposes of the exercise of any function of the specified person.

(4) "Specified person" means a person specified in Schedule 1 (persons to whom Director etc may disclose information).

(5) The Secretary of State may by regulations amend Schedule 1.

(6) In this section, "relevant staff member" means a member of staff provided to the Director under section 1(4).

7 Information gateways: supplementary

(1) A disclosure of information which is authorised by section 6 does not breach—
 (a) an obligation of confidence owed by the person making the disclosure, or
 (b) any other restriction on the disclosure of information (however imposed).

(2) But nothing in section 6 authorises the making of a disclosure which—

(a) contravenes the Data Protection Act 1998, or

(b) is prohibited by Part 1 of the Regulation of Investigatory Powers Act 2000.

(3) Section 6 does not limit the circumstances in which information may be disclosed apart from that section.

(4) Section 6(1) does not authorise a person serving in an intelligence service to disclose information to the Director or a relevant staff member.

But this does not affect the disclosures which such a person may make in accordance with intelligence service disclosure arrangements.

(5) Intelligence service information may not be disclosed by the Director or a relevant staff member without authorisation from the appropriate service chief.

(6) If the Director or a relevant staff member has disclosed intelligence service information to a person, that person may not further disclose that information without authorisation from the appropriate service chief.

(7) HMRC information may not be disclosed by the Director or a relevant staff member without authorisation from HMRC Commissioners.

(8) If the Director or a relevant staff member has disclosed HMRC information to a person, that person may not further disclose that information without authorisation from HMRC Commissioners.

(9) Subsections (7) and (8) do not apply to national minimum wage information.

(10) If a person contravenes subsection (7) or (8) by disclosing revenue and customs information relating to a person whose identity—

(a) is specified in the disclosure, or

(b) can be deduced from it,

section 19 of the Commissioners for Revenue and Customs Act 2005 (wrongful disclosure) applies in relation to that disclosure as it applies in relation to a disclosure of such information in contravention of section 20(9) of that Act.

(11) In this section—

"appropriate service chief" means—

(a) the Director-General of the Security Service (in the case of information obtained by the Director or a relevant staff member from that Service or a person acting on its behalf);

(b) the Chief of the Secret Intelligence Service (in the case of information so obtained from that Service or a person acting on its behalf);

(c) the Director of GCHQ (in the case of information so obtained from GCHQ or a person acting on its behalf);

"GCHQ" has the same meaning as in the Intelligence Services Act 1994;

"HMRC information" means information disclosed to the Director or a relevant staff member under section 6 by HMRC Commissioners or a person acting on behalf of HMRC Commissioners;

"intelligence service" means—

(a) the Security Service;

(b) the Secret Intelligence Service;

(c) GCHQ;

"intelligence service disclosure arrangements" means—

(a) arrangements made by the Director-General of the Security Service under section 2(2)(a) of the Security Service Act 1989 about the disclosure of information by that Service,

(b) arrangements made by the Chief of the Intelligence Service under section 2(2)(a) of the Intelligence Services Act 1994 about the disclosure of information by that Service, and

(c) arrangements made by the Director of GCHQ under section 4(2)(a) of that Act about the disclosure of information by GCHQ;

"intelligence service information" means information obtained from an intelligence service or a person acting on behalf of an intelligence service;

"national minimum wage information" means information obtained by an officer in the course of acting—

(a) for the purposes of the National Minimum Wage Act 1998 (see section 13 of that Act), or

(b) by virtue of section 26(2);

"relevant staff member" has the same meaning as in section 6;

"revenue and customs information relating to a person" has the meaning given in section 19(2) of the Commissioners for Revenue and Customs Act 2005.

8 Information hub

(1) The Director must gather, store, process, analyse and disseminate information relating to non-compliance in the labour market.

(2) The Director may request any person by whom, or by whose officers, labour market enforcement functions are exercisable to provide the Director with any non-compliance information specified or of a description specified in the request.

(3) "Non-compliance information" means information relating to non-compliance in the labour market which the Director considers would facilitate the exercise of any of his or her functions.

(4) A person by whom, or by whose officers, labour market enforcement functions are exercisable may request the Director to provide the person, or an officer of the person, with any enforcement information specified or of a description specified in the request.

(5) "Enforcement information" means information which the person making the request considers would facilitate the exercise of any labour market enforcement function of the person or of an officer of the person.

(6) A person who receives a request under this section must respond to it in writing within a reasonable period.

9 Restriction on exercising functions in relation to individual cases

(1) The Director must not in exercising any function make any recommendation in relation to an individual case.

(2) Subsection (1) does not prevent the Director considering individual cases and drawing conclusions about them for the purpose of, or in the context of, considering a general issue.

Gangmasters and Labour Abuse Authority

10 Renaming of Gangmasters Licensing Authority

(1) The Gangmasters Licensing Authority is renamed the Gangmasters and Labour Abuse Authority.

(2) In any enactment passed before the day on which this section comes into force, and in any instrument or other document made before that day, references to the Gangmasters Licensing Authority are to be read, in relation to any time on or after that day, as references to the Gangmasters and Labour Abuse Authority.

11 Functions in relation to labour market

(1) Schedule 2 (functions in relation to labour market) has effect.

(2) The Secretary of State may by regulations confer other functions on the Gangmasters and Labour Abuse Authority or its officers.

12 PACE powers in England and Wales for labour abuse prevention officers

(1) After section 114A of the Police and Criminal Evidence Act 1984 insert—

"114B Application of Act to labour abuse prevention officers

(1) The Secretary of State may by regulations apply any provision of this Act which relates to investigations of offences conducted by police officers to investigations of labour market offences conducted by labour abuse prevention officers.

(2) The regulations may apply provisions of this Act with any modifications specified in the regulations.

(3) In this section "labour abuse prevention officer" means an officer of the Gangmasters and Labour Abuse Authority who—

(a) falls within subsection (4), and

(b) is authorised (whether generally or specifically) by the Secretary of State for the purposes of this section.

(4) An officer of the Gangmasters and Labour Abuse Authority falls within this subsection if he or she is—

(a) acting for the purposes of the Employment Agencies Act 1973 (see section 8A of that Act),

(b) acting for the purposes of the National Minimum Wage Act 1998 (see section 13 of that Act),

(c) acting for the purposes of the Gangmasters (Licensing) Act 2004 as an enforcement officer within the meaning of section 15 of that Act,

(d) acting for the purposes of Part 1 or 2 of the Modern Slavery Act 2015 (see sections 11A and 30A of that Act), or

(e) acting for any other purpose prescribed in regulations made by the Secretary of State.

(5) The investigations for the purposes of which provisions of this Act may be applied by regulations under this section include investigations of offences committed, or suspected of having been committed, before the coming into force of the regulations or of this section.

(6) Regulations under this section are to be made by statutory instrument.

(7) Regulations under this section may make—

(a) different provision for different purposes;

(b) provision which applies generally or for particular purposes;

(c) incidental, supplementary, consequential, transitional or transitory provision or savings.

(8) Regulations under subsection (4)(e) may, in particular, make such provision amending, repealing or revoking any enactment as the Secretary of State considers appropriate in consequence of any provision made by the regulations.

(9) A statutory instrument containing regulations under subsection (4)(e) may not be made unless a draft of the instrument has been laid before, and approved by a resolution of, each House of Parliament.

(10) Any other statutory instrument containing regulations under this section is subject to annulment in pursuance of a resolution of either House of Parliament.

(11) In this section—

"enactment" includes an enactment contained in subordinate legislation within the meaning of the Interpretation Act 1978;

"labour market offence" has the meaning given in section 3 of the Immigration Act 2016."

(2) In section 18 of the Gangmasters (Licensing) Act 2004 (obstruction of officers), in subsection (1)(a), after "this Act" insert "or functions conferred by virtue of section 114B of the Police and Criminal Evidence Act 1984 (application of that Act to Authority officers)".

13 Relationship with other agencies: requests for assistance

(1) The Gangmasters (Licensing) Act 2004 is amended as follows.

(2) Before section 23 (but after the italic heading before it) insert—

"22A Relationship with other agencies: requests for assistance

(1) The Authority may request any of the following to provide assistance to the Authority or any of its officers—

(a) a chief officer of police for a police area in England and Wales;

(b) the Director General of the National Crime Agency;

(c) a person appointed as an immigration officer under paragraph 1 of Schedule 2 to the Immigration Act 1971;

(d) any other person prescribed or of a prescribed description.

(2) The Authority may make a request under subsection (1) only if it considers that the assistance would facilitate the exercise of any function by the Authority or any of its officers.

(3) Any of the following persons may request the Authority to provide assistance to the person—

(a) a chief officer of police for a police area in England and Wales;

(b) a person appointed as an immigration officer under paragraph 1 of Schedule 2 to the Immigration Act 1971;

(c) any other person prescribed or of a prescribed description.

(4) A person may make a request under subsection (3) only if the person considers that the assistance would facilitate the exercise by the person of any function.

(5) A request under this section must—

(a) set out what assistance is being requested, and

(b) explain how the assistance would facilitate the exercise of the function.

(6) A person who receives a request under this section must respond to it in writing within a reasonable period.

(7) Regulations under this section must not make provision which would be—

(a) within the legislative competence of the Scottish Parliament if contained in an Act of that Parliament,

(b) within the legislative competence of the National Assembly for Wales if contained in an Act of that Assembly, or

(c) within the legislative competence of the Northern Ireland Assembly if contained in an Act of that Assembly made without the consent of the Secretary of State."

(3) In section 25 (regulations, rules and orders), in subsection (5)—

(a) omit the "or" at the end of paragraph (a);

(b) at the end insert ", or

(c) section 22A(1)(d) or (3)(c) (regulations regarding persons whom the Authority may request to provide assistance and who may request assistance from Authority)."

Labour market enforcement undertakings

14 Power to request LME undertaking

(1) This section applies where an enforcing authority believes that a person has committed, or is committing, a trigger offence.

(2) An enforcing authority may give a notice to the person—

(a) identifying the trigger offence which the authority believes has been or is being committed;

(b) giving the authority's reasons for the belief;
(c) inviting the person to give the authority a labour market enforcement undertaking in the form attached to the notice.

(3) A labour market enforcement undertaking (an "LME undertaking") is an undertaking by the person giving it (the "subject") to comply with any prohibitions, restrictions and requirements set out in the undertaking (as to which see section 15).

(4) "Trigger offence" means—
(a) an offence under the Employment Agencies Act 1973 other than one under section 9(4)(b) of that Act;
(b) an offence under the National Minimum Wage Act 1998;
(c) an offence under the Gangmasters (Licensing) Act 2004;
(d) any other offence prescribed by regulations made by the Secretary of State;
(e) an offence of attempting or conspiring to commit an offence mentioned in paragraphs (a) to (d);
(f) an offence under Part 2 of the Serious Crime Act 2007 in relation to an offence so mentioned;
(g) an offence of inciting a person to commit an offence so mentioned;
(h) an offence of aiding, abetting, counselling or procuring the commission of an offence so mentioned.

(5) "Enforcing authority"—
(a) in relation to a trigger offence under the Employment Agencies Act 1973, means the Secretary of State or any authority whose officers are acting for the purposes of that Act (see section 8A of that Act);
(b) in relation to a trigger offence under the National Minimum Wage Act 1998, means the Secretary of State or any authority whose officers are acting for the purposes of that Act (see section 13 of that Act);
(c) in relation to a trigger offence under the Gangmasters (Licensing) Act 2004, means the Secretary of State or any authority whose officers are acting as enforcement officers for the purposes of that Act (see section 15 of that Act);
(d) in relation to an offence which is a trigger offence by virtue of subsection (4)(d) (including an offence mentioned in subsection (4)(e) to (h) in connection with such an offence), has the meaning prescribed in regulations made by the Secretary of State.

(6) In subsection (5), a reference to an offence under an Act includes a reference to an offence mentioned in subsection (4)(e) to (h) in connection with such an offence.

(7) In this section references to the Gangmasters (Licensing) Act 2004 are references to that Act only so far as it applies in relation to England and Wales and Scotland.

15 Measures in LME undertakings

(1) An LME undertaking may include a prohibition, restriction or requirement (each a "measure") if, and only if—
(a) the measure falls within subsection (2) or (3) (or both), and
(b) the enforcing authority considers that the measure is just and reasonable.

(2) A measure falls within this subsection if it is for the purpose of—

(a) preventing or reducing the risk of the subject not complying with any requirement imposed by or under the relevant enactment, or

(b) bringing to the attention of persons likely to be interested in the matter—

(i) the existence of the LME undertaking,

(ii) the circumstances in which it was given, and

(iii) any action taken (or not taken) by the subject in order to comply with the undertaking.

(3) A measure falls within this subsection if it is prescribed, or is of a description prescribed, in regulations made by the Secretary of State.

(4) The enforcing authority must not—

(a) invite the subject to give an LME undertaking, or

(b) agree to the form of an undertaking,

unless the authority believes that at least one measure in the undertaking is necessary for the purpose mentioned in subsection (5).

(5) That purpose is preventing or reducing the risk of the subject—

(a) committing a further trigger offence under the relevant enactment, or

(b) continuing to commit the trigger offence.

(6) An LME undertaking must set out how each measure included for the purpose mentioned in subsection (2)(a) is expected to achieve that purpose.

(7) In this section, the "relevant enactment" means the enactment under which the enforcing authority believes the trigger offence concerned has been or is being committed.

16 Duration

(1) An LME undertaking has effect from when it is accepted by the enforcing authority or from the later time specified in it for this purpose.

(2) An LME undertaking has effect for the period specified in it but the maximum period for which an undertaking may have effect is 2 years.

(3) The enforcing authority may release the subject from an LME undertaking.

(4) The enforcing authority must release the subject from an LME undertaking if at any time during the period for which it has effect the authority believes that no measure in it is necessary for the purpose mentioned in section 15(5).

(5) If the enforcing authority releases the subject from an LME undertaking it must take such steps as it considers appropriate to bring that fact to the attention of—

(a) the subject;

(b) any other persons likely to be interested in the matter.

17 Further provision about giving notice under section 14

(1) A notice may be given under section 14 to a person by—

(a) delivering it to the person,

(b) leaving it at the person's proper address,

(c) sending it by post to the person at that address, or

(d) subject to subsection (6), sending it to the person by electronic means.

(2) A notice to a body corporate may be given to any officer of that body.

(3) A notice to a partnership may be given to any partner.

(4) A notice to an unincorporated association (other than a partnership) may be given to any member of the governing body of the association.

(5) For the purposes of this section and of section 7 of the Interpretation Act 1978 (service of documents by post) in its application to this section, the proper address of a person is the person's last known address (whether of the person's residence or of a place where the person carries on business or is employed) and also—

(a) in the case of a body corporate or an officer of the body, the address of the body's registered or principal office in the United Kingdom;

(b) in the case of a partnership or a partner, the address of the principal office of the partnership in the United Kingdom;

(c) in the case of an unincorporated association (other than a partnership) or a member of its governing body, the principal office of the association in the United Kingdom.

(6) A notice may be sent to a person by electronic means only if—

(a) the person has indicated that notices under section 14 may be given to the person by being sent to an electronic address and in an electronic form specified for that purpose, and

(b) the notice is sent to that address in that form.

(7) A notice sent to a person by electronic means is, unless the contrary is proved, to be treated as having been given on the working day immediately following the day on which it was sent.

(8) In this section—

"electronic address" means any number or address used for the purposes of sending or receiving documents or information by electronic means;

"officer", in relation to a body corporate, means a director, manager, secretary or other similar officer of the body;

"working day" means a day other than a Saturday, a Sunday, Christmas Day, Good Friday or a bank holiday under the Banking and Financial Dealings Act 1971 in any part of the United Kingdom.

Labour market enforcement orders

18 Power to make LME order on application

(1) The appropriate court may, on an application by an enforcing authority under section 19, make a labour market enforcement order against a person if the court—

(a) is satisfied, on the balance of probabilities, that the person has committed, or is committing, a trigger offence, and

(b) considers that it is just and reasonable to make the order.

(2) A labour market enforcement order (an "LME order") is an order which—

(a) prohibits or restricts the person against whom it is made ("the respondent") from doing anything set out in the order;

(b) requires the respondent to do anything set out in the order.

See section 21.

(3) In this section "the appropriate court"—

(a) where the conduct constituting the trigger offence took or is taking place primarily in England and Wales, means a magistrates' court;

(b) where that conduct took or is taking place primarily in Scotland, means the sheriff;

(c) where that conduct took or is taking place primarily in Northern Ireland, means a court of summary jurisdiction.

(4) An application for an LME order under this section is—

(a) in England and Wales, to be made by complaint;

(b) in Northern Ireland, to be made by complaint under Part 8 of the Magistrates' Courts (Northern Ireland) Order 1981 (S.I. 1981/1675 (N.I. 26)).

19 Applications

(1) An enforcing authority may apply for an LME order to be made under section 18 against a person (the "proposed respondent") if—

(a) the authority has served a notice on the proposed respondent under section 14, and

(b) the proposed respondent—

(i) refuses to give an LME undertaking, or

(ii) otherwise fails, before the end of the negotiation period, to give an LME undertaking in the form attached to the notice or in such other form as may be agreed with the enforcing authority.

(2) An enforcing authority may also apply for an LME order if the proposed respondent—

(a) has given an LME undertaking to the enforcing authority, and

(b) has failed to comply with the undertaking.

(3) In subsection (1) "the negotiation period" means—

(a) the period of 14 days beginning with the day after that on which the notice mentioned in paragraph (a) of that subsection was given, or

(b) such longer period as may be agreed between the enforcing authority and the proposed respondent.

20 Power to make LME order on conviction

(1) This section applies where a court deals with a person in respect of a conviction for a trigger offence.

(2) The court may make an LME order against the person if the court considers it is just and reasonable to do so.

(3) An LME order must not be made under this section except—

(a) in addition to a sentence imposed in respect of the offence concerned, or

(b) in addition to an order discharging the person conditionally or, in Scotland, discharging the person absolutely.

21 Measures in LME orders

(1) An LME order may include a prohibition, restriction or requirement (each a "measure") if, and only if, the measure falls within subsection (2) or (3) (or both).

(2) A measure falls within this subsection if it is for the purpose of—

(a) preventing or reducing the risk of the respondent not complying with any requirement imposed by or under the relevant enactment, or

(b) bringing to the attention of persons likely to be interested in the matter—

(i) the existence of the LME order,

(ii) the circumstances in which it was made, and

(iii) any action taken (or not taken) by the respondent in order to comply with the order.

(3) A measure falls within this subsection if it is prescribed, or is of a description prescribed, in regulations made by the Secretary of State.

(4) Where an LME order includes a measure for the purpose mentioned in subsection (2) (a), the order must set out how the measure is expected to achieve that purpose.

(5) In this section the "relevant enactment" means the enactment under which the trigger offence concerned has been or is being committed.

22 Further provision about LME orders

(1) An LME order has effect for the period specified in it but the maximum period for which an order may have effect is 2 years.

(2) An LME order may not be made against an individual who is under 18.

(3) If a court makes an LME order, the court may also—

(a) release the respondent from any LME undertaking given in relation to the trigger offence concerned;

(b) discharge any other LME order which is in force against the respondent and which was made by the court or any other court in the same part of the United Kingdom as the court.

23 Variation and discharge

(1) The appropriate court may by order vary or discharge an LME order—

(a) on the application of the respondent;

(b) if the order was made under section 18, on the application of the enforcing authority who applied for the order;

(c) if the order was made under section 20, on the application of the enforcing authority whose officer conducted the investigation which resulted in the prosecution of the respondent for the trigger offence.

(2) In this section "the appropriate court"—

(a) in relation to an LME order made in England and Wales (whether made under section 18 or 20), means a magistrates' court;

(b) in relation to such an order made in Scotland, means the sheriff;

(c) in relation to such an order made in Northern Ireland, means a court of summary jurisdiction.

(3) An application for an order under this section is—

(a) if made to a magistrates' court in England and Wales, to be made by complaint;

(b) if made to a court of summary jurisdiction in Northern Ireland, to be made by complaint under Part 8 of the Magistrates' Courts (Northern Ireland) Order 1981 (S.I. 1981/1675 (N.I. 26)).

24 Appeals

(1) A respondent may appeal against—

(a) the making of an LME order under section 18;

(b) the making of, or refusal to make, an order under section 23.

(2) An appeal under subsection (1) is to be made—

(a) where the order was made or refused by a magistrates' court in England and Wales, to the Crown Court;

(b) where the order was made or refused by the sheriff, to the Sheriff Appeal Court;

(c) where the order was made or refused by a court of summary jurisdiction in Northern Ireland, to a county court.

(3) On an appeal under subsection (1) the court hearing the appeal may make such orders as may be necessary to give effect to its determination of the appeal, and may also make such incidental or consequential orders as appear to it to be just and reasonable.

(4) An LME order that has been varied by virtue of subsection (3) remains an order of the court that first made it for the purposes of section 23.

(5) A respondent may appeal against the making of an LME order under section 20 as if the order were a sentence passed on the respondent for the trigger offence.

LME undertakings and orders: supplementary

25 Code of practice

(1) The Secretary of State must issue a code of practice giving guidance to enforcing authorities about the exercise of their functions under sections 14 to 23.

(2) The Secretary of State may revise the code from time to time.

(3) The code and any revised code—

(a) must not be issued unless a draft has been laid before Parliament, and

(b) comes into force on such day as the Secretary of State appoints by regulations.

(4) The Secretary of State must publish the code and any revised code.

(5) An enforcing authority must have regard to the current version of the code in exercising its functions under sections 14 to 23.

26 Investigative functions

(1) An officer acting for the purposes of the Employment Agencies Act 1973—

(a) may also act for the purposes of taking action where it appears that a person has failed to comply with an LME undertaking or an LME order where the trigger offence to which the undertaking or order relates is an offence under that Act, and

(b) in doing so, has the same powers and duties as he or she has when acting for the purposes of that Act.

(2) An officer acting for the purposes of the National Minimum Wage Act 1998—

(a) may also act for the purposes of taking action where it appears that a person has failed to comply with an LME undertaking or an LME order where the trigger offence to which the undertaking or order relates is an offence under that Act, and

(b) in doing so, has the same powers and duties as he or she has when acting for the purposes of that Act.

(3) An officer acting as an enforcement officer for the purposes of the Gangmasters (Licensing) Act 2004—

(a) may also act for the purposes of taking action where it appears that a person has failed to comply with an LME undertaking or an LME order where the trigger offence to which the undertaking or order relates is an offence under that Act, and

(b) in doing so, has the same powers and duties as he or she has when acting as an enforcement officer for the purposes of that Act.

(4) In this section references to the Gangmasters (Licensing) Act 2004 are references to that Act only so far as it applies in relation to England and Wales and Scotland.

27 Offence

(1) A person against whom an LME order is made commits an offence if the person, without reasonable excuse, fails to comply with the order.

(2) A person guilty of an offence under this section is liable—

(a) on conviction on indictment, to imprisonment for a term not exceeding 2 years, to a fine or to both;

(b) on summary conviction in England and Wales, to imprisonment for a term not exceeding 12 months, to a fine or to both;

(c) on summary conviction in Scotland, to imprisonment for a term not exceeding 12 months, to a fine not exceeding the statutory maximum or to both;

(d) on summary conviction in Northern Ireland, to imprisonment for a term not exceeding 6 months, to a fine not exceeding the statutory maximum or to both.

(3) In relation to an offence committed before the commencement of section 154(1) of the Criminal Justice Act 2003, the reference in subsection (2)(b) to 12 months is to be read as a reference to 6 months.

28 Offences by bodies corporate

(1) If an offence under section 27 committed by a body corporate is proved—

(a) to have been committed with the consent or connivance of an officer of the body, or

(b) to be attributable to any neglect on the part of such an officer, the officer, as well as the body corporate, is guilty of the offence and liable to be proceeded against and punished accordingly.

(2) In subsection (1) "officer", in relation to a body corporate, means—
  (a) a director, manager, secretary or other similar officer of the body;
  (b) a person purporting to act in any such capacity.

(3) If the affairs of a body corporate are managed by its members, subsection (1) applies in relation to the acts and defaults of a member in connection with the member's functions of management as if the member were a director of the body corporate.

29 Application to unincorporated associations

(1) In a case falling within subsection (2), an unincorporated association is to be treated as a legal person for the purposes of sections 14 to 27.

(2) A case falls within this subsection if it relates to a trigger offence for which it is possible to bring proceedings against an unincorporated association in the name of the association.

(3) Proceedings for an offence under section 27 alleged to have been committed by an unincorporated association may be brought against the association in the name of the association.

(4) For the purposes of such proceedings—
  (a) rules of court relating to the service of documents have effect as if the association were a body corporate, and
  (b) the following provisions apply as they apply in relation to a body corporate—
    (i) section 33 of the Criminal Justice Act 1925 and Schedule 3 to the Magistrates' Courts Act 1980;
    (ii) sections 70 and 143 of the Criminal Procedure (Scotland) Act 1995;
    (iii) section 18 of the Criminal Justice Act (Northern Ireland) 1945 (c. 15 (N.I.)) and Schedule 4 to the Magistrates' Courts (Northern Ireland) Order 1981 (S.I. 1981/1675 (N.I. 26)).

(5) A fine imposed on the association on its conviction of an offence is to be paid out of the funds of the association.

(6) If an offence under section 27 committed by an unincorporated association is proved—
  (a) to have been committed with the consent or connivance of an officer of the association, or
  (b) to be attributable to any neglect on the part of such an officer,

the officer, as well as the association, is guilty of the offence and liable to be proceeded against and punished accordingly.

(7) In subsection (6) "officer", in relation to any association, means—
  (a) an officer of the association or a member of its governing body;
  (b) a person purporting to act in such a capacity.

30 Application to partnerships

(1) If an offence under section 27 committed by a partner of a partnership which is not regarded as a legal person is shown—

(a) to have been committed with the consent or connivance of another partner, or

(b) to be attributable to any neglect on the part of another partner,

that other partner, as well as the first-mentioned partner, is guilty of the offence and liable to be proceeded against and punished accordingly.

(2) Proceedings for an offence under section 27 alleged to have been committed by a partnership which is regarded as a legal person may be brought against the partnership in the firm name.

(3) For the purposes of such proceedings—

(a) rules of court relating to the service of documents have effect as if the partnership were a body corporate, and

(b) the following provisions apply as they apply in relation to a body corporate—

(i) section 33 of the Criminal Justice Act 1925 and Schedule 3 to the Magistrates' Courts Act 1980;

(ii) sections 70 and 143 of the Criminal Procedure (Scotland) Act 1995;

(iii) section 18 of the Criminal Justice Act (Northern Ireland) 1945 (c. 15 (N.I.)) and Schedule 4 to the Magistrates' Courts (Northern Ireland) Order 1981 (S.I. 1981/1675 (N.I. 26)).

(4) A fine imposed on a partnership on its conviction of an offence is to be paid out of the funds of the partnership.

(5) If an offence under section 27 committed by a partnership is proved—

(a) to have been committed with the consent or connivance of a partner, or

(b) to be attributable to any neglect on the part of a partner,

the partner, as well as the partnership, is guilty of the offence and liable to be proceeded against and punished accordingly.

(6) In subsections (1) and (5) "partner" includes a person purporting to act as a partner.

(7) For the purposes of this section a partnership is, or is not, "regarded as a legal person" if it is, or is not, so regarded under the law of the country or territory under which it was formed.

Supplementary provision

31 Consequential and related amendments

Schedule 3 (consequential and related amendments) has effect.

32 Regulations under Chapter 1

(1) Regulations under section 3 or 14 must not prescribe a requirement, function or offence if provision imposing the requirement, conferring the function or creating the offence falls within subsection (3).

(2) Regulations under section 11 must not confer a function if provision doing so falls within subsection (3).

(3) Provision falls within this subsection if—

(a) it would be within the legislative competence of the Scottish Parliament if contained in an Act of that Parliament,

(b) it would be within the legislative competence of the National Assembly for Wales if contained in an Act of that Assembly, or

(c) it would be within the legislative competence of the Northern Ireland Assembly if contained in an Act of that Assembly made without the consent of the Secretary of State.

(4) Regulations under section 3, 11 or 14 may make such provision amending, repealing or revoking any provision of any enactment, including this Chapter, as the Secretary of State considers appropriate in consequence of the regulations.

33 Interpretation of Chapter 1

In this Chapter—

"the Director" has the meaning given by section 1;

"enactment" includes—

(a) an enactment contained in subordinate legislation within the meaning of the Interpretation Act 1978;

(b) an enactment contained in, or in an instrument made under, an Act of the Scottish Parliament;

(c) an enactment contained in, or in an instrument made under, a Measure or Act of the National Assembly for Wales;

(d) an enactment contained in, or in an instrument made under, Northern Ireland legislation;

"enforcing authority" has the meaning given by section 14;

"financial year" means a period of 12 months ending with 31 March;

"HMRC Commissioners" means the Commissioners for Her Majesty's Revenue and Customs;

"labour market enforcement functions" has the meaning given by section 3;

"LME order" has the meaning given by section 18;

"LME undertaking" has the meaning given by section 14;

"non-compliance in the labour market" has the meaning given by section 3;

"the respondent" has the meaning given by section 18;

"strategy" has the meaning given by section 2;

"subject" has the meaning given by section 14;

"trigger offence" has the meaning given by section 14.

CHAPTER 2

ILLEGAL WORKING

Offences

34 Offence of illegal working

(1) The Immigration Act 1971 is amended as follows.

(2) In section 3(1)(c)(i) (power to grant limited leave to enter or remain in the United Kingdom subject to condition restricting employment or occupation) for "employment" substitute "work".

(3) After section 24A insert—

"24B Illegal working

(1) A person ("P") who is subject to immigration control commits an offence if—

(a) P works at a time when P is disqualified from working by reason of P's immigration status, and

(b) at that time P knows or has reasonable cause to believe that P is disqualified from working by reason of P's immigration status.

(2) For the purposes of subsection (1) a person is disqualified from working by reason of the person's immigration status if—

(a) the person has not been granted leave to enter or remain in the United Kingdom, or

(b) the person's leave to enter or remain in the United Kingdom—

(i) is invalid,

(ii) has ceased to have effect (whether by reason of curtailment, revocation, cancellation, passage of time or otherwise), or

(iii) is subject to a condition preventing the person from doing work of that kind.

(3) A person who is guilty of an offence under subsection (1) is liable on summary conviction—

(a) in England and Wales, to imprisonment for a term not exceeding 51 weeks or a fine, or both,

(b) in Scotland or Northern Ireland, to imprisonment for a term not exceeding 6 months or a fine not exceeding level 5 on the standard scale, or both.

(4) In relation to an offence committed before section 281(5) of the Criminal Justice Act 2003 comes into force, the reference in subsection (3)(a) to 51 weeks is to be read as a reference to 6 months.

(5) If a person is convicted of an offence under subsection (1) in England and Wales, the prosecutor must consider whether to ask the court to commit the person to the Crown Court under section 70 of the Proceeds of Crime Act 2002 (committal with view to confiscation order being considered).

(6) If a person is convicted of an offence under subsection (1) in Scotland, the prosecutor must consider whether to ask the court to act under section 92 of the Proceeds of Crime Act 2002 (making of confiscation order).

(7) If a person is convicted of an offence under subsection (1) in Northern Ireland, the prosecutor must consider whether to ask the court to commit the person to the Crown Court under section 218 of the Proceeds of Crime Act 2002 (committal with view to confiscation order being considered).

(8) The reference in subsection (1) to a person who is subject to immigration control is to a person who under this Act requires leave to enter or remain in the United Kingdom.

(9) Where a person is on immigration bail within the meaning of Part 1 of Schedule 10 to the Immigration Act 2016—

(a) the person is to be treated for the purposes of subsection (2) as if the person had been granted leave to enter the United Kingdom, but

(b) any condition as to the person's work in the United Kingdom to which the person's immigration bail is subject is to be treated for those purposes as a condition of leave.

(10) The reference in subsection (1) to a person working is to that person working—

(a) under a contract of employment,

(b) under a contract of apprenticeship,

(c) under a contract personally to do work,

(d) under or for the purposes of a contract for services,

(e) for a purpose related to a contract to sell goods,

(f) as a constable,

(g) in the course of Crown employment,

(h) as a relevant member of the House of Commons staff, or

(i) as a relevant member of the House of Lords staff.

(11) In subsection (10)—

"contract to sell goods" means a contract by which a person acting in the course of a trade, business, craft or profession transfers or agrees to transfer the property in goods to another person (and for this purpose "goods" means any tangible moveable items);

"Crown employment"—

(a) in relation to England and Wales and Scotland, has the meaning given by section 191(3) of the Employment Rights Act 1996;

(b) in relation to Northern Ireland, has the meaning given by Article 236(3) of the Employment Rights (Northern Ireland) Order 1996 (SI 1996/1919 (NI 16));

"relevant member of the House of Commons staff" has the meaning given by section 195(5) of the Employment Rights Act 1996;

"relevant member of the House of Lords staff" has the meaning given by section 194(6) of the Employment Rights Act 1996.

(12) Subsection (1) does not apply to—

(a) service as a member of the naval, military or air forces of the Crown, or

(b) employment by an association established for the purposes of Part 11 of the Reserve Forces Act 1996.

(13) In this section "contract" means a contract whether express or implied and, if express, whether oral or in writing."

(4) In section 28A(3)(a) (arrest without warrant) after "section" insert "24B,".

(5) In section 28B(5) (search and arrest by warrant: relevant offences) after "24A," insert "24B,".

(6) In section 28CA(1) (business premises: entry to arrest) after paragraph (b) insert—

"(ba) for an offence under section 24B,".

(7) In section 28D(4) (entry and search of premises: relevant offences) after "24A," insert "24B,".

(8) In section 28FA(1)(a) (search for personnel records: offences to which section applies) for "or 24A(1)" substitute ", 24A(1) or 24B(1)".

35 Offence of employing illegal worker

(1) Section 21 of the Immigration, Asylum and Nationality Act 2006 (offence of knowingly employing illegal worker) is amended in accordance with subsections (2) to (4).

(2) In subsection (1) for the words from "an adult" to the end of the subsection substitute "disqualified from employment by reason of the employee's immigration status."

(3) After subsection (1) insert—

"(1A) A person commits an offence if the person—

(a) employs another person ("the employee") who is disqualified from employment by reason of the employee's immigration status, and

(b) has reasonable cause to believe that the employee is disqualified from employment by reason of the employee's immigration status.

(1B) For the purposes of subsections (1) and (1A) a person is disqualified from employment by reason of the person's immigration status if the person is an adult subject to immigration control and—

(a) the person has not been granted leave to enter or remain in the United Kingdom, or

(b) the person's leave to enter or remain in the United Kingdom—

(i) is invalid,

(ii) has ceased to have effect (whether by reason of curtailment, revocation, cancellation, passage of time or otherwise), or

(iii) is subject to a condition preventing the person from accepting the employment."

(4) In subsection (2)(a)(i) (maximum term of imprisonment for conviction of offence on indictment) for "two" substitute "five".

(5) Section 22 of the Immigration, Asylum and Nationality Act 2006 (offences by bodies corporate etc) is amended in accordance with subsections (6) and (7).

(6) After subsection (1) insert—

"(1A) For the purposes of section 21(1A) a body (whether corporate or not) shall be treated as having reasonable cause to believe a fact about an employee if a person who has responsibility within the body for an aspect of the employment has reasonable cause to believe that fact."

(7) In each of subsections (2) and (4) after "21(1)" insert "or (1A)".

(8) In section 24(a) of the Immigration, Asylum and Nationality Act 2006 (immigration bail) for "21(1)" substitute "21(1B)".

(9) In section 28A of the Immigration Act 1971 (arrest without warrant)—

(a) after subsection (9A) insert—

"(9B) An immigration officer may arrest without warrant a person who, or whom the immigration officer has reasonable grounds for suspecting—

(a) has committed or attempted to commit an offence under section 21(1) or (1A) of the Immigration, Asylum and Nationality Act 2006 (employment of illegal worker etc), or

(b) is committing or attempting to commit that offence.",

(b) in subsection (10) for "and (5)" substitute ", (5) and (9B)", and

(c) in subsection (11) for "and (5)" substitute ", (5) and (9B)".

(10) In section 28AA(1) of that Act (arrest with warrant) for paragraphs (a) and (b) substitute "section 24(1)(d)".

Illegal working in licensed premises

36 Licensing Act 2003: amendments relating to illegal working

(1) Schedule 4 (Licensing Act 2003: amendments relating to illegal working) has effect.

(2) The Secretary of State may by regulations make provision which—

(a) has a similar effect to the amendments made by Schedule 4, and

(b) applies in relation to Scotland or Northern Ireland.

(3) Regulations under subsection (2) may—

(a) amend, repeal or revoke any enactment;

(b) confer functions on any person.

(4) Regulations under subsection (2) may not confer functions on—

(a) the Scottish Ministers,

(b) the First Minister and deputy First Minister in Northern Ireland,

(c) a Northern Ireland Minister, or

(d) a Northern Ireland department.

(5) In this section "enactment" includes—

(a) an enactment contained in subordinate legislation within the meaning of the Interpretation Act 1978;

(b) an enactment contained in, or in an instrument made under, an Act of the Scottish Parliament;

(c) an enactment contained in, or in an instrument made under, Northern Ireland legislation.

Illegal working in relation to private hire vehicles etc

37 Private hire vehicles etc

Schedule 5 (private hire vehicles etc) has effect.

Illegal working notices and orders

38 Illegal working closure notices and illegal working compliance orders

Schedule 6 (illegal working closure notices and illegal working compliance orders) has effect.

PART 2

ACCESS TO SERVICES

Residential tenancies

39 Offence of leasing premises

(1) The Immigration Act 2014 is amended in accordance with subsections (2) to (5).

(2) After section 33 insert—

"Offences

33A Offences: landlords

(1) The landlord under a residential tenancy agreement which relates to premises in England commits an offence if the first and second conditions are met.

(2) The first condition is that the premises are occupied by an adult who is disqualified as a result of their immigration status from occupying premises under a residential tenancy agreement.

(3) The second condition is that the landlord knows or has reasonable cause to believe that the premises are occupied by an adult who is disqualified as a result of their immigration status from occupying premises under a residential tenancy agreement.

(4) But unless subsection (5) applies the landlord does not commit an offence under subsection (1) if—

(a) the premises are located in an area in relation to which section 22 is in force,

(b) the adult mentioned in subsections (2) and (3) is a limited right occupier, and

(c) the eligibility period in relation to that occupier has not expired.

(5) This subsection applies if the Secretary of State has given a notice in writing to the landlord which—

(a) identifies the adult mentioned in subsections (2) and (3), and
(b) states that the adult is disqualified as a result of their immigration status from occupying premises under a residential tenancy agreement.

(6) It is a defence for a person charged with an offence under subsection (1) to prove that—
(a) the person has taken reasonable steps to terminate the residential tenancy agreement, and
(b) the person has taken such steps within a reasonable period beginning with the time when the person first knew or had reasonable cause to believe that the premises were occupied by the adult mentioned in subsections (2) and (3).

(7) In determining whether subsection (6)(a) or (b) applies to a person, the court must have regard to any guidance which, at the time in question, had been issued by the Secretary of State for the purposes of that subsection and was in force at that time.

(8) Guidance issued for the purposes of subsection (6)—
(a) must be laid before Parliament in draft before being issued, and
(b) comes into force in accordance with regulations made by the Secretary of State.

(9) Section 22(9) applies for the purposes of subsection (1) as it applies for the purposes of that section.

(10) A person commits an offence if—
(a) there has been a post-grant contravention in relation to a residential tenancy agreement which relates to premises in England,
(b) the person is the responsible landlord in relation to the post-grant contravention,
(c) the person knows or has reasonable cause to believe that there has been a post-grant contravention in relation to the agreement, and
(d) none of paragraphs (a), (b) and (c) of section 24(6) applies in relation to the post-grant contravention.

(11) Subsection (10) applies whether or not the landlord is given a notice under section 23 in respect of the contravention.

33B Offences: agents

(1) Subsection (2) applies to an agent who is responsible for a landlord's contravention of section 22 in relation to premises in England.

(2) The agent commits an offence if the agent—
(a) knew or had reasonable cause to believe that the landlord would contravene section 22 by entering into the residential tenancy agreement in question,
(b) had sufficient opportunity to notify the landlord of that fact before the landlord entered into the agreement, but
(c) did not do so.

(3) Subsection (4) applies where—

(a) a landlord contravenes section 22 in relation to a residential tenancy agreement relating to premises in England,

(b) the contravention is a post-grant contravention, and

(c) a person acting as the landlord's agent ("the agent") is responsible for the post-grant contravention.

(4) The agent commits an offence if—

(a) the agent knows or has reasonable cause to believe that there has been a post-grant contravention in relation to the agreement, and

(b) neither of paragraphs (a) and (b) of section 26(6) applies in relation to the post-grant contravention.

(5) Subsection (4) applies whether or not the agent is given a notice under section 25 in respect of the contravention.

33C Offences: penalties etc

(1) A person who is guilty of an offence under section 33A or 33B is liable—

(a) on conviction on indictment, to imprisonment for a term not exceeding five years, to a fine or to both;

(b) on summary conviction, to imprisonment for a term not exceeding 12 months, to a fine or to both.

(2) In the application of this section in relation to an offence committed before the coming into force of section 154(1) of the Criminal Justice Act 2003 the reference in subsection (1)(b) to 12 months is to be read as a reference to 6 months.

(3) If an offence under section 33A or 33B is committed by a body corporate with the consent or connivance of an officer of the body, the officer, as well as the body, is to be treated as having committed the offence.

(4) In subsection (3) a reference to an officer of a body includes a reference to—

(a) a director, manager or secretary,

(b) a person purporting to act as a director, manager or secretary, and

(c) if the affairs of the body are managed by its members, a member.

(5) Where an offence under section 33A or 33B is committed by a partnership (whether or not a limited partnership) subsection (3) has effect, but as if a reference to an officer of the body were a reference to—

(a) a partner, and

(b) a person purporting to act as a partner.

(6) An offence under section 33A or 33B is to be treated as—

(a) a relevant offence for the purposes of sections 28B and 28D of the Immigration Act 1971 (search, entry and arrest), and

(b) an offence under Part 3 of that Act (criminal proceedings) for the purposes of sections 28E, 28G and 28H of that Act (search after arrest)."

(3) In section 35 (transitional provision) after subsection (3) insert—

"(4) References in this section to this Chapter do not include sections 33A to 33E (offences and eviction).

(5) Sections 33A to 33C apply in relation to a residential tenancy agreement entered into before or after the coming into force of section 39 of the Immigration Act 2016 (which inserted those sections into this Act).

(6) But sections 33A(10) and (11) and 33B apply only in relation to a contravention of section 22 which occurs after the coming into force of section 39 of the Immigration Act 2016."

(4) In section 36 (Crown application) at the end insert "or the landlord for the purposes of section 33A."

(5) In section 37(4)(a) (provisions in which references to the landlord are to any of them) —

(a) omit the "and" at the end of sub-paragraph (ii), and
(b) at the end of sub-paragraph (iii) insert—
"(iv) section 33A,".

(6) In section 28A of the Immigration Act 1971 (arrest without warrant)—
(a) after subsection (9B) insert—

"(9C) An immigration officer may arrest without warrant a person who, or whom the immigration officer has reasonable grounds for suspecting—
(a) has committed or attempted to commit an offence under section 33A or 33B of the Immigration Act 2014 (offences relating to residential tenancies), or
(b) is committing or attempting to commit that offence.",

(b) in subsection (10) for "and (9B)" substitute ", (9B) and (9C)", and
(c) in subsection (11) for "and (9B)" substitute ", (9B) and (9C)".

40 Eviction

(1) The Immigration Act 2014 is amended in accordance with subsections (2) to (4).

(2) After section 33C (inserted by section 39) insert—

"Eviction

33D Termination of agreement where all occupiers disqualified

(1) The landlord under a residential tenancy agreement relating to premises in England may terminate the agreement in accordance with this section if the condition in subsection (2) is met.

(2) The condition is that the Secretary of State has given one or more notices in writing to the landlord which, taken together,—
(a) identify the occupier of the premises or (if there is more than one occupier) all of them, and

(b) state that the occupier or occupiers are disqualified as a result of their immigration status from occupying premises under a residential tenancy agreement.

(3) The landlord may terminate the residential tenancy agreement by giving notice in writing and in the prescribed form to the tenant or, in the case of a joint tenancy, all of the tenants specifying the date on which the agreement comes to an end.

(4) That date must not be earlier than the end of the period of 28 days beginning with the day specified in the notice as the day on which it is given.

(5) The notice may be given—

(a) by delivering it to the tenant or tenants,

(b) by leaving it at the premises,

(c) by sending it by post to the tenant or tenants at the address of the premises, or

(d) in any other prescribed manner.

(6) The notice is to be treated as a notice to quit in a case where a notice to quit would otherwise be required to bring the residential tenancy agreement to an end.

(7) The notice is enforceable as if it were an order of the High Court.

(8) In this section "occupier", in relation to premises to which a residential tenancy agreement applies, means—

(a) a tenant,

(b) a person who, under the agreement, otherwise has the right to occupy the premises and is named in the agreement, and

(c) any other person who the landlord knows is occupying the premises.

33E Other procedures for ending agreement

(1) It is an implied term of a residential tenancy agreement to which this subsection applies that the landlord may terminate the tenancy if the premises to which it relates are occupied by an adult who is disqualified as a result of their immigration status from occupying premises under a residential tenancy agreement.

(2) Subsection (1) applies to a residential tenancy agreement relating to premises in England if—

(a) it is a tenancy or sub-tenancy or an agreement for a tenancy or sub-tenancy, but

(b) it is not a protected or statutory tenancy within the meaning of the Rent Act 1977 or an assured tenancy within the meaning of the Housing Act 1988.

(3) For provision relating to a residential tenancy agreement which is a protected or statutory tenancy where a tenant or occupier is disqualified as a result of their immigration status from occupying premises under a residential tenancy agreement, see Case 10A in Part 1 of Schedule 15 to the Rent Act 1977.

(4) For provision relating to a residential tenancy agreement which is an assured tenancy where a tenant or occupier is disqualified as a result of their immigration status from occupying premises under a residential tenancy agreement, see Ground 7B in Part 1 of Schedule 2 to the Housing Act 1988."

(3) In section 35 (transitional provision) after subsection (6) (inserted by section 39(3)) insert—

"(7) Sections 33D and 33E apply in relation to a residential tenancy agreement entered into before or after the coming into force of section 40 of the Immigration Act 2016 (which inserted those sections into this Act)."

(4) In section 37(4)(a) (provisions in which references to the landlord are to any of them) after sub-paragraph (iv) (inserted by section 39(5)(b)) insert—

"(v) section 33D, and

(vi) section 33E,".

(5) In section 3A of the Protection from Eviction Act 1977 (excluded tenancies and licences) after subsection (7C) insert—

"(7D) A tenancy or licence is excluded if—

(a) it is a residential tenancy agreement within the meaning of Chapter 1 of Part 3 of the Immigration Act 2014, and

(b) the condition in section 33D(2) of that Act is met in relation to that agreement."

(6) In section 5 of the Housing Act 1988 (security of tenure)—

(a) in subsection (1) omit the "or" at the end of paragraph (b) and at the end of paragraph (c) insert ", or

(d) in the case of an assured tenancy—

(i) which is a residential tenancy agreement within the meaning of Chapter 1 of Part 3 of the Immigration Act 2014, and

(ii) in relation to which the condition in section 33D(2) of that Act is met,

giving a notice in accordance with that section,", and

(b) in subsection (2) omit the "or" at the end of paragraph (a) and at the end of paragraph (b) insert ", or

(c) the giving of a notice under section 33D of the Immigration Act 2014,".

(7) The amendments made by subsections (5) and (6) apply in relation to a tenancy or (in the case of subsection (5)) a licence entered into before or after the coming into force of this section.

41 Order for possession of dwelling-house

(1) The Housing Act 1988 is amended in accordance with subsections (2) to (5).

(2) In Part 1 of Schedule 2 (assured tenancies: grounds on which court must order possession) after Ground 7A insert—

"Ground 7B

Both of the following conditions are met in relation to a dwelling-house in England.

Condition 1 is that the Secretary of State has given a notice in writing to the landlord or, in the case of joint landlords, one or more of them which identifies—

(a) the tenant or, in the case of joint tenants, one or more of them, or

(b) one or more other persons aged 18 or over who are occupying the dwelling-house,

as a person or persons disqualified as a result of their immigration status from occupying the dwelling-house under the tenancy.

Condition 2 is that the person or persons named in the notice—

(a) fall within paragraph (a) or (b) of condition 1, and

(b) are disqualified as a result of their immigration status from occupying the dwelling-house under the tenancy.

For the purposes of this ground a person ("P") is disqualified as a result of their immigration status from occupying the dwelling-house under the tenancy if—

(a) P is not a relevant national, and

(b) P does not have a right to rent in relation to the dwelling-house.

P does not have a right to rent in relation to the dwelling-house if—

(a) P requires leave to enter or remain in the United Kingdom but does not have it, or

(b) P's leave to enter or remain in the United Kingdom is subject to a condition preventing P from occupying the dwelling-house.

But P is to be treated as having a right to rent in relation to a dwelling-house if the Secretary of State has granted P permission for the purposes of this ground to occupy a dwelling-house under an assured tenancy.

In this ground "relevant national" means—

(a) a British citizen,

(b) a national of an EEA State other than the United Kingdom, or

(c) a national of Switzerland."

(3) In section 7 (orders for possession)—

(a) in subsection (3) after "subsections (5A) and (6)" insert "and section 10A",

(b) in subsection (5A)(a) for "and 7A" substitute ", 7A and 7B",

(c) in subsection (6)(a) after "Ground 7A" insert ", Ground 7B", and

(d) after subsection (6A) insert—

"(6B) The requirement in subsection (6)(b) that would otherwise apply to an order for possession of a dwelling-house let on an assured fixed term tenancy does not apply where the ground for possession is Ground 7B in Part 1 of Schedule 2 to this Act."

(4) In section 8(5) (cases where court may not dispense with notice of proceedings for possession) after "Ground 7A" insert ", 7B".

(5) After section 10 insert—

"10A Power to order transfer of tenancy in certain cases

(1) This section applies on an application for an order for possession of a dwelling-house let on an assured tenancy if the court is satisfied that—

(a) Ground 7B in Schedule 2 is established,

(b) no other ground in that Schedule is established, or one or more grounds in Part 2 of that Schedule are established but it is not reasonable to make an order for possession on that ground or those grounds,

(c) the tenancy is a joint tenancy, and

(d) one or more of the tenants is a qualifying tenant.

(2) In subsection (1)(d) "qualifying tenant" means a person who (within the meaning of Ground 7B) is not disqualified as a result of the person's immigration status from occupying the dwelling-house under the tenancy.

(3) The court may, instead of making an order for possession, order that the tenant's interest under the tenancy is to be transferred so that it is held—

(a) if there is one qualifying tenant, by the qualifying tenant as sole tenant, or

(b) if there is more than one qualifying tenant, by all of them as joint tenants.

(4) The effect of an order under this section is that, from the time the order takes effect, the qualifying tenant or tenants—

(a) are entitled to performance of the landlord's covenants under the tenancy, and

(b) are liable to perform the tenant's covenants under the tenancy.

(5) The effect of an order under this section is that, from the time it takes effect, any other person who was a tenant under the tenancy before the order took effect—

(a) ceases to be entitled to performance of the landlord's covenants under the tenancy, or

(b) ceases to be liable to perform the tenant's covenants under the tenancy.

(6) Subsection (5) does not remove any right or liability of the person which accrued before the order took effect.

(7) An order under this section does not operate to create a new tenancy as between the landlord and the qualifying tenant or tenants.

(8) In particular, if the tenancy is a fixed term tenancy, the term comes to an end at the same time as if the order had not been made."

(6) In Part 1 of Schedule 15 to the Rent Act 1977 (grounds for possession of dwelling-houses let on or subject to protected or statutory tenancies) after Case 10 insert—

"Case 10A

Both of the following conditions are met in relation to a dwelling-house in England.

Condition 1 is that the Secretary of State has given a notice in writing to the landlord or, in the case of joint landlords, one or more of them which identifies—

(a) the tenant or, in the case of joint tenants, one or more of them, or

(b) one or more other persons aged 18 or over who are occupying the dwelling-house,

as a person or persons disqualified as a result of their immigration status from occupying the dwelling-house under the tenancy.

Condition 2 is that the person or persons named in the notice—

(a) fall within paragraph (a) or (b) of condition 1, and

(b) are disqualified as a result of their immigration status from occupying the dwelling-house under the tenancy.

For the purposes of this case a person ("P") is disqualified as a result of their immigration status from occupying the dwelling-house under the tenancy if—

(a) P is not a relevant national, and

(b) P does not have a right to rent in relation to the dwelling-house.

P does not have a right to rent in relation to the dwelling-house if—

(a) P requires leave to enter or remain in the United Kingdom but does not have it, or

(b) P's leave to enter or remain in the United Kingdom is subject to a condition preventing P from occupying the dwelling-house.

But P is to be treated as having a right to rent in relation to a dwelling-house if the Secretary of State has granted P permission for the purposes of this case to occupy a dwelling-house which is for the time being let on a protected tenancy or subject to a statutory tenancy.

In this case "relevant national" means—

(a) a British citizen,

(b) a national of an EEA State other than the United Kingdom, or

(c) a national of Switzerland."

(7) The amendments made by this section apply in relation to a tenancy entered into before or after the coming into force of this section.

42 Extension to Wales, Scotland and Northern Ireland

(1) The Secretary of State may by regulations make such provision as the Secretary of State considers appropriate for enabling any of the residential tenancies provisions to apply in relation to Wales, Scotland or Northern Ireland.

(2) The Secretary of State may by regulations make provision which—

(a) has a similar effect to any of the residential tenancies provisions, and

(b) applies in relation to Wales, Scotland or Northern Ireland.

(3) Regulations under subsection (1) or (2) may—

(a) amend, repeal or revoke any enactment;

(b) confer functions on any person.

(4) Regulations under subsection (1) or (2) may not confer functions on—

(a) the Welsh Ministers,

(b) the Scottish Ministers,
(c) the First Minister and deputy First Minister in Northern Ireland,
(d) a Northern Ireland Minister, or
(e) a Northern Ireland department.

(5) In this section—

"enactment" includes—

(a) an enactment contained in subordinate legislation within the meaning of the Interpretation Act 1978;
(b) an enactment contained in, or in an instrument made under, an Act or Measure of the National Assembly for Wales;
(c) an enactment contained in, or in an instrument made under, an Act of the Scottish Parliament;
(d) an enactment contained in, or in an instrument made under, Northern Ireland legislation;

"the residential tenancies provisions" means sections 39 to 41 and the amendments made by those sections.

Driving

43 Powers to carry out searches relating to driving licences

(1) Schedule 2 to the Immigration Act 1971 (administrative provisions as to control of entry etc) is amended in accordance with subsections (2) and (3).

(2) After paragraph 25C insert—

"*25CA Entry of premises to search for driving licence*

25CA (1) An authorised officer may exercise the powers in this section if the officer has reasonable grounds for believing that a person—

(a) is in possession of a driving licence, and
(b) is not lawfully resident in the United Kingdom.

(2) The authorised officer may enter and search any premises—

(a) occupied or controlled by the person, or
(b) in which the person was when the person was encountered by the officer,

for the driving licence.

(3) The power conferred by sub-paragraph (2) may be exercised—

(a) only if the authorised officer has reasonable grounds for believing that the driving licence is on the premises,
(b) only to the extent that it is reasonably required for the purpose of discovering the driving licence, and
(c) unless the authorised officer is a constable, only if a senior officer has authorised its exercise in writing.

(4) Sub-paragraph (3)(c) does not apply where it is not reasonably practicable for the authorised officer to obtain the authorisation of a senior officer before exercising the power.

(5) An authorised officer who has conducted a search in reliance on sub-paragraph (4) must inform a senior officer as soon as is practicable.

(6) The senior officer authorising a search, or who is informed of one under sub-paragraph (5), must make a record in writing of the grounds for the search.

(7) In this paragraph and paragraphs 25CB and 25CC—

"authorised officer" means—

(a) an immigration officer,

(b) a constable, or

(c) a person of a kind authorised for the purposes of this paragraph and paragraphs 25CB and 25CC by the Secretary of State;

"driving licence"—

(a) means a licence to drive a motor vehicle granted under Part 3 of the Road Traffic Act 1988 or Part II of the Road Traffic (Northern Ireland) Order 1981 (SI 1981/154 (NI 1)), and

(b) includes a licence of that kind which has been revoked;

"senior officer" means—

(a) in relation to an authorised officer who is an immigration officer, an immigration officer not below the rank of chief immigration officer;

(b) in relation to an authorised officer other than an immigration officer, a person of a kind designated by the Secretary of State for the purposes of this paragraph in relation to an authorised officer of that kind.

(8) For the purposes of this paragraph and paragraphs 25CB and 25CC a person is not lawfully resident in the United Kingdom if the person requires leave to enter or remain in the United Kingdom but does not have it.

25CB Searching persons for driving licences

25CB (1) An authorised officer may exercise the powers in this section if the officer has reasonable grounds for believing that a person—

(a) is in possession of a driving licence, and

(b) is not lawfully resident in the United Kingdom.

(2) The authorised officer may search the person for the driving licence.

(3) The power conferred by sub-paragraph (2) may be exercised—

(a) only if the authorised officer has reasonable grounds for believing that the driving licence may be concealed on the person, and

(b) only to the extent that it is reasonably required for the purpose of discovering the driving licence.

(4) An intimate search may not be carried out under sub-paragraph (2).

(5) In sub-paragraph (4) "intimate search" has the same meaning as in section 28H(11).

25CC Seizure and retention of driving licence

25CC (1) If an authorised officer who is exercising a power to search a person or premises finds a driving licence to which this sub-paragraph applies in the course of the search, the officer may seize and retain the licence.

(2) Sub-paragraph (1) applies to a driving licence if—

(a) the authorised officer finds the licence in the possession of a person who the authorised officer has reasonable grounds for believing is not lawfully resident in the United Kingdom, or

(b) the authorised officer has reasonable grounds for believing that the holder of the licence is not lawfully resident in the United Kingdom.

(3) A driving licence seized under sub-paragraph (1) must, as soon as practicable, be given to—

(a) the Secretary of State, in the case of a licence granted by the Secretary of State, or

(b) the Department for Infrastructure for Northern Ireland, in the case of a licence granted by the Department.

(4) A person who is in possession of a driving licence by virtue of sub-paragraph (3) must retain it if—

(a) it has not been revoked,

(b) it has been revoked but the time limit for an appeal against revocation of the licence has not expired, or

(c) it has been revoked, such an appeal has been brought but the appeal has not been determined.

(5) A driving licence which is required to be retained under sub-paragraph (4) must be retained—

(a) until a decision is taken not to revoke it, or

(b) if it has been or is subsequently revoked—

(i) until the time limit for an appeal against revocation of the licence expires without an appeal being brought, or

(ii) until such an appeal is determined.

(6) A driving licence which is in the possession of a person by virtue of sub-paragraph (3) but which is not required to be retained under sub-paragraphs (4) and (5) must be returned to the holder if—

(a) a decision is taken not to revoke the licence, or

(b) an appeal against revocation of the licence is determined in favour of the holder.

(7) Otherwise the driving licence may be dealt with in such manner as that person thinks fit.

(8) Neither the Secretary of State nor the Department for Infrastructure for Northern Ireland is obliged to re-issue a licence which has been seized and retained under this paragraph.

(9) References in this paragraph to an appeal against the revocation of a licence are to—

(a) an appeal under section 100 of the Road Traffic Act 1988, in the case of a licence granted by the Secretary of State, or

(b) an appeal under Article 16 of the Road Traffic (Northern Ireland) Order 1981 (SI 1981/154 (NI 1)), in the case of a licence granted by the Department for Infrastructure for Northern Ireland.

(10) References in this paragraph to the holder of a driving licence, in relation to a licence that has been revoked, include the person who was the holder of the licence before it was revoked."

(3) In paragraph 25D(8) (access and copying: meaning of seized material) at the end insert "other than a driving licence seized under paragraph 25CC."

(4) In section 146(2) of the Immigration and Asylum Act 1999 (use of reasonable force) after paragraph (a) insert—

"(aa) paragraph 25CA, 25CB or 25CC of Schedule 2 to the 1971 Act (powers to search for and seize driving licences),".

(5) In the period (if any) between the coming into force of subsection (2) and the coming into force of the Departments Act (Northern Ireland) 2016, references to the Department for Infrastructure for Northern Ireland in paragraph 25CC(3)(b), (8) and (9)(b) of Schedule 2 to the Immigration Act 1971 (as inserted by subsection (2)) are to be read as references to the Department of the Environment for Northern Ireland.

44 Offence of driving when unlawfully in the United Kingdom

(1) The Immigration Act 1971 is amended in accordance with subsections (2) to (6).

(2) Before section 25 insert—

"24C Driving when unlawfully in the United Kingdom

(1) A person commits an offence if—

(a) the person drives a motor vehicle on a road or other public place at a time when the person is not lawfully resident in the United Kingdom, and

(b) at that time the person knows or has reasonable cause to believe that the person is not lawfully resident in the United Kingdom.

(2) A person who is guilty of an offence under subsection (1) is liable on summary conviction—

(a) in England and Wales, to imprisonment for a term not exceeding 51 weeks, to a fine or to both;

(b) in Scotland or Northern Ireland, to imprisonment for a term not exceeding 6 months, to a fine not exceeding level 5 on the standard scale or to both.

(3) In relation to an offence committed before section 281(5) of the Criminal Justice Act 2003 comes into force, the reference in subsection (2)(a) to 51 weeks is to be read as a reference to 6 months.

(4) In this section "motor vehicle" and "road"—

(a) in relation to England and Wales and Scotland, have the same meanings as in the Road Traffic Act 1988;

(b) in relation to Northern Ireland, have the same meanings as in the Road Traffic (Northern Ireland) Order 1995 (SI 1995/2994 (NI 18)).

(5) For the purposes of this section a person is not lawfully resident in the United Kingdom if the person requires leave to enter or remain in the United Kingdom but does not have it.

24D Detention of motor vehicles

(1) If a person ("P") has been arrested for an offence under section 24C committed in England and Wales or Northern Ireland, a senior officer or a constable may detain a relevant vehicle.

(2) Subject to regulations under subsection (8), a vehicle detained under subsection (1) must be released—

(a) when a decision is taken not to charge P with the offence, or

(b) if P is charged with the offence—

(i) when P is acquitted, the charge against P is dismissed or the proceedings are discontinued, or

(ii) if P is convicted, when the court decides not to order forfeiture of the vehicle.

(3) If a person ("P") has been arrested for an offence under section 24C committed in Scotland, a senior officer or a constable may detain a relevant vehicle.

(4) Subject to regulations under subsection (8) a vehicle detained under subsection (3) must be released—

(a) when a decision is taken not to institute criminal proceedings against P for the offence, or

(b) if criminal proceedings are instituted against P for the offence—

(i) when P is acquitted or, under section 147 of the Criminal Procedure (Scotland) Act 1995, liberated or the trial diet is deserted simpliciter, or

(ii) if P is convicted, when the court decides not to order forfeiture of the vehicle.

(5) For the purposes of subsection (4) criminal proceedings are instituted against a person ("P") at whichever is the earliest of P's first appearance before the sheriff or the service on P of a complaint.

(6) A power in subsection (1) or (3) may be exercised by a senior officer or constable at any place at which the senior officer or constable is lawfully present.

(7) A vehicle is a relevant vehicle in relation to P if the officer or constable concerned has reasonable grounds for believing it was used in the commission by P of an offence under section 24C.

(8) The Secretary of State may by regulations make provision about the release of a vehicle detained under subsection (1) or (3).

(9) Regulations under subsection (8) may in particular make provision—

- (a) for the release of a vehicle before the time mentioned in subsection (2) or (4);
- (b) about the procedure by which a person may seek to have a vehicle released before or after that time;
- (c) about the persons to whom a vehicle may or must be released before or after that time;
- (d) prescribing conditions to be met before a vehicle may be released before or after that time (including a condition requiring the payment of costs in relation to detention of the vehicle and any application for its release);
- (e) as to the destination of payments made in compliance with such a condition;
- (f) enabling a person specified in the regulations to waive compliance with such a condition;
- (g) as to the disposal of a vehicle in a case where such a condition is not met;
- (h) as to the destination of the proceeds arising from the disposal of a vehicle in such a case.

(10) Regulations under subsection (8)—

- (a) are to be made by statutory instrument;
- (b) may make different provision for different cases;
- (c) may make incidental, supplementary, consequential, transitional, transitory or saving provision.

(11) A statutory instrument containing regulations under subsection (8) is subject to annulment in pursuance of a resolution of either House of Parliament.

(12) In this section "senior officer" means an immigration officer not below the rank of chief immigration officer.

24E Powers to enter premises to detain motor vehicle

(1) A senior officer or a constable may enter and search any premises for the purposes of detaining a vehicle under section 24D.

(2) The power in subsection (1) may be exercised—

- (a) only to the extent that it is reasonably required for that purpose, and
- (b) only if the senior officer or constable knows that a vehicle which may be detained under section 24D is to be found on the premises.

(3) The power in subsection (1) may be exercised—

- (a) by a senior officer ("S") only if S produces identification showing that S is an immigration officer (whether or not S is asked to do so);
- (b) by a constable ("C") only if C produces identification showing that C is a constable (whether or not C is asked to do so).

(4) Subsection (5) applies if, on an application by a senior officer or constable, a justice of the peace is satisfied that there are reasonable grounds for suspecting

that a vehicle which may be detained under section 24D may be found on premises mentioned in subsection (6).

(5) The justice of the peace may issue a warrant authorising any senior officer or constable to enter, if need be by force, the premises for the purpose of searching for and detaining the vehicle.

(6) The premises referred to in subsection (4) are—

(a) one or more sets of premises specified in the application, or

(b) subject to subsection (10), any premises occupied or controlled by a person specified in the application, including such sets of premises as are so specified (in which case the application is for an "all premises warrant").

(7) If the application is for an all premises warrant, the justice of the peace must also be satisfied—

(a) that there are reasonable grounds for believing that it is necessary to search premises occupied or controlled by the person in question which are not specified in the application in order to find the vehicle, and

(b) that it is not reasonably practicable to specify in the application all the premises which the person occupies or controls and which might need to be searched.

(8) Subject to subsection (10), the warrant may authorise entry to and search of premises on more than one occasion if, on the application, the justice of the peace is satisfied that it is necessary to authorise multiple entries in order to achieve the purpose for which the justice issues the warrant.

(9) If it authorises multiple entries, the number of entries authorised may be unlimited, or limited to a maximum.

(10) A justice of the peace in Scotland may not issue—

(a) an all premises warrant under this section, or

(b) a warrant under this section authorising multiple entries.

(11) In the application of this section to Scotland, references to a justice of the peace are to be read as references to the sheriff or a justice of the peace.

(12) In this section "senior officer" means an immigration officer not below the rank of chief immigration officer.

24F Orders following conviction of offence under section 24C

(1) If a person is convicted of an offence under section 24C, the court may order the forfeiture of the vehicle used in the commission of the offence.

(2) Where a person who claims to have an interest in the vehicle applies to the court to make representations on the question of forfeiture, the court may not make an order under this section in respect of the vehicle unless the person has been given an opportunity to make representations.

(3) For the purposes of subsection (2) the persons who have an interest in a vehicle include—

(a) a person who owns it,

(b) the person in whose name the vehicle is registered under the Vehicle Excise and Registration Act 1994, and

(c) a person who is in possession of it under a hire purchase agreement (or, in the case of a detained vehicle, was in possession of it under a hire purchase agreement immediately before its detention).

(4) The Secretary of State may by regulations make provision about—

(a) the disposal of a vehicle forfeited under this section;

(b) the destination of the proceeds arising from the disposal of such a vehicle.

(5) Regulations under subsection (4)—

(a) are to be made by statutory instrument;

(b) may make different provision for different cases;

(c) may make incidental, supplementary, consequential, transitional, transitory or saving provision.

(6) A statutory instrument containing regulations under subsection (4) is subject to annulment in pursuance of a resolution of either House of Parliament."

(3) In section 28A(3)(a) (arrest without warrant) before "25" insert "24C,".

(4) In section 28B(5) (search and arrest by warrant: relevant offences) before "26A" insert "24C,".

(5) In section 28CA(1) (business premises: entry to arrest) for the "or" at the end of paragraph (b) substitute—

"(bb) for an offence under section 24C, or".

(6) In section 28D(4) (entry and search of premises: relevant offences) before "25" insert "24C,".

(7) In section 16(2A)(b) of the Police and Criminal Evidence Act 1984 (powers of persons accompanying constables in execution of warrants) after "seizure" insert "or detention".

(8) In Article 18(2A)(b) of the Police and Criminal Evidence (Northern Ireland) Order 1989 (SI 1989/1341 (NI 12)) (powers of persons accompanying constables in execution of warrants) after "seizure" insert "or detention".

(9) In section 146(2) of the Immigration and Asylum Act 1999 (use of reasonable force) before paragraph (a) insert—

"(za) section 24E(1) (powers to enter premises to detain motor vehicle) of the 1971 Act,".

Bank accounts

45 Bank accounts

(1) Schedule 7 (bank accounts) has effect.

(2) Before the end of the period mentioned in subsection (3), the Secretary of State must—

(a) review the operation of sections 40A to 40G of the Immigration Act 2014 (inserted by Schedule 7),

(b) prepare a report of the review, and
(c) lay a copy of the report before Parliament.

(3) The period referred to in subsection (2) is the period of 5 years beginning with the day on which Schedule 7 comes fully into force.

PART 3

ENFORCEMENT

Powers of immigration officers etc

46 Powers in connection with examination, detention and removal

(1) Schedule 2 to the Immigration Act 1971 (administrative provisions as to control on entry etc) is amended as follows.

(2) In paragraph 2(1) (examination by immigration officers) at the end of paragraph (c) insert "; and

(d) whether, if he has been given leave which is still in force, his leave should be curtailed."

(3) After paragraph 15 insert—

"15A Search of premises in connection with removal

15A (1) This paragraph applies if—

(a) an immigration officer is lawfully on any premises, and
(b) a person who is liable to be detained under paragraph 16(2) is on the premises.

(2) The immigration officer may search the premises for documents which—

(a) relate to the person, and
(b) may be evidence for a ground on which the person's leave to enter or remain in the United Kingdom may be curtailed.

(3) The power may be exercised—

(a) only if the immigration officer has reasonable grounds for believing there are documents within sub-paragraph (2) on the premises, and
(b) only to the extent that it is reasonably required for the purpose of discovering such documents.

(4) An immigration officer searching premises under this paragraph may seize any document the officer finds which the officer has reasonable grounds for believing is a document within sub-paragraph (2).

(5) Sub-paragraph (6) applies where—

(a) an immigration officer is searching premises under this paragraph, and

(b) any document the officer has reasonable grounds for believing is a document within sub-paragraph (2) is stored in any electronic form and is accessible from the premises.

(6) The immigration officer may require the document to be produced in a form in which it can be taken away and in which it is visible and legible or from which it can readily be produced in a visible and legible form.

(7) If a requirement under sub-paragraph (6) is not complied with or a document to which that sub-paragraph applies cannot be produced in a form of the kind mentioned in that sub-paragraph, the immigration officer may seize the device or medium on which it is stored.

(8) But sub-paragraphs (4) to (7) do not apply to a document which the immigration officer has reasonable grounds for believing is an item subject to legal privilege.

(9) An immigration officer may retain a document seized under this paragraph while—

(a) the person to whom the document relates is liable to be detained under paragraph 16(2), and

(b) the document falls within sub-paragraph (2)(b).

(10) But a document may not be retained for the purpose mentioned in sub-paragraph (9) if a photograph or copy would be sufficient for that purpose."

(4) In paragraph 25A (entry and search of premises where person arrested or detained under Schedule 2)—

(a) after sub-paragraph (7) insert—

"(7A) Sub-paragraph (7B) applies where—

(a) an officer is searching premises under this paragraph, and

(b) any document the officer has reasonable grounds for believing is a relevant document is stored in any electronic form and is accessible from the premises.

(7B) The officer may require the document to be produced in a form in which it can be taken away and in which it is visible and legible or from which it can readily be produced in a visible and legible form.

(7C) If a requirement under sub-paragraph (7B) is not complied with or a document to which that sub-paragraph applies cannot be produced in a form of the kind mentioned in that sub-paragraph, the officer may seize the device or medium on which it is stored.",

(b) in sub-paragraph (8) for "sub-paragraph (7)(a) does" substitute "sub-paragraphs (7) to (7C) do", and

(c) in sub-paragraph (8A) for "sub-paragraph (7)" substitute "this paragraph".

(5) In paragraph 25B (search of person arrested under Schedule 2) after sub-paragraph (8) insert—

"(8A) Sub-paragraph (8B) applies where—

(a) an officer is searching a person under this paragraph, and

(b) any document the officer has reasonable grounds for believing is a document within sub-paragraph (3)(b) is stored in any electronic form on a device or medium found on the person.

(8B) The officer may require the document to be produced in a form in which it can be taken away and in which it is visible and legible or from which it can readily be produced in a visible and legible form.

(8C) If a requirement under sub-paragraph (8B) is not complied with or a document to which that sub-paragraph applies cannot be produced in a form of the kind mentioned in that sub-paragraph, the officer may seize the device or medium on which it is stored.

(8D) Sub-paragraphs (8B) and (8C) do not apply to a document which the officer has reasonable grounds for believing is an item subject to legal privilege."

47 Search of premises in connection with imposition of civil penalty

(1) This section applies if an immigration officer is lawfully on any premises.

(2) The immigration officer may search the premises for documents which might be of assistance in determining whether a person is liable to the imposition of a penalty under—

(a) section 15 of the Immigration, Asylum and Nationality Act 2006 (penalty for employing illegal worker etc), or

(b) section 23 or 25 of the Immigration Act 2014 (penalty for leasing premises to disqualified person etc).

(3) The power may be exercised—

(a) only if the immigration officer has reasonable grounds for believing there are documents within subsection (2) on the premises, and

(b) only to the extent that it is reasonably required for the purpose of discovering such documents.

(4) An immigration officer searching premises under this section may seize any document the officer finds which the officer has reasonable grounds for believing is a document within subsection (2).

(5) Subsection (6) applies where—

(a) an immigration officer is searching premises under this section, and

(b) any document the officer has reasonable grounds for believing is a document within subsection (2) is stored in any electronic form and is accessible from the premises.

(6) The immigration officer may require the document to be produced in a form in which it can be taken away and in which it is visible and legible or from which it can readily be produced in a visible and legible form.

(7) If a requirement under subsection (6) is not complied with or a document to which that subsection applies cannot be produced in a form of the kind mentioned in that subsection, the immigration officer may seize the device or medium on which it is stored.

(8) But subsections (4) to (7) do not apply to a document or item which the immigration officer has reasonable grounds for believing is an item subject to legal privilege.

(9) An immigration officer may retain a document or item seized under this section while the officer has reasonable grounds for believing that the document may be required—

(a) for the purposes of determining whether a person is liable to the imposition of a penalty under a provision mentioned in subsection (2),

(b) for the purposes of any objection relating to the imposition of such a penalty, or

(c) for the purposes of any appeal or other legal proceedings relating to the imposition of such a penalty.

(10) But a document or item may not be retained for a purpose mentioned in subsection (9) if a photograph or copy would be sufficient for that purpose.

(11) Section 28I of the Immigration Act 1971 (seized material: access and copying) applies to a document seized and retained under this section as it applies to anything seized and retained under Part 3 of that Act.

48 Seizure and retention in relation to offences

(1) This section applies if an immigration officer is lawfully on any premises.

(2) The immigration officer may seize anything which the officer finds in the course of exercising a function under the Immigration Acts if the officer has reasonable grounds for believing—

(a) that it has been obtained in consequence of the commission of an offence, and

(b) that it is necessary to seize it in order to prevent it being concealed, lost, damaged, altered or destroyed.

(3) The immigration officer may seize anything which the officer finds in the course of exercising a function under the Immigration Acts if the officer has reasonable grounds for believing—

(a) that it is evidence in relation to an offence, and

(b) that it is necessary to seize it in order to prevent the evidence being concealed, lost, altered or destroyed.

(4) The immigration officer may require any information which is stored in any electronic form and is accessible from the premises to be produced if the officer has reasonable grounds for believing—

(a) that—

(i) it is evidence in relation to an offence, or

(ii) it has been obtained in consequence of the commission of an offence, and

(b) that it is necessary to seize it in order to prevent it being concealed, lost, tampered with or destroyed.

(5) The reference in subsection (4) to information which is stored in any electronic form being produced is to such information being produced in a form—

(a) in which it can be taken away, and

(b) in which it is visible and legible or from which it can readily be produced in a visible and legible form.

(6) This section does not authorise an immigration officer to seize an item which the officer has reasonable grounds for believing is an item subject to legal privilege.

(7) Anything seized by an immigration officer under this section which relates to an immigration offence may be retained so long as is necessary in all the circumstances and in particular—

(a) may be retained, except as provided for by subsection (8)—

(i) for use as evidence at a trial for an offence, or

(ii) for forensic examination or for investigation in connection with an offence, and

(b) may be retained in order to establish its lawful owner, where there are reasonable grounds for believing that it has been obtained in consequence of the commission of an offence.

(8) Nothing may be retained for a purpose mentioned in subsection (7)(a) if a photograph or copy would be sufficient for that purpose.

(9) Section 28I of the Immigration Act 1971 (seized material: access and copying) applies to anything seized and retained under this section which relates to an immigration offence as it applies to anything seized and retained by an immigration officer under Part 3 of that Act.

(10) This section does not apply in relation to anything which may be seized by an immigration officer under—

(a) section 19 of the Police and Criminal Evidence Act 1984 as applied by an order under section 23 of the Borders, Citizenship and Immigration Act 2009, or

(b) Article 21 of the Police and Criminal Evidence (Northern Ireland) Order 1989 (SI 1989/1341 (NI 12) as applied by that section.

(11) In this section and section 49 "immigration offence" means an offence which relates to an immigration or nationality matter.

49 Duty to pass on items seized under section 48

(1) This section applies if an immigration officer exercises—

(a) the power under section 48 to seize or take away an item on the basis that the item or information contained in it has been obtained in consequence of the commission of, or is evidence in relation to, an offence other than an immigration offence (a "relevant offence"), or

(b) a power to that effect in Part 3 of the Immigration Act 1971 as applied by section 14(3) of the Asylum and Immigration (Treatment of Claimants etc) Act 2004.

(2) Subject to subsection (3), the immigration officer must, as soon as is reasonably practicable after the power is exercised, notify a person who the immigration officer thinks has functions in relation to the investigation of the relevant offence.

(3) If the immigration officer has reasonable grounds for believing that the item referred to in subsection (1) has also been obtained in consequence of the commission of, or is evidence in relation to, an immigration offence, the immigration officer may notify a person who the immigration officer thinks has functions in relation to the investigation of the relevant offence.

(4) A person notified under this section of the exercise of a power mentioned in subsection (1) in relation to an item must, as soon as is reasonably practicable after

being so notified, inform the immigration officer whether the person will accept the item.

(5) The person may inform the immigration officer that the person will not accept the item only if—

(a) the person does not think the item or information contained in it has been obtained in consequence of the commission of, or is evidence in relation to, an offence,

(b) the person does not have functions in relation to the investigation of the relevant offence, or

(c) the person thinks that it would be more appropriate for the relevant offence to be investigated by another person with such functions.

(6) If the person informs the immigration officer that the person will accept the item, the immigration officer must give it to the person as soon as is reasonably practicable.

(7) Once the item has been given as mentioned in subsection (6), any provision of an enactment which applies to items seized or taken away by the person applies to the item as if it had been seized or taken away by the person for the purposes of the investigation of the relevant offence.

(8) If the person informs the immigration officer that the person will not accept the item because subsection (5)(a) applies, the immigration officer must, as soon as is reasonably practicable, return the item in accordance with subsection (10).

(9) If the person informs the immigration officer that the person will not accept the item because subsection (5)(b) or (c) applies, the immigration officer must, as soon as is reasonably practicable—

(a) notify the exercise of a power mentioned in subsection (1) in relation to the item to another person (if any) who the immigration officer thinks has functions in relation to the investigation of the relevant offence, or

(b) if there is no such person, return the item in accordance with subsection (10).

(10) An item which must be returned in accordance with this subsection must be returned—

(a) to the person from whom it was seized, or

(b) if there is no such person, to the place from which it was seized or taken away.

(11) Where an item to which this section applies or information contained in such an item has been obtained in consequence of the commission of, or is evidence in relation to, more than one offence, references in this section to the relevant offence are to any of those offences.

(12) A function conferred or imposed by this section on an immigration officer may be exercised by any other immigration officer.

(13) In this section "enactment" includes—

(a) an enactment contained in subordinate legislation within the meaning of the Interpretation Act 1978,

(b) an enactment contained in, or in an instrument made under, an Act of the Scottish Parliament,

(c) an enactment contained in, or in an instrument made under, a Measure or Act of the National Assembly for Wales, and

(d) an enactment contained in, or in an instrument made under, Northern Ireland legislation.

50 Retention of things seized under Part 3 of the Immigration Act 1971

After section 28H of the Immigration Act 1971 insert—

"28ZI Retention of seized material

(1) This section applies to anything seized by an immigration officer under this Part for the purposes of the investigation of an offence or on the basis that it may be evidence relating to an offence.

(2) Anything seized as mentioned in subsection (1) may be retained so long as is necessary in all the circumstances and in particular—

(a) may be retained, except as provided for by subsection (3)—

(i) for use as evidence at a trial for an offence, or

(ii) for forensic examination or for investigation in connection with an offence, and

(b) may be retained in order to establish its lawful owner, where there are reasonable grounds for believing that it has been obtained in consequence of the commission of an offence.

(3) Nothing may be retained for a purpose mentioned in subsection (2)(a) if a photograph or copy would be sufficient for that purpose."

51 Search for nationality documents by detainee custody officers etc

(1) The Secretary of State may direct a detainee custody officer, prison officer or prisoner custody officer to exercise any of the powers in subsection (6) in relation to—

(a) a detained person who is detained in a removal centre, prison or young offender institution, or

(b) a person who is detained in a short-term holding facility.

(2) The Secretary of State may direct a prison officer or prisoner custody officer to exercise any of the powers in subsection (6) in relation to a person detained in a prison or young offender institution—

(a) who has been recommended for deportation by a court under section 3(6) of the Immigration Act 1971,

(b) in respect of whom the Secretary of State has made a deportation order under section 5(1) of that Act,

(c) to whom a notice has been given in accordance with regulations under section 105 of the Nationality, Immigration and Asylum Act 2002 (notice of decision) of a decision to make a deportation order against that person, or

(d) in respect of whom the Secretary of State must make, or has made, a deportation order under section 32(5) of the UK Borders Act 2007.

(3) In this section and section 52 "relevant officer" means a detainee custody officer, prison officer or prisoner custody officer.

(4) The Secretary of State may give a direction in relation to a person detained as mentioned in subsection (1) or (2) only if the Secretary of State has reasonable grounds to believe a relevant nationality document will be found if a power in subsection (6) is exercised in relation to the person.

(5) A relevant officer to whom a direction is given under subsection (1) or (2) must (if able to do so) comply with it.

(6) The powers referred to in subsections (1), (2) and (4) are—

(a) to require the person to hand over to the relevant officer all relevant nationality documents in his or her possession,

(b) to search for such documents and to take possession of any that the relevant officer finds,

(c) to inspect any relevant nationality documents obtained in the course of the exercise of a power in paragraph (a) or (b), and

(d) to seize and retain any such documents so obtained.

(7) The power in subsection (6)(b) is a power to search any of the following—

(a) the person;

(b) anything the person has with him or her;

(c) the person's accommodation in the removal centre, short-term holding facility, prison or young offender institution;

(d) any item of the person's property in the removal centre, short-term holding facility, prison or young offender institution.

(8) A full search may be carried out under subsection (7)(a); but such a search may not be carried out in the presence of—

(a) another person detained as mentioned in subsection (1) or (2), or

(b) a person of the opposite sex.

(9) An intimate search may not be carried out under subsection (7)(a).

(10) A relevant officer may if necessary use reasonable force for the purposes of exercising a power in subsection (6)(a) or (b).

(11) A relevant officer must pass a relevant nationality document seized and retained under subsection (6)(d) to the Secretary of State as soon as is reasonably practicable.

(12) The Secretary of State may retain a relevant nationality document which comes into the Secretary of State's possession under subsection (11) while the Secretary of State suspects that—

(a) a person to whom the document relates may be liable to removal from the United Kingdom in accordance with a provision of the Immigration Acts, and

(b) retention of the document may facilitate the removal.

(13) If subsection (12) does not apply to a document which comes into the Secretary of State's possession under this section, the Secretary of State may—

(a) arrange for the document to be returned in accordance with subsection (14), or

(b) if the Secretary of State thinks that it would not be appropriate to return the document, dispose of the document in such manner as the Secretary of State thinks appropriate.

(14) A document which is required to be returned in accordance with this subsection must be returned to—

(a) the person who was previously in possession of it, or

(b) if it was not found in the possession of a person, the location in which it was found.

(15) In this section and section 52—

"full search" means a search which involves the removal of an item of clothing which—

(a) is being worn wholly or partly on the trunk, and

(b) is being so worn either next to the skin or next to an article of underwear;

"intimate search" means a search which consists of a physical examination of a person's body orifices other than the mouth;

"nationality document" means a document which might—

(a) establish a person's identity, nationality or citizenship, or

(b) indicate the place from which a person has travelled to the United Kingdom or to which a person is proposing to go.

(16) For the purposes of this section and section 52 a nationality document is "relevant" if it relates to a person who is liable to removal from the United Kingdom in accordance with a provision of the Immigration Acts.

(17) In this section the following expressions have the same meaning as in Part 8 of the Immigration and Asylum Act 1999 (see section 147)—

"detained person";

"detainee custody officer";

"prisoner custody officer";

"removal centre";

"short-term holding facility".

52 Seizure of nationality documents by detainee custody officers etc

(1) A relevant officer may seize a nationality document which the relevant officer finds in the course of the exercise of a power to search other than one conferred by section 51.

(2) Where a relevant officer seizes a nationality document under subsection (1), the relevant officer—

(a) must seek the consent of the Secretary of State to retain the document, and

(b) if the relevant officer obtains the Secretary of State's consent, must pass the document to the Secretary of State as soon as is practicable.

(3) The Secretary of State may give consent under subsection (2) only if the Secretary of State has reasonable grounds to believe that—

(a) the document is a relevant nationality document, and

(b) the document may facilitate the removal of the person to whom it relates from the United Kingdom in accordance with a provision of the Immigration Acts.

(4) If the Secretary of State does not give consent under subsection (2), the Secretary of State must—

(a) direct the relevant officer to return the document as mentioned in subsection (5), or

(b) if the Secretary of State thinks that it would not be appropriate to return the document, direct the relevant officer to dispose of the document in such manner as the Secretary of State may direct.

(5) A document which is required to be returned in accordance with this subsection must be returned to—

(a) the person who was previously in possession of it, or

(b) if it was not found in the possession of a person, the location in which it was found.

(6) The Secretary of State may retain a relevant nationality document which comes into the Secretary of State's possession under this section while the Secretary of State suspects that—

(a) a person to whom the document relates may be liable to removal from the United Kingdom in accordance with a provision of the Immigration Acts, and

(b) retention of the document may facilitate the removal.

(7) If subsection (6) does not apply to a document which comes into the Secretary of State's possession under this section, the Secretary of State may—

(a) arrange for the document to be returned in accordance with subsection (5), or

(b) if the Secretary of State thinks that it would not be appropriate to return the document, dispose of the document in such manner as the Secretary of State thinks appropriate.

53 Amendments relating to sections 51 and 52

(1) Schedule 11 to the Immigration and Asylum Act 1999 (detainee custody officers) is amended as follows.

(2) In paragraph 4 (offence of assaulting detainee custody officer)—

(a) omit the "or" at the end of paragraph (b), and

(b) at the end of paragraph (c) insert "or

(d) performing functions under section 51 of the Immigration Act 2016 (search for nationality documents),".

(3) In paragraph 5 (offence of obstructing detainee custody officer)—

(a) omit the "or" at the end of paragraph (b), and

(b) at the end of paragraph (c) insert "or

(d) performing functions under section 51 of the Immigration Act 2016 (search for nationality documents),".

(4) After paragraph 8 insert—

"9 A reference in paragraph 4(d) or 5(d) to a detainee custody officer performing functions under section 51 of the Immigration Act 2016 includes a reference to a prison officer or prisoner custody officer performing such functions."

54 Amendments to search warrant provisions

Schedule 8 (amendments to search warrant provisions) has effect.

55 Supply of information to Secretary of State

(1) Section 20 of the Immigration and Asylum Act 1999 (supply of information to Secretary of State) is amended in accordance with subsections (2) to (10).

(2) For the heading substitute "Power to supply information etc to Secretary of State".

(3) In subsection (1) for paragraphs (a) to (f) substitute—

"(a) a public authority, or

(b) any specified person, for purposes specified in relation to that person."

(4) In subsection (1A) in each of paragraphs (a) and (b) for "a person listed in subsection (1) or someone acting on his behalf" substitute "a public authority or someone acting on behalf of a public authority".

(5) After subsection (1A) insert—

"(1B) This section does not apply to—

(a) information which is held by the Crown Prosecution Service, or

(b) a document or article which comes into the possession of, or is discovered by, the Crown Prosecution Service, or someone acting on behalf of the Crown Prosecution Service,

if section 40 of the UK Borders Act 2007 applies to the information, document or article."

(6) After subsection (2A) insert—

"(2B) Subsection (2A)(a) does not affect any other power of the Secretary of State to retain a document or article."

(7) In subsection (3) after paragraph (d) insert—

"(da) anything else that is done in connection with the exercise of a function under any of the Immigration Acts;".

(8) After subsection (3) insert—

"(3A) Public authority" means a person with functions of a public nature but does not include—

(a) Her Majesty's Revenue and Customs,

(b) either House of Parliament or a person exercising functions in connection with proceedings in Parliament,

(c) the Scottish Parliament or a person exercising functions in connection with proceedings in the Scottish Parliament,

(d) the National Assembly for Wales or a person exercising functions in connection with proceedings in that Assembly, or

(e) the Northern Ireland Assembly or a person exercising functions in connection with proceedings in that Assembly."

(9) Omit subsection (4).

(10) After subsection (6) insert—

"(7) Nothing in this section authorises information, a document or an article to be supplied if to do so would contravene a restriction on the disclosure of information (however imposed)."

(11) After section 20 of the Immigration and Asylum Act 1999 insert—

"20A Duty to supply nationality documents to Secretary of State

(1) This section applies to a nationality document which the Secretary of State has reasonable grounds for believing is lawfully in the possession of a person listed in Schedule A1.

(2) The Secretary of State may direct the person to supply the document to the Secretary of State if the Secretary of State suspects that—

   (a) a person to whom the document relates may be liable to removal from the United Kingdom in accordance with a provision of the Immigration Acts, and

   (b) the document may facilitate the removal.

(3) A person to whom a direction is given must, as soon as is practicable, supply the document to the Secretary of State.

(4) If the document was originally created in hard copy form and the person possesses the original document, it must be supplied to the Secretary of State unless it is required by the person for the performance of any of the person's functions.

(5) If the original document is required by the person for the performance of any of the person's functions—

   (a) the person must, as soon as is practicable, supply a copy of the document to the Secretary of State, and

   (b) if subsequently the person no longer requires the original document, the person must supply it to the Secretary of State as soon as is practicable after it is no longer required.

(6) Subsection (5)(b) does not apply if the Secretary of State notifies the person that the original document is no longer required.

(7) If subsection (5) applies the person may make a copy of the original document before supplying it to the Secretary of State.

(8) The Secretary of State may retain a nationality document supplied under this section while the Secretary of State suspects that—

   (a) a person to whom the document relates may be liable to removal from the United Kingdom in accordance with a provision of the Immigration Acts, and

   (b) retention of the document may facilitate the removal.

(9) Subsection (8) does not affect any other power of the Secretary of State to retain a document.

(10) The Secretary of State may dispose of a nationality document supplied under this section in such manner as the Secretary of State thinks appropriate.

(11) Nothing in this section authorises or requires a document to be supplied if to do so would contravene a restriction on the disclosure of information (however imposed).

(12) The Secretary of State may by regulations amend Schedule A1 so as to add, modify or remove a reference to a person or description of person.

(13) Regulations under subsection (12) may not amend Schedule A1 so as to apply this section to—

(a) either House of Parliament or a person exercising functions in connection with proceedings in Parliament,

(b) the Scottish Parliament or a person exercising functions in connection with proceedings in the Scottish Parliament,

(c) the National Assembly for Wales or a person exercising functions in connection with proceedings in that Assembly, or

(d) the Northern Ireland Assembly or a person exercising functions in connection with proceedings in that Assembly.

(14) In this section "nationality document" means a document which might—

(a) establish a person's identity, nationality or citizenship, or

(b) indicate the place from which a person has travelled to the United Kingdom or to which a person is proposing to go."

(12) In section 166 of the Immigration and Asylum Act 1999 (regulations and orders)—

(a) after subsection (5) insert—

"(5A) No regulations under section 20A(12) which amend Schedule A1 so as to—

(a) add a reference to a person or description of person, or

(b) modify a reference to a person or description of person otherwise than in consequence of a change of name or transfer of functions,

are to be made unless a draft of the regulations has been laid before Parliament and approved by a resolution of each House.", and

(b) in subsection (6), before the "or" at the end of paragraph (a) insert—

"(ab) under section 20A(12) and which falls within subsection (5A),".

(13) Before Schedule 1 to the Immigration and Asylum Act 1999 insert the Schedule A1 set out in Schedule 9.

56 Detention etc. by immigration officers in Scotland

(1) The Criminal Law (Consolidation) (Scotland) Act 1995 is amended as follows.

(2) In section 24A (extension of period of detention under section 24) for subsection (7) substitute—

"(7) In this section and section 24B, "custody review officer" means—

(a) an officer who—

(i) is of a rank at least equivalent to that of police inspector, and

(ii) has not been involved in the investigation in connection with which the person is detained, or

(b) in relation to the detention of a person under section 24 by an immigration officer, a constable—

(i) of the rank of inspector or above, and

(ii) who has not been involved in the investigation in connection with which the person is detained."

(3) In section 26A(2) (power of arrest of authorised immigration officers) omit "or immigration enforcement offence".

(4) Section 26B(1) (interpretation of Part 3) is amended as follows.

(5) In the definition of "immigration offence"—

(a) after "means" insert "— (a)", and

(b) at the end of paragraph (a) insert ", or

(b) (insofar as it is not an offence within paragraph (a)) an offence under the Immigration Acts or in relation to which a power of arrest is conferred on an immigration officer by the Immigration Acts;".

(6) Omit the definition of "immigration enforcement offence".

57 Powers to take fingerprints etc. from dependants

(1) Section 141 of the Immigration and Asylum Act 1999 (powers to take fingerprints from certain persons and their dependants) is amended as follows.

(2) In subsection (7) for paragraph (f) substitute—

"(f) any person ("F") who is—

(i) a member of the family of a person within any of paragraphs (a), (b) or (ca) to (e), or

(ii) a dependant of a person within paragraph (c)(i)."

(3) In subsection (8)(f) after "person" insert "of whose family he is a member or".

(4) In subsection (9)(f) after "person" insert "of whose family he is a member or".

(5) After subsection (13) insert—

"(13A) For the purposes of subsection (7)(f)(i), a person is a member of the family of another person ("P") if—

(a) the person is—

(i) P's partner,

(ii) P's child, or a child living in the same household as P in circumstances where P has care of the child,

(iii) in a case where P is a child, P's parent, or

(iv) an adult dependant relative of P, and

(b) the person does not have a right of abode in the United Kingdom or indefinite leave to enter or remain in the United Kingdom.

(13B) In subsection (13A) "child" means a person who is under the age of 18."

(6) In subsection (14) for "(7)(f)" substitute "(7)(f)(ii)".

(7) Section 142 of the Immigration and Asylum Act 1999 (attendance for fingerprinting) is amended as follows.

(8) In subsection (2) for "a dependant of" substitute "a member of the family of, or a dependant of,".

(9) In subsection (2A) for "a dependant of" substitute "a member of the family of".

(10) Until the commencement of the repeal of section 143 of the Immigration and Asylum Act 1999 (destruction of fingerprints) by paragraph 17(2) of Schedule 9 to the Immigration Act 2014, subsection (9) of that section has effect as if after "the person" there were inserted "of whose family he is a member or".

(11) In section 144A(2) of the Immigration and Asylum Act 1999 (application of regulations about use and retention of fingerprints etc to dependants) after "the person" insert "of whose family F is a member or".

58 Interpretation of Part

(1) In this Part "immigration officer" means a person appointed by the Secretary of State as an immigration officer under paragraph 1 of Schedule 2 to the Immigration Act 1971.

(2) In this Part "premises" and "item subject to legal privilege" have the same meaning—
- (a) in relation to England and Wales, as in the Police and Criminal Evidence Act 1984;
- (b) in relation to Northern Ireland, as in the Police and Criminal Evidence (Northern Ireland) Order 1989 (SI 1989/1341 (NI 12));
- (c) in relation to Scotland, as in section 412 of the Proceeds of Crime Act 2002.

Detention and bail

59 Guidance on detention of vulnerable persons

(1) The Secretary of State must issue guidance specifying matters to be taken into account by a person to whom the guidance is addressed in determining—
- (a) whether a person ("P") would be particularly vulnerable to harm if P were to be detained or to remain in detention, and
- (b) if P is identified as being particularly vulnerable to harm in those circumstances, whether P should be detained or remain in detention.

(2) In subsection (1) "detained" means detained under—
- (a) the Immigration Act 1971,
- (b) section 62 of the Nationality, Immigration and Asylum Act 2002, or
- (c) section 36 of the UK Borders Act 2007,

and "detention" is to be construed accordingly.

(3) A person to whom guidance under this section is addressed must take the guidance into account.

(4) Before issuing guidance under this section the Secretary of State must lay a draft of the guidance before Parliament.

(5) Guidance under this section comes into force in accordance with regulations made by the Secretary of State.

(6) The Secretary of State may from time to time review guidance under this section and may revise and re-issue it.

(7) References in this section to guidance under this section include revised guidance.

60 Limitation on detention of pregnant women

(1) This section applies to a woman if the Secretary of State is satisfied that the woman is pregnant.

(2) A woman to whom this section applies may not be detained under a relevant detention power unless the Secretary of State is satisfied that—

(a) the woman will shortly be removed from the United Kingdom, or

(b) there are exceptional circumstances which justify the detention.

(3) In determining whether to authorise the detention under a relevant detention power of a woman to whom this section applies, a person who, apart from this section, has power to authorise the detention must have regard to the woman's welfare.

(4) A woman to whom this section applies may not be detained under a relevant detention power for a period of—

(a) more than 72 hours from the relevant time, or

(b) more than seven days from the relevant time, in a case where the longer period of detention is authorised personally by a Minister of the Crown (within the meaning of the Ministers of the Crown Act 1975).

(5) In subsection (4) "the relevant time" means the later of—

(a) the time at which the Secretary of State is first satisfied that the woman is pregnant, and

(b) the time at which the detention begins.

(6) A woman to whom this section applies who has been released following detention under a relevant detention power may be detained again under such a power in accordance with this section.

(7) This section does not apply to the detention under paragraph 16(2) of Schedule 2 to the Immigration Act 1971 of an unaccompanied child to whom paragraph 18B of that Schedule applies.

(8) In this section—

"relevant detention power" means a power to detain under—

(a) paragraph 16(2) of Schedule 2 to the Immigration Act 1971 (detention of persons liable to examination or removal),

(b) paragraph 2(1), (2) or (3) of Schedule 3 to that Act (detention pending deportation),

(c) section 62 of the Nationality, Immigration and Asylum Act 2002 (detention of persons liable to examination or removal), or

(d) section 36(1) of the UK Borders Act 2007 (detention pending deportation);

"woman" means a female of any age.

(9) The Immigration Act 1971 is amended in accordance with subsections (10) and (11).

(10) In paragraph 16 of Schedule 2 (detention of persons liable to examination or removal) after sub-paragraph (2A) insert—

"(2B) The detention under sub-paragraph (2) of a person to whom section 60 (limitation on detention of pregnant women) of the Immigration Act 2016 applies is subject to that section."

(11) In paragraph 2 of Schedule 3 (detention or control pending deportation) after sub-paragraph (4) insert—

"(4ZA) The detention under sub-paragraph (1), (2) or (3) of a person to whom section 60 (limitation on detention of pregnant women) of the Immigration Act 2016 applies is subject to that section."

(12) In section 62 of the Nationality, Immigration and Asylum Act 2002 (detention by Secretary of State) after subsection (7) insert—

"(7A) The detention under this section of a person to whom section 60 (limitation on detention of pregnant women) of the Immigration Act 2016 applies is subject to that section."

(13) In section 36 of the UK Borders Act 2007 (detention) after subsection (2) insert—

"(2A) The detention under subsection (1) of a person to whom section 60 (limitation on detention of pregnant women) of the Immigration Act 2016 applies is subject to that section."

61 Immigration bail

(1) Schedule 10 (immigration bail) has effect.

(2) In that Schedule—

(a) Part 1 contains the main provisions about immigration bail, and

(b) Part 2 contains amendments to other Acts.

(3) A person may be released and remain on bail under paragraph 22 or 29 of Schedule 2 to the Immigration Act 1971 even if the person can no longer be detained under a provision of the Immigration Acts to which that paragraph applies, if the person is liable to detention under such a provision.

(4) The reference in subsection (3) to paragraph 22 or 29 of Schedule 2 to the Immigration Act 1971 includes that paragraph as applied by any other provision of the Immigration Acts.

(5) Subsections (3) and (4) are to be treated as always having had effect.

(6) Subsections (3) to (5) are repealed on the coming into force of the repeal of paragraphs 22 and 29 of Schedule 2 to the Immigration Act 1971 by paragraph 20 of Schedule 10.

Power to cancel leave

62 Power to cancel leave extended under section 3C of the Immigration Act 1971

(1) In section 3C of the Immigration Act 1971 (continuation of leave pending variation decision) after subsection (3) insert—

"(3A) Leave extended by virtue of this section may be cancelled if the applicant—

(a) has failed to comply with a condition attached to the leave, or

(b) has used or uses deception in seeking leave to remain (whether successfully or not)."

(2) In section 4(1) of that Act (persons by whom and means by which powers are to be exercised) after "conditions)" insert "or to cancel any leave under section 3C(3A)".

PART 4

APPEALS

63 Appeals within the United Kingdom: certification of human rights claims

(1) Section 94B of the Nationality, Immigration and Asylum Act 2002 (appeals from within the United Kingdom: certification of human rights claims made by persons liable to deportation) is amended in accordance with subsections (2) to (5).

(2) In the heading omit "made by persons liable to deportation".

(3) In subsection (1) omit the words from "who is liable" to the end of paragraph (b).

(4) In subsection (2) for the words from "removal" to "removed" substitute "refusing P entry to, removing P from or requiring P to leave the United Kingdom".

(5) In subsection (3) for the words from "removed" in the first place it appears to "removed" in the second place it appears substitute "refused entry to, removed from or required to leave the United Kingdom".

(6) In section 92(3)(a) of that Act (cases where human rights claim appeal must be brought from outside the United Kingdom) omit "made by persons liable to deportation".

64 Continuation of leave: repeals

(1) In the Immigration Act 1971 omit section 3D (continuation of leave following revocation).

(2) In section 2(2)(a) of the Special Immigration Appeals Commission Act 1997 (jurisdiction: appeals) omit "or 3D".

(3) In section 120(4)(b) of the Nationality, Immigration and Asylum Act 2002 (requirement to state additional grounds for application etc) omit "or 3D".

(4) In consequence of the repeals made by this section, the following are repealed—
- (a) paragraph 14(b)(i) of Schedule 1 to the Immigration, Asylum and Nationality Act 2006, and
- (b) paragraph 22 of Schedule 9 to the Immigration Act 2014.

(5) The repeals made by this section do not apply in relation to a person ("P") where—
- (a) P's leave was extended by virtue of section 3D of the Immigration Act 1971 immediately before 6 April 2015, and
- (b) immediately before the coming into force of this section an appeal by P against the variation or revocation of P's leave to enter or remain in the United Kingdom was pending within the meaning of section 104 of the Nationality, Immigration and Asylum Act 2002.

65 Deemed refusal of leave to enter: repeals

(1) In the Immigration Act 1971 omit paragraph 2A(9) of Schedule 2 (deemed refusal of leave to enter).

(2) In consequence of the repeal made by this section, paragraph 23 of Schedule 9 to the Immigration Act 2014 is repealed.

(3) The repeals made by this section do not apply in relation to a person if, immediately before the coming into force of this section, the person's appeal by virtue of paragraph 2A(9) of Schedule 2 to the Immigration Act 1971 against the cancellation of the person's leave to enter under paragraph 2A(8) of that Schedule was pending within the meaning of section 104 of the Nationality, Immigration and Asylum Act 2002.

PART 5

SUPPORT ETC FOR CERTAIN CATEGORIES OF MIGRANT

Support

66 Support for certain categories of migrant

Schedule 11 (support for certain categories of migrant) has effect.

67 Unaccompanied refugee children: relocation and support

(1) The Secretary of State must, as soon as possible after the passing of this Act, make arrangements to relocate to the United Kingdom and support a specified number of unaccompanied refugee children from other countries in Europe.

(2) The number of children to be resettled under subsection (1) shall be determined by the Government in consultation with local authorities.

(3) The relocation of children under subsection (1) shall be in addition to the resettlement of children under the Vulnerable Persons Relocation Scheme.

68 Availability of local authority support

Schedule 12 (availability of local authority support) has effect.

Transfer of responsibility for relevant children

69 Transfer of responsibility for relevant children

(1) This section applies in relation to a local authority in England ("the first authority") if—

(a) the authority has functions under any of the provisions of or made under Part 3, 4 or 5 of the Children Act 1989 (support for children and families and care, supervision and protection of children) ("the relevant provisions") in relation to a relevant child, or

(b) functions under any of the relevant provisions may be conferred on the authority in relation to a relevant child.

(2) The first authority may make arrangements with another local authority in England ("the second authority") under which—

(a) if this section applies to the authority by virtue of paragraph (a) of subsection (1), the functions mentioned in that paragraph become functions of the second authority in relation to the relevant child, and

(b) if this section applies to the authority by virtue of paragraph (b) of subsection (1), the functions mentioned in that paragraph become functions that may be conferred on the second authority in relation to the relevant child.

(3) The effect of arrangements under this section is that, from the time at which the arrangements have effect in accordance with their terms—

(a) functions under the relevant provisions cease to be functions of, and may not be conferred on, the first authority in relation to the relevant child ("C"),

(b) any of the relevant provisions which immediately before that time applied in relation to C as a result of C's connection with the first authority or the area of the first authority have effect as if C had that connection with the second authority or the area of the second authority (if that would not otherwise be the case), and

(c) C is to be treated for the purposes of the relevant provisions as if C were not and had never been ordinarily resident in the area of the first authority (if that would otherwise be the case).

(4) Subsection (3)(b) is subject to any change in C's circumstances after the time at which the arrangements have effect.

(5) Nothing in subsection (3) affects any liability of the first authority in relation to C for any act or omission of the first authority before the time at which the arrangements have effect.

(6) The Secretary of State may by regulations make further provision about the effect of arrangements under this section.

(7) Arrangements under this section may not be brought to an end by the first or second authority once they have come into effect.

(8) In this section "local authority" means a local authority within the meaning of the Children Act 1989 (see section 105(1) of that Act).

(9) In this section "relevant child" means—

(a) a person under the age of 18 who is unaccompanied and has made a protection claim which has not been determined,

(b) a person under the age of 18 who is unaccompanied and who—

(i) requires leave to enter or remain in the United Kingdom but does not have it, and

(ii) is a person of a kind specified in regulations made by the Secretary of State, or

(c) a person under the age of 18 who is unaccompanied and who—

(i) has leave to enter or remain in the United Kingdom, and

(ii) is a person of a kind specified in regulations made by the Secretary of State.

(10) The Secretary of State may by regulations make provision about the meaning of "unaccompanied" for the purposes of subsection (9).

(11) In subsection (9)—

(a) "protection claim" has the meaning given by section 82(2) of the Nationality, Immigration and Asylum Act 2002, and

(b) the reference to a protection claim having been determined is to be construed in accordance with section 94(3) of the Immigration and Asylum Act 1999.

70 Duty to provide information for the purposes of transfers of responsibility

(1) The Secretary of State may direct a local authority in England to provide information of the kind specified in subsection (2) to the Secretary of State for the purposes of enabling—

(a) arrangements to be made under section 69, or

(b) the Secretary of State to exercise functions under section 72.

(2) The information mentioned in subsection (1) is—

(a) information about the support or accommodation provided to children who are looked after by the local authority within the meaning of the Children Act 1989;

(b) such other information as may be specified in regulations made by the Secretary of State.

(3) A local authority which is directed to provide information under this section must provide it—

(a) in such form and manner as the Secretary of State may direct, and

(b) before such time or before the end of such period as the Secretary of State may direct.

(4) In this section "local authority" has the same meaning as in section 69.

71 Request for transfer of responsibility for relevant children

(1) Subsection (2) applies if—

(a) a local authority in England ("the first authority") requests another local authority in England ("the second authority") to enter into arrangements under section 69, and

(b) the second authority does not comply with the first authority's request.

(2) The Secretary of State may direct the second authority to provide the first authority and the Secretary of State with written reasons for its failure to comply with the request.

(3) In this section "local authority" has the same meaning as in section 69.

72 Scheme for transfer of responsibility for relevant children

(1) The Secretary of State may prepare a scheme for functions of, or which may be conferred on, a local authority in England ("the transferring authority") to become functions of, or functions which may be conferred on, one or more other local authorities in England (a "receiving authority") in accordance with arrangements under section 69.

(2) A scheme under this section—

(a) must specify the local authorities to which it relates, and

(b) unless it relates to all relevant children who may be the subject of arrangements under section 69 between the transferring authority and each receiving authority, must specify the relevant child or children, or descriptions of relevant children, to which it relates.

(3) The Secretary of State may direct the transferring authority and each receiving authority under a scheme under this section to comply with the scheme.

(4) A direction may not be given under subsection (3) unless the Secretary of State is satisfied that compliance with the direction will not unduly prejudice the discharge by each receiving authority of any of its functions.

(5) Before giving a direction under subsection (3) to a local authority, the Secretary of State must give the authority notice in writing of the proposed direction.

(6) The Secretary of State may not give a direction to a local authority before the end of the period of 14 days beginning with the day on which notice under subsection (5) was given to it.

(7) The local authority may make written representations to the Secretary of State about the proposed direction within that period.

(8) The Secretary of State may modify or withdraw a direction under subsection (3) by notice in writing to the local authorities to which it was given.

(9) A modification or withdrawal of a direction does not affect any arrangements made under section 69 pursuant to the direction before it was modified or withdrawn.

(10) Subsections (5) to (7) apply to the modification or withdrawal of a direction as they apply to the giving of a direction, but as if—

(a) the reference to the proposed direction were to the proposed modification or proposal to withdraw the direction, and

(b) subsection (6) permitted the Secretary of State to withdraw the direction before the end of the 14 day period with the agreement of the local authorities to which it applies.

(11) In this section "local authority" and "relevant child" have the same meanings as in section 69.

73 Extension to Wales, Scotland and Northern Ireland

(1) The Secretary of State may by regulations make such provision as the Secretary of State considers appropriate for enabling any of the provisions of sections 69 to 72 to apply in relation to Wales, Scotland or Northern Ireland.

(2) The Secretary of State may by regulations make provision which—

(a) has a similar effect to—

(i) any of the provisions mentioned in subsection (1), or

(ii) provision which may be made under section 69(6) or (10), and

(b) applies in relation to Wales, Scotland or Northern Ireland.

(3) Regulations under subsection (1) may amend, repeal or revoke any enactment (including an enactment contained in this Act).

(4) Regulations under subsection (1) or (2) may not confer functions on—

(a) the Welsh Ministers,

(b) the Scottish Ministers,

(c) the First Minister and deputy First Minister in Northern Ireland,

(d) a Northern Ireland Minister, or

(e) a Northern Ireland department.

(5) In this section "enactment" includes—

(a) an enactment contained in subordinate legislation within the meaning of the Interpretation Act 1978;

(b) an enactment contained in, or in an instrument made under, an Act or Measure of the National Assembly for Wales;

(c) an enactment contained in, or in an instrument made under, an Act of the Scottish Parliament;

(d) an enactment contained in, or in an instrument made under, Northern Ireland legislation.

PART 6

BORDER SECURITY

74 Penalties relating to airport control areas

(1) In paragraph 26 of Schedule 2 to the Immigration Act 1971 (supplementary duties of those connected with ships or aircraft or with ports) after sub-paragraph (3A) insert—

> "(4) Part 1A of this Schedule makes provision for and in connection with the imposition of a penalty for certain breaches of sub-paragraph (2) or (3)."

(2) In that Schedule after Part 1 insert the Part 1A set out in Schedule 13.

75 Maritime enforcement

Schedule 14 (maritime enforcement) has effect.

76 Persons excluded from the United Kingdom under international obligations

(1) In section 8 of the Immigration Act 1971 (exceptions for seamen, aircrews and other special cases) in subsection (5) after "expired" insert "or otherwise ceased to be in force".

(2) In section 8A of that Act (persons ceasing to be exempt) after subsection (3) insert—

> "(4) References in this section to a person who ceases to be exempt do not include a person who ceases to be exempt by virtue of section 8B(3)."

(3) Section 8B of that Act (persons excluded from the United Kingdom under international obligations) is amended as follows.

(4) In subsection (1) after paragraph (b) insert—

"(and any leave given to a person who is an excluded person is invalid)".

(5) For subsection (3) substitute—

"(3) Any exemption of a person from the provisions of this Act under section 8(1), (2) or (3) does not apply while the person is an excluded person."

(6) In subsection (4) for "a designated instrument" substitute "an instrument falling within subsection (5)".

(7) In subsection (5) for "The Secretary of State may by order designate an instrument" substitute "An instrument falls within this subsection".

(8) After subsection (5) insert—

"(5A) Subsection (1), (2) or (3) does not apply to a person if—

(a) the application of that subsection to that person would be contrary to the United Kingdom's obligations under—

(i) the Human Rights Convention (within the meaning given by section 167(1) of the Immigration and Asylum Act 1999), or

(ii) the Refugee Convention (within the meaning given by that provision), or

(b) the person has been exempted from the application of that subsection under a process applying by virtue of the instrument falling within subsection (5)."

(9) Omit subsections (6) to (8).

PART 7

LANGUAGE REQUIREMENTS FOR PUBLIC SECTOR WORKERS

77 English language requirements for public sector workers

(1) A public authority must ensure that each person who works for the public authority in a customer-facing role speaks fluent English.

(2) In determining how to comply with subsection (1), a public authority must have regard to the code of practice under section 80 that is for the time being applicable to that authority.

(3) A public authority must operate an adequate procedure for enabling complaints to be made to the authority about breaches by the authority of subsection (1) and for the consideration of such complaints.

(4) In determining whether a procedure is adequate for the purposes of subsection (3), a public authority must have regard to the code of practice under section 80 that is for the time being applicable to that authority.

(5) For the purposes of this Part a person works for a public authority if the person works—

(a) under a contract of employment with the public authority,

(b) under a contract of apprenticeship with the public authority,

(c) under a contract to do work personally with the public authority,

(d) in England and Wales or Scotland, as an agency worker within the meaning of the Agency Workers Regulations 2010 (SI 2010/93) in respect of whom the public authority is the hirer within the meaning of those regulations,

(e) in Northern Ireland, as an agency worker within the meaning of the Agency Workers Regulations (Northern Ireland) 2011 (SR 2011/350) in respect of whom the public authority is the hirer within the meaning of those regulations,

(f) for the public authority as a constable, or

(g) for the public authority in the course of Crown employment.

(6) In subsection (5) "Crown employment"—

(a) in relation to England and Wales and Scotland, has the meaning given by section 191(3) of the Employment Rights Act 1996,

(b) in relation to Northern Ireland, has the meaning given by Article 236(3) of the Employment Rights (Northern Ireland) Order 1996 (SI 1996/1919 (NI 16)), and

(c) includes service as a member of the armed forces of the Crown and employment by an association established for the purposes of Part 11 of the Reserve Forces Act 1996.

(7) References in this Part to a person who works in a customer-facing role are to a person who, as a regular and intrinsic part of the person's role, is required to speak to members of the public in English.

(8) For the purposes of this Part a person speaks fluent English if the person has a command of spoken English which is sufficient to enable the effective performance of the person's role.

(9) This section applies in relation to a person who is working in a customer-facing role for a public authority when this section comes into force as well as to a person who begins to work in such a role after that time.

(10) This section does not apply in relation to a person whose work is carried out wholly or mainly outside the United Kingdom.

78 Meaning of "public authority"

(1) Subject as follows, in this Part "public authority" means a person with functions of a public nature.

(2) A person is not a public authority for the purposes of this Part if, apart from this subsection, the person would be a public authority for those purposes merely because the person exercises functions on behalf of another public authority.

(3) A person who exercises functions in relation to Scotland is a public authority for the purposes of this Part in relation to those functions only if and to the extent that those functions relate to a reserved matter.

(4) In subsection (3) "Scotland" and "reserved matter" have the same meanings as in the Scotland Act 1998.

(5) A person who exercises functions in relation to Wales is a public authority for the purposes of this Part in relation to those functions only if and to the extent that those

functions relate to a matter which is outside the legislative competence of the National Assembly for Wales.

(6) A person who exercises functions in relation to Northern Ireland is a public authority for the purposes of this Part in relation to those functions only if and to the extent that those functions relate to an excepted matter.

(7) In subsection (6) "Northern Ireland" and "excepted matter" have the same meanings as in the Northern Ireland Act 1998.

(8) The following are not public authorities for the purposes of this Part—
 (a) the Security Service;
 (b) the Secret Intelligence Service;
 (c) the Government Communications Headquarters.

(9) The relevant Minister may by regulations amend subsection (8) so as to add, modify or remove a reference to a person or description of person with functions of a public nature.

79 Power to expand meaning of person working for public authority

(1) The relevant Minister may by regulations amend section 77 with the effect that a person who works for a contractor of a public authority is a person who works for the authority for the purposes of this Part.

(2) In subsection (1) "contractor", in relation to a public authority, means a person who—
 (a) provides a service to members of the public as a result of an arrangement made with a public authority (whether or not by that person), but
 (b) is not a public authority.

(3) For the purposes of subsection (1) a person works for a contractor if the person works—
 (a) under a contract of employment with the contractor,
 (b) under a contract of apprenticeship with the contractor,
 (c) under a contract to do work personally with the contractor,
 (d) in England and Wales or Scotland, as an agency worker within the meaning of the Agency Workers Regulations 2010 (SI 2010/93) in respect of whom the contractor is the hirer within the meaning of those regulations, or
 (e) in Northern Ireland, as an agency worker within the meaning of the Agency Workers Regulations (Northern Ireland) 2011 (SR 2011/350) in respect of whom the contractor is the hirer within the meaning of those regulations.

80 Duty to issue codes of practice

(1) The relevant Minister must issue a code or codes of practice for the purposes of section 77.

(2) A code of practice must include provision about the following matters—
 (a) the standard of spoken English to be met by a person working for a public authority to which the code applies in a customer-facing role;
 (b) the action available to such a public authority where such a person does not meet that standard;

(c) the procedure to be operated by such a public authority for enabling complaints to be made to the authority about breaches by the authority of section 77(1) and for the consideration of such complaints;

(d) how the public authority is to comply with its other legal obligations as well as complying with the duty in section 77(1).

(3) A code of practice may make such other provision as the relevant Minister considers appropriate for securing that a person who works for a public authority to which the code applies in a customer-facing role speaks fluent English.

(4) A code of practice may make provision in relation to—

(a) all public authorities,

(b) particular descriptions of public authority, or

(c) particular public authorities.

(5) But the relevant Minister must ensure that there is at all times a code of practice in force which applies to each public authority.

(6) A code of practice may make different provision for different purposes, including different provision for different public authorities or descriptions of public authority.

81 Procedure for codes of practice

(1) In preparing a code of practice the relevant Minister must consult such persons as the relevant Minister thinks appropriate.

(2) Before issuing a code of practice the relevant Minister must lay a draft of the code before Parliament.

(3) A code of practice comes into force in accordance with provision made by regulations made by the relevant Minister.

(4) After a code of practice has come into force the relevant Minister must publish it in such manner as the relevant Minister thinks appropriate.

(5) The relevant Minister may from time to time review a code of practice and may revise and re-issue it following a review.

(6) References in subsections (1) to (4) to a code of practice include a revised code.

82 Application of Part to Wales

(1) Subsection (2) makes provision about the application of this Part in relation to—

(a) a public authority that exercises functions only in Wales, and

(b) a public authority that exercises functions outside Wales and in Wales, to the extent that it exercises functions in Wales.

(2) In the provisions of this Part listed in subsection (3) references to English are to be read as references to English or Welsh.

(3) Those provisions are—

(a) section 77(1), (7) and (8), and

(b) section 80(2)(a) and (3).

83 Interpretation of Part

In this Part—

"contract" means a contract whether express or implied and, if express, whether oral or in writing;

"public authority" has the meaning given by section 78;

"relevant Minister" means the Secretary of State or the Chancellor of the Duchy of Lancaster;

"Wales" has the same meaning as in the Government of Wales Act 2006.

84 Crown application

This Part binds the Crown.

PART 8

FEES AND CHARGES

Immigration

85 Immigration skills charge

(1) The Immigration Act 2014 is amended as follows.

(2) After section 70 insert—

"70A Immigration skills charge

(1) The Secretary of State may by regulations provide for a charge to be imposed on—

(a) persons who make immigration skills arrangements, or

(b) any description of such persons.

(2) "Immigration skills arrangements" are arrangements made by a person ("the sponsor") with the Secretary of State with a view to securing that an individual who is not exempt for the purposes of this section is granted entry clearance or leave to remain in the United Kingdom to enable the individual to work for the sponsor in the United Kingdom.

(3) Regulations under this section may in particular—

(a) impose a separate charge on a sponsor in respect of each individual in relation to whom the sponsor makes immigration skills arrangements;

(b) specify the amount of any charge (and different amounts may be specified for different purposes);

(c) make provision about when or how a charge may or must be paid to the Secretary of State;

(d) make provision about the consequences of a sponsor failing to pay a charge;

(e) provide for exemptions from a charge;

(f) provide for the reduction, waiver or refund of part or all of a charge (whether by conferring a discretion or otherwise).

(4) Sums paid by virtue of regulations under this section must—

(a) be paid into the Consolidated Fund, or

(b) be applied in such other way as the regulations may specify.

(5) Regulations under this section may be made only with the consent of the Treasury.

(6) An individual is exempt for the purposes of this section if he or she is—

(a) a British citizen;

(b) a national of an EEA State other than the United Kingdom;

(c) a national of Switzerland;

(d) otherwise entitled to enter or remain in the United Kingdom by virtue of an enforceable EU right or of any provision made under section 2(2) of the European Communities Act 1972.

(7) In this section "entry clearance" has the meaning given by section 33(1) of the Immigration Act 1971."

(3) In section 74(2) (orders and regulations which are subject to affirmative resolution procedure) after paragraph (j) insert—

"(ja) regulations under section 70A;".

Passports and civil registration

86 Power to make passport fees regulations

(1) The Secretary of State may by regulations provide for fees to be charged in respect of the exercise by the Secretary of State of such functions in connection with applications for the issue of a passport or other travel document as may be specified.

(2) Regulations under subsection (1) are referred to in this section and section 87 as "passport fees regulations".

(3) Passport fees regulations must provide for the fee in respect of the exercise of each specified function to comprise one or more amounts each of which is—

(a) a specified fixed amount, or

(b) an amount calculated by reference to a specified hourly rate or other specified factor.

(4) Provision made under subsection (3) may be intended to result in a fee in respect of a specified function which exceeds the costs of exercising the function.

(5) In specifying the amount of any fee, or hourly rate or other factor, the Secretary of State may have regard only to the costs of exercising—

(a) the function;

(b) any other function of the Secretary of State in connection with United Kingdom passports or other UK travel documents;

(c) any consular function.

This is subject to section 87(5).

(6) In respect of any fee provided for under this section, passport fees regulations may—

(a) provide for exceptions;

(b) provide for the reduction, waiver or refund of part or all of a fee (whether by conferring a discretion or otherwise);

(c) make provision about—

(i) the consequences of failure to pay a fee;

(ii) enforcement;

(iii) when a fee may or must be paid.

(7) In this section—

"consular function" means—

(a) any of the functions described in Article 5 of the Vienna Convention on Consular Relations set out in Schedule 1 to the Consular Relations Act 1968;

(b) any function in the United Kingdom which corresponds to a function mentioned in paragraph (a);

in each case regardless of whether the function is exercised by a consular officer or by another person authorised by the Secretary of State;

"costs" includes—

(a) the costs of the Secretary of State, and

(b) the costs of any other person (whether or not funded from public money);

"function" includes a power or a duty;

"specified" means specified in passport fees regulations;

"travel document" means a document which enables or facilitates travel from one state to another and a "UK travel document" means such a document issued by the Secretary of State;

"United Kingdom passport" has the same meaning as in the Immigration Act 1971 (see section 33 of that Act).

(8) Any reference in this section to the exercise of a function includes a reference to its exercise in particular circumstances, including its exercise—

(a) at particular times or in a particular place;

(b) under particular arrangements;

(c) otherwise in particular ways,

and, for this purpose, "arrangements" includes arrangements for the convenience of applicants or persons making requests for the exercise of a function.

87 Passport fees regulations: supplemental

(1) Passport fees regulations may be made only with the consent of the Treasury.

(2) A fee under section 86 may relate to something done outside the United Kingdom.

(3) Fees payable by virtue of section 86 may be recovered as a debt due to the Secretary of State.

(4) Fees paid to the Secretary of State by virtue of section 86 must be—

(a) paid into the Consolidated Fund, or

(b) applied in such other way as passport fees regulations may specify.

(5) Section 86 is without prejudice to—
   (a) section 1 of the Consular Fees Act 1980 (fees for consular acts etc),
   (b) section 102 of the Finance (No 2) Act 1987 (government fees and charges), or
   (c) any other power to charge a fee.

88 Power to charge for passport validation services

(1) The Secretary of State may charge a fee in respect of the provision of passport validation services to persons on request.

(2) "Passport validation services" are services in connection with confirming the validity of United Kingdom passports or the accuracy of the information contained in them which are provided for the purpose of preventing or detecting crime.

(3) In this section "United Kingdom passport" has the same meaning as in the Immigration Act 1971 (see section 33 of that Act).

(4) A fee payable under this section may be recovered as a debt due to the Secretary of State.

(5) Fees paid to the Secretary of State under this section must be—
   (a) paid into the Consolidated Fund, or
   (b) applied in such other way as the Secretary of State may by regulations specify.

(6) Regulations under subsection (5) may be made only with the consent of the Treasury.

(7) This section is without prejudice to—
   (a) section 1 of the Consular Fees Act 1980 (fees for consular acts etc),
   (b) section 102 of the Finance (No 2) Act 1987 (government fees and charges), or
   (c) any other power to charge a fee.

89 Civil registration fees

(1) Schedule 15 (civil registration fees) has effect.

(2) In that Schedule—
   (a) Part 1 amends enactments about civil registration in connection with powers to make regulations for the charging of fees, and
   (b) Part 2 makes consequential and related amendments.

PART 9

MISCELLANEOUS AND GENERAL

Welfare of children

90 Duty regarding the welfare of children

For the avoidance of doubt, this Act does not limit any duty imposed on the Secretary of State or any person by section 55 of the Borders, Citizenship and Immigration Act 2009 (duty regarding welfare of children).

Final provisions

91 Financial provisions

The following are to be paid out of money provided by Parliament—

(a) any expenditure incurred under or by virtue of this Act by a Minister of the Crown, a person holding office under Her Majesty or a government department, and

(b) any increase attributable to the Act in the sums payable under any other Act out of money so provided.

92 Transitional and consequential provision

(1) The Secretary of State may by regulations make such transitional, transitory or saving provision as the Secretary of State considers appropriate in connection with the coming into force of any provision of this Act.

(2) The Secretary of State may by regulations make such provision as the Secretary of State considers appropriate in consequence of this Act.

(3) The provision that may be made by regulations under subsection (2) includes provision amending, repealing or revoking any enactment.

(4) "Enactment" includes—

(a) an enactment contained in subordinate legislation within the meaning of the Interpretation Act 1978;

(b) an enactment contained in, or in an instrument made under, an Act of the Scottish Parliament;

(c) an enactment contained in, or in an instrument made under, a Measure or Act of the National Assembly for Wales;

(d) an enactment contained in, or in an instrument made under, Northern Ireland legislation.

(5) In section 61(2) of the UK Borders Act 2007 (meaning of "the Immigration Acts")—

(a) omit the "and" at the end of paragraph (i), and

(b) at the end of paragraph (j) insert ", and

(k) the Immigration Act 2016."

93 Regulations

(1) Regulations made by the Secretary of State or the Chancellor of the Duchy of Lancaster under this Act are to be made by statutory instrument.

(2) A statutory instrument containing (whether alone or with other provision) any of the following regulations may not be made unless a draft of the instrument has been laid before, and approved by a resolution of, each House of Parliament—

(a) regulations under section 3 which amend or repeal primary legislation,

(b) regulations under section 6,

(c) regulations under section 11 which amend or repeal primary legislation,

(d) regulations under section 14, 15 or 21,

(e) regulations under section 36(2),

(f) regulations under section 42(1) or (2),
(g) regulations under section 73(1) or (2),
(h) regulations under section 78(9),
(i) regulations under section 79(1),
(j) passport fees regulations within the meaning of section 86 which include provision specifying functions as mentioned in subsection (1) of that section,
(k) regulations under section 92(2) which amend or repeal primary legislation,
(l) regulations under paragraph 1(13) of Schedule 6, and
(m) regulations under paragraph 2(7) of that Schedule.

(3) Primary legislation means any of the following—
(a) an Act of Parliament;
(b) an Act of the Scottish Parliament;
(c) a Measure or Act of the National Assembly for Wales;
(d) Northern Ireland legislation.

(4) A statutory instrument—
(a) containing any other regulations made by the Secretary of State or the Chancellor of the Duchy of Lancaster under this Act, and
(b) to which subsection (2) does not apply,

is subject to annulment in pursuance of a resolution of either House of Parliament.

(5) Subsection (4) does not apply to regulations under section 92(1) or 94(1).

(6) Regulations made by the Secretary of State or the Chancellor of the Duchy of Lancaster under this Act—
(a) may make different provision for different purposes or areas,
(b) may make provision which applies generally or for particular purposes or areas,
(c) may make transitional, transitory or saving provision, or
(d) may make incidental, supplementary or consequential provision.

94 Commencement

(1) Subject to subsections (3) to (5) this Act comes into force on such day as the Secretary of State appoints by regulations.

(2) Regulations under subsection (1) may appoint different days for different purposes or areas.

(3) Subsections (3) to (5) of section 61 come into force on the day on which this Act is passed.

(4) Section 85 comes into force at the end of the period of two months beginning with the day on which this Act is passed.

(5) This Part comes into force on the day on which this Act is passed.

95 Extent

(1) This Act extends to England and Wales, Scotland and Northern Ireland, subject as follows.

(2) Sections 69 to 72 extend to England and Wales only.

(3) Any amendment, repeal or revocation made by this Act has the same extent within the United Kingdom as the provision to which it relates.

(4) But subsection (3) does not apply to the amendments made to the Modern Slavery Act 2015 by paragraphs 30 and 35 of Schedule 3 (for the extent of which, see the amendments to section 60 of that Act made by paragraph 33 of that Schedule).

(5) Her Majesty may by Order in Council provide for any of the provisions of this Act to extend, with or without modifications, to any of the Channel Islands or the Isle of Man.

(6) A power under any provision listed in subsection (7) may be exercised so as to extend (with or without modifications) to any of the Channel Islands or the Isle of Man any amendment or repeal made by or under this Act of any part of an Act to which the provision listed in subsection (7) relates.

(7) Those provisions are—

- (a) section 36 of the Immigration Act 1971,
- (b) section 52(2) of the Civil Jurisdiction and Judgments Act 1982,
- (c) section 9(3) of the Special Immigration Appeals Commission Act 1997,
- (d) section 170(7) of the Immigration and Asylum Act 1999,
- (e) section 163(4) of the Nationality, Immigration and Asylum Act 2002,
- (f) section 49(3) of the Asylum and Immigration (Treatment of Claimants, etc) Act 2004,
- (g) section 63(3) of the Immigration, Asylum and Nationality Act 2006,
- (h) section 60(4) of the UK Borders Act 2007,
- (i) section 76(6) of the Immigration Act 2014, and
- (j) section 60(6) of the Modern Slavery Act 2015.

96 Short title

This Act may be cited as the Immigration Act 2016.

SCHEDULES

SCHEDULE 1

Section 6

PERSONS TO WHOM DIRECTOR ETC MAY DISCLOSE INFORMATION

Authorities with functions in connection with the labour market or the work place etc

The Secretary of State.

HMRC Commissioners.

A person by whom, or by whose officers, labour market enforcement functions are exercisable.

The Health and Safety Executive.

An enforcing authority within the meaning of Part 1 of the Health and Safety at Work etc. Act 1974 (see section 18(7) of that Act).

An inspector appointed by such an enforcing authority (see section 19 of that Act).

An enforcement authority within the meaning of regulation 28 of the Working Time Regulations 1998 (S.I. 1998/1833).

An inspector appointed by such an enforcement authority (see Schedule 3 to those Regulations).

The Low Pay Commission.

The Pensions Regulator.

Law enforcement and border security

A chief officer of police for a police area in England and Wales.

A local policing body within the meaning given by section 101(1) of the Police Act 1996.

The chief constable of the British Transport Police Force.

The chief constable of the Police Service of Scotland.

The Chief Constable of the Police Service of Northern Ireland.

A person appointed as an immigration officer under paragraph 1 of Schedule 2 to the Immigration Act 1971.

Local government

A county or district council in England.

A London borough council.

The Greater London Authority.

The Common Council of the City of London.

The Council of the Isles of Scilly.

A county or county borough council in Wales.

A council constituted under section 2 of the Local Government etc. (Scotland) Act 1994.

A district council in Northern Ireland.

Health bodies

The Care Quality Commission.

A National Health Service trust established under section 25 of the National Health Service Act 2006 or section 18 of the National Health Service (Wales) Act 2006.

An NHS foundation trust within the meaning given by section 30 of the National Health Service Act 2006.

A Local Health Board established under section 11 of the National Health Service (Wales) Act 2006.

Other

The Independent Anti-slavery Commissioner.

A Northern Ireland department.

SCHEDULE 2

Section 11

FUNCTIONS IN RELATION TO LABOUR MARKET

Employment Agencies Act 1973 (c. 35)

1 The Employment Agencies Act 1973 is amended as follows.

2 Before section 9 insert—

"8A Appointment of officers

"8A Appointment of officers

(1) The Secretary of State may—

(a) appoint officers to act for the purposes of this Act, and

(b) instead of or in addition to appointing any officers under this section, arrange with any relevant authority for officers of that authority to act for those purposes.

(2) The following are relevant authorities—

(a) any Minister of the Crown or government department;

(b) any body performing functions on behalf of the Crown;

(c) the Gangmasters and Labour Abuse Authority."

3 (1) Section 9 (inspection) is amended as follows.

(2) Before subsection (1) insert—

"(A1) This section does not apply to an officer acting for the purposes of this Act in relation to England and Wales if the officer is a labour abuse prevention officer within the meaning of section 114B of the Police and Criminal Evidence Act 1984 (PACE powers for labour abuse prevention officers)."

(3) In subsection (1), for "duly authorised in that behalf by the Secretary of State" substitute "acting for the purposes of this Act".

(4) In subsection (4)(a), in each of sub-paragraphs (ii) and (iii), for "or servant appointed by, or person exercising functions on behalf of, the Secretary of State" substitute "acting for the purposes of this Act,".

National Minimum Wage Act 1998 (c. 39)

4 The National Minimum Wage Act 1998 is amended as follows.

5 In section 13 (appointment of officers for enforcement)—

(a) in subsection (1)(b), for the words from "Minister of the Crown" to "body shall" substitute "relevant authority for officers of that authority to";

(b) after subsection (1) insert—

"(1A) The following are relevant authorities—

(a) any Minister of the Crown or government department;

(b) any body performing functions on behalf of the Crown;

(c) the Gangmasters and Labour Abuse Authority."

6 In section 14 (powers of officers) before subsection (1) insert—

"(A1) This section does not apply to an officer acting for the purposes of this Act in relation to England and Wales if the officer is a labour abuse prevention officer within the meaning of section 114B of the Police and Criminal Evidence Act 1984 (PACE powers for labour abuse prevention officers)."

7 In section 15 (information obtained by officers)—

(a) in subsection (3)(b), after "any" insert "eligible";

(b) in subsection (4)(a), after "to any" insert "eligible";

(c) in subsection (8), for the words from ""relevant" to "body which," substitute ""eligible relevant authority" means any relevant authority within the meaning given by section 13(1A) which".

Modern Slavery Act 2015 (c.30)

8 The Modern Slavery Act 2015 is amended as follows.

9 Before section 12 (but after the italic heading before it) insert—

"11A Enforcement by Gangmasters and Labour Abuse Authority

"11A Enforcement by Gangmasters and Labour Abuse Authority

(1) The Secretary of State may make arrangements with the Gangmasters and Labour Abuse Authority for officers of the Authority to act for the purposes of this Part in taking action in circumstances in which it appears that an offence under this Part which is a labour market offence (within the meaning of section 3 of the Immigration Act 2016) has been, is being or may be committed.

(2) For provision about the powers of such an officer who is acting for the purposes of this Part, see section 114B of the Police and Criminal Evidence Act 1984 (PACE powers for labour abuse prevention officers)."

10 (1) Section 15 (slavery and trafficking prevention orders on application) is amended as follows.

(2) In subsection (1)—

(a) omit the "or" after paragraph (b);

(b) after paragraph (c) insert ", or

(d) the Gangmasters and Labour Abuse Authority."

(3) In subsection (7)—

(a) for "or the Director General", in the first place it occurs, substitute ", the Director General or the Gangmasters and Labour Abuse Authority";

(b) for "or the Director General", in the second place it occurs, substitute ", the Director General or the Authority".

(4) In subsection (8)(b)—

(a) for "or the Director General", in the first place it occurs, substitute ", the Director General or the Gangmasters and Labour Abuse Authority";

(b) for "or the Director General", in the second place it occurs, substitute ", the Director General or the Authority".

11 In section 19(7) (requirement to provide name and address)—

(a) for "or an immigration officer" substitute ", an immigration officer or the Gangmasters and Labour Abuse Authority";

(b) for "or the officer" substitute ", the officer or the Authority".

12 (1) Section 20 (variation, renewal and discharge) is amended as follows.

(2) In subsection (2), after paragraph (f) insert—

"(g) where the order was made on an application under section 15 by the Gangmasters and Labour Abuse Authority, the Authority."

(3) In subsection (9)—

(a) for "or the Director General", in the first place it occurs, substitute ", the Director General or the Gangmasters and Labour Abuse Authority";

(b) for "or the Director General", in the second and third places it occurs, substitute ", the Director General or the Authority".

13 (1) Section 23 (slavery and trafficking risk orders) is amended as follows.

(2) In subsection (1)—

(a) omit the "or" after paragraph (b);

(b) after paragraph (c) insert ", or

(d) the Gangmasters and Labour Abuse Authority."

(3) In subsection (6)—

(a) for "or the Director General", in the first place it occurs, substitute ", the Director General or the Gangmasters and Labour Abuse Authority";

(b) for "or the Director General", in the second place it occurs, substitute ", the Director General or the Authority".

(4) In subsection (7)(b)—

(a) for "or the Director General" substitute ", the Director General or the Gangmasters and Labour Abuse Authority";

(b) for "or Director General" substitute ", the Director General or the Authority".

14 In section 26(7) (requirement to provide name and address)—

(a) for "or an immigration officer" substitute ", an immigration officer or the Gangmasters and Labour Abuse Authority";

(b) for "or the officer" substitute ", the officer or the Authority".

15 (1) Section 27 (variation, renewal and discharge) is amended as follows.

(2) In subsection (2), after paragraph (f) insert—

"(g) where the order was made on an application by the Gangmasters and Labour Abuse Authority, the Authority."

(3) In subsection (7)—

(a) for "or the Director General" in the first place it occurs, substitute ", the Director General or the Gangmasters and Labour Abuse Authority";

(b) for "or the Director General" in the second and third places it occurs, substitute ", the Director General or the Authority".

16 After section 30 (offences) insert—

"30A Enforcement by Gangmasters and Labour Abuse Authority

"30A Enforcement by Gangmasters and Labour Abuse Authority

(1) The Secretary of State may make arrangements with the Gangmasters and Labour Abuse Authority for officers of the Authority to act for the purposes of this Part in taking action in circumstances in which it appears that an offence under this Part which is a labour market offence (within the meaning of section 3 of the Immigration Act 2016) has been, is being or may be committed.

(2) For provision about the powers of such an officer who is acting for the purposes of this Part, see section 114B of the Police and Criminal Evidence Act 1984 (PACE powers for labour abuse prevention officers)."

17 In section 33 (guidance), in subsection (1) for "and the Director General of the National Crime Agency" substitute ", the Director General of the National Crime Agency and the Gangmasters and Labour Abuse Authority".

SCHEDULE 3

Section 31

CONSEQUENTIAL AND RELATED AMENDMENTS

Public Records Act 1958 (c. 51)

1 In the Public Records Act 1958, in Schedule 1 (definition of public records), in Part 2 of the Table at the end of paragraph 3 (other establishments and organisations), for "Gangmasters Licensing Authority" substitute "Gangmasters and Labour Abuse Authority".

Parliamentary Commissioner Act 1967 (c. 13)

2 In the Parliamentary Commissioner Act 1967, in Schedule 2 (departments etc subject to investigation)—

(a) at the appropriate place insert "Director of Labour Market Enforcement";

(b) for "Gangmasters Licensing Authority" substitute "Gangmasters and Labour Abuse Authority".

Superannuation Act 1972 (c. 11)

3 In the Superannuation Act 1972, in Schedule 1 (kinds of employment to which that Act applies)—

(a) under the heading "Other bodies", for "Gangmasters Licensing Authority" substitute "Gangmasters and Labour Abuse Authority";

(b) under the heading "Offices", at the appropriate place insert "Director of Labour Market Enforcement".

Employment Agencies Act 1973 (c. 35)

4 (1) Section 9 of the Employment Agencies Act 1973 (inspection) is amended as follows.

(2) In subsection (4)—

(a) in paragraph (a), for the words before sub-paragraph (i) substitute "No information to which this subsection applies shall be disclosed except—";

(b) at the end of paragraph (a) insert "; or

(vii) to an officer acting by virtue of section 26 of the Immigration Act 2016 (investigative functions in connection with labour market enforcement undertakings and orders); or

(viii) to an officer acting for the purposes of Part 2 of the Employment (Miscellaneous Provisions) (Northern Ireland) Order 1981 for any purpose relating to that Part; or

(ix) to the Pensions Regulator for the purposes of the exercise of any function of the Regulator; or

(x) to the Care Quality Commission for the purposes of the exercise of any function of the Commission."

(3) After subsection (4) insert—

"(5) Subsection (4) applies to—

(a) information obtained in the course of exercising the powers conferred by this section,

(b) information obtained pursuant to section 15(5A) of the National Minimum Wage Act 1998, and

(c) information obtained in the course of exercising powers by virtue of section 26(1) of the Immigration Act 2016 (investigative functions in connection with labour market enforcement undertakings and orders)."

House of Commons Disqualification Act 1975 (c. 24)

5 In the House of Commons Disqualification Act 1975, in Schedule 1 (offices disqualifying for membership)—

(a) in Part 2 (bodies of which all members are disqualified), for "Gangmasters Licensing Authority" substitute "Gangmasters and Labour Abuse Authority";

(b) in Part 3 (other disqualifying offices), at the appropriate place insert "Director of Labour Market Enforcement".

Northern Ireland Assembly Disqualification Act 1975 (c. 25)

6 In the Northern Ireland Assembly Disqualification Act 1975, in Schedule 1 (offices disqualifying for membership)—

(a) in Part 2 (bodies of which all members are disqualified), for "Gangmasters Licensing Authority" substitute "Gangmasters and Labour Abuse Authority";

(b) in Part 3 (other disqualifying offices), at the appropriate place insert "Director of Labour Market Enforcement".

National Minimum Wage Act 1998 (c. 39)

7 (1) Section 15 of the National Minimum Wage Act 1998 (information obtained by officers) is amended as follows.

(2) In subsection (1)—

(a) after "to" insert "—

(a)";

(b) at the end insert ", and

(b) any information obtained by an officer acting by virtue of section 26(2) of the Immigration Act 2016 (investigative functions in connection with labour market enforcement undertakings and orders)."

(3) After subsection (5B) insert—

"(5C) Information to which this section applies—

(a) may be supplied by, or with the authorisation of, the Secretary of State to an officer acting by virtue of section 26 of the Immigration Act 2016 (investigative functions in connection with labour market enforcement undertakings and orders); and

(b) may be used by an officer so acting for any purpose for which the officer is so acting."

Regulation of Investigatory Powers Act 2000 (c. 23)

8 In the Regulation of Investigatory Powers Act 2000, in Schedule 1 (relevant public authorities), in Part 1 (relevant authorities for purposes of sections 28 and 29 of that Act) in paragraph 20E for "Gangmasters Licensing Authority" substitute "Gangmasters and Labour Abuse Authority".

Freedom of Information Act 2000 (c. 36)

9 In the Freedom of Information Act 2000, in Schedule 1 (public authorities), in Part 6 (other public bodies and offices: general)—

(a) at the appropriate place insert "Director of Labour Market Enforcement";

(b) for "Gangmasters Licensing Authority" substitute "Gangmasters and Labour Abuse Authority".

Police Reform Act 2002 (c. 30)

10 The Police Reform Act 2002 is amended as follows.

11 In section 10 (general functions of the Independent Police Complaints Commission) —

(a) in subsection (1), after paragraph (g) insert—

"(ga) to carry out such corresponding functions in relation to officers of the Gangmasters and Labour Abuse Authority in their capacity as labour abuse prevention officers (see section 114B of the Police and Criminal Evidence Act 1984 (PACE powers for labour abuse prevention officers)).";

(b) in subsection (3), after paragraph (bc) insert—

"(bd) any regulations under section 26D of this Act (labour abuse prevention officers);".

12 After section 26C insert—

"26D Labour abuse prevention officers

"26D Labour abuse prevention officers

(1) The Secretary of State may make regulations conferring functions on the Commission in relation to the exercise of functions by officers of the Gangmasters and Labour Abuse Authority (the "Authority") in their capacity as labour abuse prevention officers (see section 114B of the Police and Criminal Evidence Act 1984 (PACE powers for labour abuse prevention officers)).

(2) Regulations under this section may, in particular—

(a) apply (with or without modifications), or make provision similar to, any provision of or made under this Part;

(b) make provision for payment by the Authority to, or in respect of, the Commission.

(3) The Commission and the Parliamentary Commissioner for Administration may jointly investigate a matter in relation to which—

(a) the Commission has functions by virtue of this section, and

(b) the Parliamentary Commissioner for Administration has functions by virtue of the Parliamentary Commissioner Act 1967.

(4) An officer of the Authority may disclose information to the Commission, or to a person acting on the Commission's behalf, for the purposes of the exercise by the Commission, or by any person acting on the Commission's behalf, of an Authority complaints function.

(5) The Commission and the Parliamentary Commissioner for Administration may disclose information to each other for the purposes of the exercise of a function—

(a) by virtue of this section, or

(b) under the Parliamentary Commissioner Act 1967.

(6) Regulations under this section may, in particular, make—

(a) further provision about the disclosure of information under subsection (4) or (5);

(b) provision about the further disclosure of information that has been so disclosed.

(7) In this section "Authority complaints function" means a function in relation to the exercise of functions by officers of the Authority."

Gangmasters (Licensing) Act 2004 (c. 11)

13 The Gangmasters (Licensing) Act 2004 is amended as follows.

14 In the italic heading before section 1, for "Gangmasters Licensing Authority" substitute "Gangmasters and Labour Abuse Authority".

15 In section 1 (Gangmasters Licensing Authority)—

(a) in the heading, for "Gangmasters Licensing Authority" substitute "Gangmasters and Labour Abuse Authority";

(b) for subsection (1) substitute—

"(1) The body known as the Gangmasters Licensing Authority is to continue to exist and is to be known as the Gangmasters and Labour Abuse Authority (in this Act referred to as "the Authority").";

(c) after subsection (3) insert—

"(3A) When carrying out functions during a year to which a labour market enforcement strategy approved under section 2 of the Immigration Act 2016 relates, the Authority and its officers must carry out those functions in accordance with the strategy."

16 In section 2 (directions etc by the Secretary of State), in subsection (2) after "the Authority" insert "and the Director of Labour Market Enforcement".

17 In section 3 (work to which Act applies)—

(a) in subsection (5)(b), for the words from "the following nature" to the end substitute "a prescribed description as being work to which this Act applies";

(b) after subsection (5) insert—

"(6) The Secretary of State must consult the Authority and the Director of Labour Market Enforcement before making regulations under subsection (5)."

18 In section 8 (general power of Authority to make rules)—

(a) in subsection (1), after "may" insert "with the approval of the Secretary of State";

(b) omit subsection (3).

19 In section 14 (offences: supplementary provisions) after subsection (2) insert—

"(2A) Subsections (1) and (2) do not apply to an enforcement officer who is acting for the purposes of this Act in relation to England and Wales if the officer is a labour abuse prevention officer within the meaning of section 114B of the Police and Criminal Evidence Act 1984 (PACE powers for labour abuse prevention officers)."

20 In section 15 (enforcement and compliance officers) after subsection (6) insert—

"(6A) Subsections (5) and (6) do not apply to an enforcement officer who is acting for the purposes of this Act in relation to England and Wales if the officer is a labour abuse prevention officer within the meaning of section 114B of the Police and Criminal Evidence Act 1984 (PACE powers for labour abuse prevention officers)."

21 In section 16 (powers of officers) before subsection (1) insert—

"(A1) This section does not apply to an enforcement officer who is acting for the purposes of this Act in relation to England and Wales if the officer is a labour abuse prevention officer within the meaning of section 114B of the Police and Criminal Evidence Act 1984 (PACE powers for labour abuse prevention officers)."

22 In section 17 (entry by warrant) before subsection (1) insert—

"(A1) This section does not apply to an enforcement officer who is acting for the purposes of this Act in relation to England and Wales if the officer is a labour abuse prevention officer within the meaning of section 114B of the Police and Criminal Evidence Act 1984 (PACE powers for labour abuse prevention officers)."

23 (1) Section 19 (information relating to gangmasters) is amended as follows.

(2) In subsection (1)—

(a) for the words before paragraph (a) substitute "Information to which this subsection applies—";

(b) for paragraph (a) substitute—

"(a) may be supplied to any person for use for the purposes of, or for any purpose connected with, the exercise of functions under this Act,

(aa) may be supplied to any person by whom, or by whose officers, labour market enforcement functions are exercisable for the purposes of, or for any purpose connected with, the exercise of such functions, and".

(3) After subsection (1) insert—

"(1A) Subsection (1) applies to—

(a) information held by any person for the purposes of, or for any purpose connected with, the exercise of functions under this Act, and

(b) information held by any officer acting by virtue of section 26(3) of the Immigration Act 2016 (investigative functions in connection with labour market enforcement undertakings and orders).

(1B) In subsection (1) "labour market enforcement functions" has the same meaning as in Chapter 1 of Part 1 of the Immigration Act 2016 (see section 3 of that Act)."

(4) In subsection (2)—

(a) omit "relating to the operations of a person acting as a gangmaster";

(b) for "(1)(b)" substitute "(1)(aa) or (b)".

24 (1) Schedule 2 (application of Act to Northern Ireland) is amended as follows.

(2) In the italic heading before paragraph 3, for "Gangmasters Licensing Authority" substitute "Gangmasters and Labour Abuse Authority".

(3) In paragraph 6—

(a) after "work in Northern Ireland," insert "—

(a)";

(b) at the end insert ", and

(b) the requirement under subsection (2) of that section to consult the Director of Labour Market Enforcement is to be ignored."

(4) In paragraph 7, for paragraph (b) substitute—

"(b) paragraph (b) is to be read as if for "work of a prescribed description as being work to which this Act applies" there were substituted "work of the following nature as being work to which this Act applies—

(i) the gathering (by any manner) of wild creatures, or wild plants, of a prescribed description and the processing and packaging of anything so gathered, and

(ii) the harvesting of fish from a fish farm (within the meaning of the Fisheries Act (NI) 1966 (c 17 (NI))."

(5) In paragraph 10, for sub-paragraph (2) substitute—

"(2) Section 8(1) as it applies in relation to Northern Ireland licences is to be read as if the words "with the approval of the Secretary of State" were omitted.

(3) The Authority must consult the relevant Northern Ireland department before making any Northern Ireland rules about fees."

(6) After paragraph 16 insert—

"16A Section 19: Information relating to gangmasters

16A (1) Section 19 as it applies in relation to Northern Ireland functions is to be read as if—

(a) paragraph (aa) of subsection (1) (and the reference to it in subsection (2)) were omitted,

(b) subsections (1A)(b) and (1B) were omitted, and

(c) in subsection (2), after "Information" there were inserted the words "relating to the operations of a person acting as a gangmaster".

(2) In this paragraph "Northern Ireland functions" means functions under this Act in connection with persons acting as gangmasters in Northern Ireland or persons acting as gangmasters in relation to work in Northern Ireland.

16B Section 22A: Relationship with other agencies: requests for assistance

16B Section 22A does not apply in relation to the Authority's functions in connection with persons acting as gangmasters in Northern Ireland or persons acting as gangmasters in relation to work in Northern Ireland."

Pensions Act 2004 (c. 35)

25 In the Pensions Act 2004, in Schedule 3 (certain permitted disclosures of restricted information held by the Pensions Regulator), at the end of the table insert—

"Director of Labour Market Enforcement or a member of staff provided to the Director under section 1(4) of the Immigration Act 2016.	Any of the Director's functions."

Natural Environment and Rural Communities Act 2006 (c. 16)

26 In the Natural Environment and Rural Communities Act 2006, in Schedule 7 (designated bodies), in paragraph 13, for "Gangmasters' Licensing Authority" substitute "Gangmasters and Labour Abuse Authority".

Regulatory Enforcement and Sanctions Act 2008 (c. 13)

27 In the Regulatory Enforcement and Sanctions Act 2008, in Schedule 5 (designated regulators), for "Gangmasters Licensing Authority" substitute "Gangmasters and Labour Abuse Authority".

Modern Slavery Act 2015 (c. 30)

28 The Modern Slavery Act 2015 is amended as follows.

29 In section 52 (duty to notify Secretary of State about suspected victims of slavery or human trafficking), in subsection (5)(k), for "Gangmasters Licensing Authority" substitute "Gangmasters and Labour Abuse Authority".

30 At the beginning of Part 7, after the italic heading "Miscellaneous" insert—

"54A Gangmasters and Labour Abuse Authority: information gateways

"54A Gangmasters and Labour Abuse Authority: information gateways

(1) A specified person may disclose information to the Gangmasters and Labour Abuse Authority (the "Authority") or a relevant officer if the disclosure is made for the purposes of the exercise of any function of the Authority or the officer under this Act.

(2) Information obtained by the Authority or a relevant officer in connection with the exercise of any function of the Authority or the officer under this Act may be used by the Authority or the officer in connection with the exercise of any other such function of the Authority or the officer.

(3) The Authority or a relevant officer may disclose to a specified person information obtained in connection with the exercise of any function of the Authority or the officer under this Act if the disclosure is made for the purposes of the exercise of any function of the specified person.

(4) A disclosure of information which is authorised by this section does not breach—

(a) an obligation of confidence owed by the person making the disclosure, or

(b) any other restriction on the disclosure of information (however imposed).

(5) But nothing in this section authorises the making of a disclosure which—

(a) contravenes the Data Protection Act 1998, or

(b) is prohibited by Part 1 of the Regulation of Investigatory Powers Act 2000.

(6) This section does not limit the circumstances in which information may be disclosed apart from this section.

(7) "Specified person" means a person specified in Schedule 4A (information gateways: specified persons).

(8) The Secretary of State may by regulations amend Schedule 4A.

(9) In this section, "relevant officer" means an officer of the Authority who is acting for the purposes of Part 1 or 2 of this Act (see sections 11A and 30A)."

31 Omit section 55 (review of Gangmasters Licensing Authority).

32 In section 58 (regulations), in subsection (4), after paragraph (j) insert—

"(ja) regulations under section 54A(8) (power to amend Schedule 4A);".

33 In section 60 (extent)—

(a) in subsection (1), after "section 53)" insert "and section 54A, and Schedule 4A, in Part 7";

(b) in subsection (3), after "and 7" insert "(except for section 54A and Schedule 4A)".

34 In Schedule 3 (public authorities under duty to co-operate with the Independent Anti-slavery Commissioner), for "Gangmasters Licensing Authority" substitute "Gangmasters and Labour Abuse Authority".

35 After Schedule 4 insert—

"SCHEDULE 4A

Section 54A

INFORMATION GATEWAYS: SPECIFIED PERSONS

Authorities with functions in connection with the labour market etc

The Secretary of State.

A person by whom, or by whose officers, labour market enforcement functions (within the meaning given by section 3 of the Immigration Act 2016) are exercisable.

Law enforcement and border security

A chief officer of police for a police area in England and Wales.

The chief constable of the British Transport Police Force.

An immigration officer.

Local government

A county council in England or Wales.

A county borough council in Wales.

A district council in England.

A London borough council.

The Greater London Authority.

The Common Council of the City of London.

The Council of the Isles of Scilly.

Health bodies

A National Health Service trust established under section 25 of the National Health Service Act 2006 or section 18 of the National Health Service (Wales) Act 2006.

An NHS foundation trust within the meaning given by section 30 of the National Health Service Act 2006.

A Local Health Board established under section 11 of the National Health Service (Wales) Act 2006.

Other

The Independent Anti-slavery Commissioner."

Human Trafficking and Exploitation (Criminal Justice and Support for Victims) Act (Northern Ireland) 2015 (c. 2) (N.I.)

36 In the Human Trafficking and Exploitation (Criminal Justice and Support for Victims) Act (Northern Ireland) 2015, in Schedule 3 (slavery and trafficking prevention orders), in Part 3 (supplementary) in paragraph 18(7)(e), for "Gangmasters Licensing Authority" substitute "Gangmasters and Labour Abuse Authority".

SCHEDULE 4

Section 36

LICENSING ACT 2003: AMENDMENTS RELATING TO ILLEGAL WORKING

PART 1

ENTITLEMENT TO WORK IN THE UNITED KINGDOM

1 After section 192 of the Licensing Act 2003 insert—

"192A Entitlement to work in the United Kingdom

"192A "192A Entitlement to work in the United Kingdom

(1) For the purposes of this Act an individual is entitled to work in the United Kingdom if—

(a) the individual does not under the Immigration Act 1971 require leave to enter or remain in the United Kingdom, or

(b) the individual has been granted such leave and the leave—

(i) is not invalid,

(ii) has not ceased to have effect (whether by reason of curtailment, revocation, cancellation, passage of time or otherwise), and

(iii) is not subject to a condition preventing the individual from doing work relating to the carrying on of a licensable activity within section 1(1)(a) or (d).

(2) Where an individual is on immigration bail within the meaning of Part 1 of Schedule 10 to the Immigration Act 2016—

(a) the individual is to be treated for the purposes of subsection (1) as if the individual had been granted leave to enter the United Kingdom, but

(b) any condition as to the individual's work in the United Kingdom to which the individual's immigration bail is subject is to be treated for those purposes as a condition of leave."

PART 2

PREMISES LICENCES

2 Part 3 of the Licensing Act 2003 (premises licences) is amended as follows.

3 In section 13(4) (meaning of "responsible authority"), after paragraph (h) insert—

"(ha) where the premises (not being a vessel) are being, or are proposed to be, used for a licensable activity within section 1(1)(a) or (d), the Secretary of State,".

4 (1) Section 16 (applicant for premises licence) is amended as follows.

(2) In subsection (1), at the beginning insert "Subject to subsections (2) and (2A),".

(3) In subsection (2), omit "But".

(4) After subsection (2) insert—

"(2A) An individual who is resident in the United Kingdom may not apply for a premises licence authorising premises to be used for a licensable activity within section 1(1)(a) or (d) unless the individual is entitled to work in the United Kingdom."

5 In section 27 (death, incapacity, insolvency etc of licence holder), after subsection (1) insert—

"(1A) A premises licence that authorises premises to be used for a licensable activity within section 1(1)(a) or (d) also lapses if the holder of the licence ceases to be entitled to work in the United Kingdom at a time when the holder of the licence is resident in the United Kingdom (or becomes so resident without being entitled to work in the United Kingdom)."

6 (1) Section 42 (application for transfer of premises licence) is amended as follows.

(2) After subsection (2) insert—

"(2A) Where the applicant is an individual who is resident in the United Kingdom and the premises licence authorises premises to be used for a licensable activity within section 1(1)(a) or (d) he must also be entitled to work in the United Kingdom."

(3) After subsection (5) insert—

"(5ZA) Where the premises licence authorises premises to be used for a licensable activity within section 1(1)(a) or (d), the relevant person must also give notice of the application to the Secretary of State."

(4) In subsection (5A), for "subsection (5)" substitute "subsections (5) and (5ZA)".

(5) After subsection (7) insert—

"(8) Where the Secretary of State is given notice under subsection (5ZA) and is satisfied that the exceptional circumstances of the case are such that granting the application would be prejudicial to the prevention of illegal working in licensed premises, the Secretary of State must give the relevant licensing authority a notice stating the reasons for being so satisfied.

(9) The Secretary of State must give that notice within the period of 14 days beginning with the day on which the Secretary of State is notified of the application under subsection (5ZA)."

7 (1) Section 44(5) (determination of transfer application) is amended as follows.

(2) In the words before paragraph (a), after "section 42(6)" insert "or (8)".

(3) In paragraph (a), for "chief officer of police" substitute "person".

(4) For paragraph (b) substitute—

"(b) having regard to the notice—

(i) where the notice is given under section 42(6), reject the application if it considers it appropriate for the promotion of the crime prevention objective to do so, or

(ii) where the notice is given under section 42(8), reject the application if it considers it appropriate for the prevention of illegal working in licensed premises to do so."

8 (1) Section 45 (notification of determination under section 44) is amended as follows.

(2) In subsection (2)—

(a) after "that section" insert "or the Secretary of State gave a notice under subsection (8) of that section";

(b) for "(and it" substitute "(which, in either case,".

(3) After subsection (2) insert—

"(2A) Where the Secretary of State gave a notice under subsection (8) of section 42 (which was not withdrawn), the notice under subsection (1) of this section must also be given to the Secretary of State."

9 (1) Section 47 (interim authority notice following death etc of licence holder) is amended as follows.

(2) In subsection (1)—

(a) after "or (c)" insert "or (1A)";

(b) after "holder" insert "or change of immigration status".

(3) In subsection (3), after "subject to" insert "subsection (3A) and".

(4) After subsection (3) insert—

"(3A) Where the premises licence authorises premises to be used for a licensable activity within section 1(1)(a) or (d), a person falling within subsection (2) (a) or (b) who is an individual who is resident in the United Kingdom may give an interim authority notice only if the person is entitled to work in the United Kingdom."

(5) In subsection (7), after paragraph (a) insert—

"(aa) where the premises licence authorises premises to be used for a licensable activity within section 1(1)(a) or (d), at the end of the initial 28 day period unless before that time the person who gave the interim authority notice has given a copy of the notice to the Secretary of State;".

(6) In subsection (7A)—

(a) in paragraph (a), for "subsection (7)(a) does" substitute "paragraphs (a) and (aa) of subsection (7) do";

(b) in paragraph (b), at the end insert "and, where the premises licence authorises premises to be used for a licensable activity within section 1(1)(a) or (d), to the Secretary of State."

10 (1) Section 48 (cancellation of interim authority notice following police objections) is amended as follows.

(2) In the heading, omit "police".

(3) In subsection (1), for "This section" substitute "Subsection (2)".

(4) After subsection (2) insert—

"(2A) Subsection (2B) applies where—

(a) an interim authority notice by a person ("the relevant person") is given in accordance with section 47,

(b) the Secretary of State is given a copy of the interim authority notice before the end of the initial 28 day period (within the meaning of that section), and

(c) the Secretary of State is satisfied that the exceptional circumstances of the case are such that a failure to cancel the interim authority notice would be prejudicial to the prevention of illegal working in licensed premises.

(2B) The Secretary of State must before the end of the second working day following receipt of the copy of the interim authority notice give the relevant licensing authority a notice stating why the Secretary of State is so satisfied."

(5) In subsection (3)—

(a) in the words before paragraph (a), for "by the chief officer of police" substitute "under subsection (2) or (2B)";

(b) in paragraph (a), for "chief officer of police" substitute "person who gave the notice";

(c) for paragraph (b) substitute—

"(b) having regard to the notice—

(i) where the notice is given under subsection (2), cancel the interim authority notice if it considers it appropriate for the promotion of the crime prevention objective to do so, or

(ii) where the notice is given under subsection (2B), cancel the interim authority notice if it considers it appropriate for the prevention of illegal working in licensed premises to do so."

(6) After subsection (5) insert—

"(5A) Where an interim authority notice is cancelled under subsection (3)(b)(ii), the licensing authority must also give a copy of the notice under subsection (4) to the Secretary of State."

11 In section 50 (reinstatement of licence on transfer following death etc of holder), in subsection (3), for "(who, in the case of an individual, is aged 18 or over)" substitute "(and who would, where applicable, satisfy subsections (2) and (2A) of section 42)".

PART 3

PERSONAL LICENCES

12 Part 6 of the Licensing Act 2003 (personal licences) is amended as follows.

13 (1) Section 113 (meaning of "relevant offence" and "foreign offence") is amended as follows.

(2) In the heading, for "and "foreign offence"" substitute ", "immigration offence", "foreign offence" and "immigration penalty"".

(3) After subsection (2) insert—

"(2A) In this Part "immigration offence" means—

(a) an offence referred to in paragraph 7A of Schedule 4, or

(b) an offence listed in paragraph 24 or 25 of Schedule 4 that is committed in relation to an offence referred to in paragraph 7A of that Schedule."

(4) At the end insert—

"(4) In this Part "immigration penalty" means a penalty under—

(a) section 15 of the Immigration, Asylum and Nationality Act 2006 ("the 2006 Act"), or

(b) section 23 of the Immigration Act 2014 ("the 2014 Act").

(5) For the purposes of this Part a person to whom a penalty notice under section 15 of the 2006 Act has been given is not to be treated as having been required to pay an immigration penalty if—

(a) the person is excused payment by virtue of section 15(3) of that Act, or

(b) the penalty is cancelled by virtue of section 16 or 17 of that Act.

(6) For the purposes of this Part a person to whom a penalty notice under section 15 of the 2006 Act has been given is not to be treated as having been required to pay an immigration penalty until such time as—

(a) the period for giving a notice of objection under section 16 of that Act has expired and the Secretary of State has considered any notice given within that period, and

(b) if a notice of objection was given within that period, the period for appealing under section 17 of that Act has expired and any appeal brought within that period has been finally determined, abandoned or withdrawn.

(7) For the purposes of this Part a person to whom a penalty notice under section 23 of the 2014 Act has been given is not to be treated as having been required to pay an immigration penalty if—

(a) the person is excused payment by virtue of section 24 of that Act, or

(b) the penalty is cancelled by virtue of section 29 or 30 of that Act.

(8) For the purposes of this Part a person to whom a penalty notice under section 23 of the 2014 Act has been given is not to be treated as having been required to pay an immigration penalty until such time as—

(a) the period for giving a notice of objection under section 29 of that Act has expired and the Secretary of State has considered any notice given within that period, and

(b) if a notice of objection was given within that period, the period for appealing under section 30 of that Act has expired and any appeal brought within that period has been finally determined, abandoned or withdrawn."

14 (1) Section 115 (period of validity of personal licence) is amended as follows.

(2) In subsection (2), after "subsections" insert "(2A),".

(3) After subsection (2) insert—

"(2A) A personal licence ceases to have effect if the holder of the licence ceases to be entitled to work in the United Kingdom."

15 (1) Section 120 (determination of application for grant) is amended as follows.

(2) In subsection (2)—

(a) after paragraph (a) insert—

"(aa) he is entitled to work in the United Kingdom,";

(b) in paragraph (d), at the end insert "or required to pay an immigration penalty".

(3) In subsection (3), for "paragraph (a), (b) or (c)" substitute "any of paragraphs (a) to (c)".

(4) In subsection (4), for "(a), (b) and (c)" substitute "(a) to (c)".

(5) In subsection (5)—

(a) omit the "and" at the end of paragraph (a);

(b) at the end of paragraph (b) insert "and

(c) the applicant having been required to pay any immigration penalty,".

(6) After subsection (5) insert—

"(5A) If it appears to the authority that the applicant meets the conditions in paragraphs (a) to (c) of subsection (2) but fails to meet the condition in paragraph (d) of that subsection by virtue of having been—

(a) convicted of an immigration offence,

(b) convicted of a foreign offence that the authority considers to be comparable to an immigration offence, or

(c) required to pay an immigration penalty,

the authority must give the Secretary of State a notice to that effect.

(5B) Where, having regard to—

(a) any conviction of the applicant for an immigration offence,

(b) any conviction of the applicant for a foreign offence which the Secretary of State considers to be comparable to an immigration offence, and

(c) the applicant having been required to pay any immigration penalty,

the Secretary of State is satisfied that granting the licence would be prejudicial to the prevention of illegal working in licensed premises, the Secretary of State must, within the period of 14 days beginning with the day the Secretary of State received the notice under subsection (5A), give the authority a notice stating the reasons for being so satisfied (an "immigration objection notice")."

(7) In subsection (6), for "is given within that period (or the notice is withdrawn)" substitute "or immigration objection notice is given within the period of 14 days referred to in subsection (5) or (5B) (as the case may be), or any such notice given is withdrawn,".

(8) In subsection (7)—

(a) in the words before paragraph (a), for "In any other case," substitute "Where an objection notice or an immigration objection notice is given within the period of 14 days referred to in subsection (5) or (5B) (as the case may be), and not withdrawn,";

(b) in paragraph (a)—

(i) omit "objection";

(ii) for "chief officer of police" substitute "person who gave the notice";

(c) for paragraph (b) substitute—

"(b) having regard to the notice, must—

(i) where the notice is an objection notice, reject the application if it considers it appropriate for the promotion of the crime prevention objective to do so, or

(ii) where the notice is an immigration objection notice, reject the application if it considers it appropriate for the prevention of illegal working in licensed premises to do so."

(9) After subsection (7) insert—

"(7A) An application that is not rejected by the authority under subsection (7)(b) must be granted by it."

16 (1) Section 122 (notification of determinations) is amended as follows.

(2) In subsection (1)—

(a) after "objection notice" insert "or the Secretary of State gave an immigration objection notice";

(b) after "(which" insert ", in either case,".

(3) After subsection (2) insert—

"(2A) Where the Secretary of State gave an immigration objection notice (which was not withdrawn) the notice under subsection (1)(a) or (2), as the case may be, must also be given to the Secretary of State."

(4) In subsection (3), in the definition of "objection notice", for "has" substitute "and "immigration objection notice" have".

17 (1) Section 123 (duty to notify licensing authority of convictions during application period) is amended as follows.

(2) In the heading, after "convictions" insert "etc".

(3) In subsection (1)—

(a) after "application period" insert ", or is required to pay an immigration penalty during that period";

(b) after "conviction" insert "or the requirement to pay (as the case may be)".

18 (1) Section 124 (convictions coming to light after grant) is amended as follows.

(2) In subsection (1)—

(a) for "("the offender")" substitute "("the licence holder")";

(b) at the end insert "or was required during that period to pay an immigration penalty".

(3) In subsection (3)—

(a) in paragraph (a)—

(i) for "applicant" substitute "licence holder";

(ii) for ", and" substitute "which occurred before the end of the application period,";

(b) in paragraph (b), after "relevant offence" insert "and which occurred before the end of the application period";

(c) at the end of paragraph (b) insert "and

(c) the licence holder having been required before the end of the application period to pay any immigration penalty,";

(d) in the words after paragraph (b), omit "which occurred before the end of the application period,".

(4) After subsection (3) insert—

"(3A) Where the licence holder was (during the application period)—

(a) convicted of an immigration offence,

(b) convicted of a foreign offence that the licensing authority considers to be comparable to an immigration offence, or

(c) required to pay an immigration penalty,

the authority must give the Secretary of State a notice to that effect.

(3B) Where, having regard to—

(a) any conviction of the licence holder for an immigration offence which occurred before the end of the application period,

(b) any conviction of the licence holder for a foreign offence which the Secretary of State considers to be comparable to an immigration offence and which occurred before the end of the application period, and

(c) the licence holder having been required before the end of the application period to pay any immigration penalty,

the Secretary of State is satisfied that continuation of the licence would be prejudicial to the prevention of illegal working in licensed premises, the Secretary of State must, within the period of 14 days beginning with the day the Secretary of State received the notice under subsection (3A), give the authority a notice stating the reasons for being so satisfied (an "immigration objection notice")."

(5) In subsection (4)—

(a) in the words before paragraph (a), for "is given within that period" substitute "or an immigration objection notice is given within the period of 14 days referred to in subsection (3) or (3B), as the case may be,";

(b) in paragraph (a)—

(i) omit "objection";

(ii) for "holder of the licence, the chief officer of police" substitute "licence holder, the person who gave the notice";

(c) in paragraph (b), for the words from "revoke" to the end of the paragraph substitute "—

(i) where the notice is an objection notice, revoke the licence if it considers it appropriate for the promotion of the crime prevention objective to do so, or

(ii) where the notice is an immigration objection notice, revoke the licence if it considers it appropriate for the prevention of illegal working in licensed premises to do so."

(6) After subsection (5) insert—

"(5A) Where the authority revokes or decides not to revoke a licence under subsection (4)(b)(ii) it must also notify the Secretary of State of the decision and its reasons for making it."

19 (1) Section 125(3) (form of personal licence) is amended as follows.

(2) For "of each" substitute "of—

(a) each".

(3) At the end insert—

"(b) each immigration penalty that the holder has been required to pay and the date of each notice by which such a penalty was imposed."

20 (1) Section 132 (licence holder's duty to notify licensing authority of convictions) is amended as follows.

(2) In the heading, after "convictions" insert "etc".

(3) After subsection (2) insert—

"(2A) Subsection (2B) applies where the holder of a personal licence is required to pay an immigration penalty.

(2B) The holder must, as soon as reasonably practicable after being required to pay the penalty, give the relevant licensing authority a notice containing details of the penalty, including the date of the notice by which the penalty was imposed."

(4) In subsection (3), after "(2)" insert "or (2B)".

21 In Schedule 4 (personal licence: relevant offences), after paragraph 7 insert—

"7A An offence under any of the Immigration Acts."

PART 4

RIGHTS OF ENTRY

22 (1) Section 179 of the Licensing Act 2003 (rights of entry to investigate licensable activities) is amended as follows.

(2) After subsection (1) insert—

"(1A) Where an immigration officer has reason to believe that any premises are being used for a licensable activity within section 1(1)(a) or (d), the officer may enter the premises with a view to seeing whether an offence under any of the Immigration Acts is being committed in connection with the carrying on of the activity."

(3) In subsection (2)—

(a) after "authorised person" insert "or an immigration officer";

(b) for "the power", in the first place it occurs, substitute "a power".

(4) In subsection (3), for "the power" substitute "a power".

(5) In subsection (4), after "authorised person" insert "or an immigration officer".

(6) In subsection (6)—

(a) omit "and" at the end of the definition of "authorisation";

(b) at the end of the subsection insert—

""""immigration officer" means a person appointed as an immigration officer under paragraph 1 of Schedule 2 to the Immigration Act 1971."

PART 5

APPEALS

23 Schedule 5 to the Licensing Act 2003 (appeals) is amended as follows.

24 (1) Paragraph 6 (transfer of licence) is amended as follows.

(2) In sub-paragraph (1)—

(a) after "42(6)" insert "or the Secretary of State gave a notice under section 42(8)";

(b) after "(which" insert ", in either case,".

(3) In sub-paragraph (2), after "police" insert "or the Secretary of State, as the case may be,".

25 (1) Paragraph 7 (interim authority notice) is amended as follows.

(2) In sub-paragraph (1)(b)—

(a) after "48(2)" insert "or the Secretary of State gives a notice under section 48(2B)";

(b) after "(which" insert ", in either case,".

(3) In sub-paragraph (3), for "the notice under that subsection," substitute "the interim authority notice under section 48(3) after the giving of a notice by a chief officer of police under section 48(2),".

(4) After sub-paragraph (3) insert—

"(3A) Where the relevant licensing authority decides not to cancel the interim authority notice under section 48(3) after the giving of a notice by the Secretary of State under section 48(2B), the Secretary of State may appeal against that decision."

26 In paragraph 9 (general provision about appeals under Part 1 of Schedule 5), in sub-paragraph (4), after "paragraph 7(3)" insert "or (3A)".

27 (1) Paragraph 17 (personal licences) is amended as follows.

(2) In sub-paragraph (2)—

(a) for "section 120(7)" substitute "120(7A) after the giving of a notice under section 120(5)";

(b) for "objection notice (within the meaning of section 120(5))" substitute "notice".

(3) After sub-paragraph (2) insert—

"(2A) Where a licensing authority grants an application for a personal licence under section 120(7A) after the giving of a notice under section 120(5B), the Secretary of State may appeal against that decision."

(4) After sub-paragraph (5) insert—

"(5A) Where in a case to which section 124 applies—

(a) the Secretary of State gives a notice under subsection (3B) of that section (and does not later withdraw it), and

(b) the licensing authority decides not to revoke the licence,

the Secretary of State may appeal against the decision."

(5) In sub-paragraph (8), for "(2), (3) or (5)" substitute "(2), (2A), (5) or (5A)".

28 At the end insert—

"PART 4

QUESTIONS ABOUT LEAVE TO ENTER OR REMAIN IN THE UK

19 On an appeal under this Schedule, a magistrates' court is not entitled to entertain any question as to whether—

(a) an individual should be, or should have been, granted leave to enter or remain in the United Kingdom, or

(b) an individual has, after the date of the decision being appealed against, been granted leave to enter or remain in the United Kingdom."

PART 6

GENERAL

29 In section 10 of the Licensing Act 2003, (sub-delegation of functions by licensing committee etc), in subsection (4)(a), in sub-paragraphs (v), (vi) and (x), omit "police".

30 (1) Section 193 of the Licensing Act 2003 (other definitions) is amended as follows.

(2) The existing text becomes subsection (1).

(3) After that subsection insert—

"(2) For the purposes of references in this Act to the prevention of illegal working in licensed premises, a person is working illegally if by doing that work at that time the person is committing an offence under section 24B of the Immigration Act 1971."

31 In section 194 of the Licensing Act 2003 (index of defined expressions), insert the following entries at the appropriate places—

"entitled to work in the United Kingdom	section 192A"
"immigration offence	section 113"
"immigration penalty (and required to pay, in relation to an immigration penalty)	section 113"
"working illegally, in relation to the prevention of illegal working in licensed premises	section 193"

32 In the Police Reform and Social Responsibility Act 2011, omit sections 109(9) and (10) and 111(3) and (5).

PART 7

TRANSITIONAL PROVISION

33 The amendments of sections 13, 16, 42, 47 and 120 of the Licensing Act 2003 made by paragraphs 3, 4, 6, 9 and 15 respectively of this Schedule do not apply in relation to applications made, or interim authority notices given, before the coming into force of the respective paragraph.

34 The amendment of section 27 of the Licensing Act 2003 made by paragraph 5 of this Schedule does not apply in relation to a premises licence granted pursuant to an application made before the coming into force of that paragraph.

35 The amendments of section 115 of the Licensing Act 2003 made by paragraph 14 of this Schedule do not apply in relation to a personal licence granted pursuant to an application made before the coming into force of that paragraph.

36 The amendment of Schedule 4 to the Licensing Act 2003 made by paragraph 21 of this Schedule applies on and after the coming into force of that paragraph in relation to—

(a) personal licences granted before, on or after the coming into force of that paragraph, and

(b) offences committed before, on or after the coming into force of that paragraph.

SCHEDULE 5

Section 37

PRIVATE HIRE VEHICLES ETC

London Hackney Carriages Act 1843 (c. 86)

1 (1) Section 18 of the London Hackney Carriages Act 1843 (licences and badges to be delivered up on the discontinuance of licences) is amended as follows.

(2) At the beginning insert "(1)".

(3) At the end of subsection (1) insert—

"(2) Subsection (1) does not require the delivery of a licence and badge on the expiry of the licence if the licence was granted in accordance with section 8A(2) or (4) of the Metropolitan Public Carriage Act 1869 (but see section 8A(6) of that Act)."

Metropolitan Public Carriage Act 1869 (c. 115)

2 The Metropolitan Public Carriage Act 1869 is amended as follows.

3 In section 8(7) (driver's licence to be in force for three years unless suspended or revoked) for "A" substitute "Subject to section 8A, a".

4 After section 8 insert—

"8A Drivers' licences for persons subject to immigration control

"8A Drivers' licences for persons subject to immigration control

(1) Subsection (2) applies if—

(a) a licence under section 8 is to be granted to a person who has been granted leave to enter or remain in the United Kingdom for a limited period ("the leave period"),

(b) the person's leave has not been extended by virtue of section 3C of the Immigration Act 1971 (continuation of leave pending variation decision), and

(c) apart from subsection (2), the period for which the licence would have been in force would have ended after the end of the leave period.

(2) Transport for London must grant the licence for a period which ends at or before the end of the leave period.

(3) Subsection (4) applies if—

(a) a licence under section 8 is to be granted to a person who has been granted leave to enter or remain in the United Kingdom for a limited period, and

(b) the person's leave has been extended by virtue of section 3C of the Immigration Act 1971 (continuation of leave pending variation decision).

(4) Transport for London must grant the licence for a period that does not exceed six months.

(5) A licence under section 8 ceases to be in force if the person to whom it was granted becomes disqualified by reason of the person's immigration status from driving a hackney carriage.

(6) If a licence granted in accordance with subsection (2) or (4) expires, the person to whom it was granted must, within the period of 7 days beginning with the day after that on which it expired, return to Transport for London—

(a) the licence,

(b) the person's copy of the licence (if any), and

(c) the person's driver's badge.

(7) If subsection (5) applies to a licence, the person to whom it was granted must, within the period of 7 days beginning with the day after the day on which the person first became disqualified, return to Transport for London—

(a) the licence,

(b) the person's copy of the licence (if any), and

(c) the person's driver's badge.

(8) A person who, without reasonable excuse, contravenes subsection (6) or (7) is guilty of an offence and liable on summary conviction—

(a) to a fine not exceeding level 3 on the standard scale, and

(b) in the case of a continuing offence, to a fine not exceeding ten pounds for each day during which an offence continues after conviction.

(9) The Secretary of State may by regulations made by statutory instrument amend the amount for the time being specified in subsection (8)(b).

(10) Regulations under subsection (9) may make transitional, transitory or saving provision.

(11) A statutory instrument containing regulations under subsection (9) may not be made unless a draft of the instrument has been laid before, and approved by a resolution of, each House of Parliament.

(12) For the purposes of this section a person is disqualified by reason of the person's immigration status from driving a hackney carriage if the person is subject to immigration control and—

(a) the person has not been granted leave to enter or remain in the United Kingdom, or

(b) the person's leave to enter or remain in the United Kingdom—

(i) is invalid,

(ii) has ceased to have effect (whether by reason of curtailment, revocation, cancellation, passage of time or otherwise), or

(iii) is subject to a condition preventing the person from driving a hackney carriage.

(13) Where a person is on immigration bail within the meaning of Part 1 of Schedule 10 to the Immigration Act 2016—

(a) the person is to be treated for the purposes of this section as if the person had been granted leave to enter the United Kingdom, but

(b) any condition as to the person's work in the United Kingdom to which the person's immigration bail is subject is to be treated for those purposes as a condition of leave.

(14) For the purposes of this section a person is subject to immigration control if under the Immigration Act 1971 the person requires leave to enter or remain in the United Kingdom."

Plymouth City Council Act 1975 (c. xx)

5 The Plymouth City Council Act 1975 is amended as follows.

6 After section 2 insert—

"2A Persons disqualified by reason of immigration status

"2A Persons disqualified by reason of immigration status

(1) For the purposes of this Act a person is disqualified by reason of the person's immigration status from carrying on a licensable activity if the person is subject to immigration control and—

(a) the person has not been granted leave to enter or remain in the United Kingdom, or

(b) the person's leave to enter or remain in the United Kingdom—

(i) is invalid,

(ii) has ceased to have effect (whether by reason of curtailment, revocation, cancellation, passage of time or otherwise), or

(iii) is subject to a condition preventing the person from carrying on the licensable activity.

(2) Where a person is on immigration bail within the meaning of Part 1 of Schedule 10 to the Immigration Act 2016—

(a) the person is to be treated for the purposes of this Act as if the person had been granted leave to enter the United Kingdom, but

(b) any condition as to the person's work in the United Kingdom to which the person's immigration bail is subject is to be treated for those purposes as a condition of leave.

(3) For the purposes of this section a person is subject to immigration control if under the Immigration Act 1971 the person requires leave to enter or remain in the United Kingdom.

(4) For the purposes of this section a person carries on a licensable activity if the person—

(a) drives a private hire vehicle,

(b) operates a private hire vehicle, or

(c) drives a hackney carriage.

2B Immigration offences and immigration penalties

2B Immigration offences and immigration penalties

(1) In this Act "immigration offence" means—

(a) an offence under any of the Immigration Acts,

(b) an offence under section 1 of the Criminal Attempts Act 1981 of attempting to commit an offence within paragraph (a), or

(c) an offence under section 1 of the Criminal Law Act 1977 of conspiracy to commit an offence within paragraph (a).

(2) In this Act "immigration penalty" means a penalty under—

(a) section 15 of the Immigration, Asylum and Nationality Act 2006 ("the 2006 Act"), or

(b) section 23 of the Immigration Act 2014 ("the 2014 Act").

(3) For the purposes of this Act a person to whom a penalty notice under section 15 of the 2006 Act has been given is not to be treated as having been required to pay an immigration penalty if—

(a) the person is excused payment by virtue of section 15(3) of that Act, or

(b) the penalty is cancelled by virtue of section 16 or 17 of that Act.

(4) For the purposes of this Act a person to whom a penalty notice under section 15 of the 2006 Act has been given is not to be treated as having been required to pay an immigration penalty until such time as—

(a) the period for giving a notice of objection under section 16 of that Act has expired and the Secretary of State has considered any notice given within that period, and

(b) if a notice of objection was given within that period, the period for appealing under section 17 of that Act has expired and any appeal brought within that period has been finally determined, abandoned or withdrawn.

(5) For the purposes of this Act a person to whom a penalty notice under section 23 of the 2014 Act has been given is not to be treated as having been required to pay an immigration penalty if—

(a) the person is excused payment by virtue of section 24 of that Act, or

(b) the penalty is cancelled by virtue of section 29 or 30 of that Act.

(6) For the purposes of this Act a person to whom a penalty notice under section 23 of the 2014 Act has been given is not to be treated as having been required to pay an immigration penalty until such time as—

(a) the period for giving a notice of objection under section 29 of that Act has expired and the Secretary of State has considered any notice given within that period, and

(b) if a notice of objection was given within that period, the period for appealing under section 30 of that Act has expired and any appeal brought within that period has been finally determined, abandoned or withdrawn."

7 (1) Section 9 (licensing of drivers of private hire vehicles) is amended as follows.

(2) In subsection (1)—

(a) in paragraph (a) after "satisfied" insert "—(i)", and

(b) for the "or" at the end of paragraph (a) substitute "and

(ii) that the applicant is not disqualified by reason of the applicant's immigration status from driving a private hire vehicle; or".

(3) After subsection (1) insert—

"(1A) In determining for the purposes of subsection (1) whether an applicant is disqualified by reason of the applicant's immigration status from driving a private hire vehicle, the Council must have regard to any guidance issued by the Secretary of State."

8 In section 11(1) (drivers' licences for hackney carriages and private hire vehicles)—

(a) in paragraph (a) for "Every" substitute "Subject to section 11A, every", and

(b) in paragraph (b) after "1889," insert "but subject to section 11A,".

9 After section 11 insert—

"11A Drivers' licences for persons subject to immigration control

"11A Drivers' licences for persons subject to immigration control

(1) Subsection (2) applies if—

(a) a licence within section 11(1)(a) or (b) is to be granted to a person who has been granted leave to enter or remain in the United Kingdom for a limited period ("the leave period"),
(b) the person's leave has not been extended by virtue of section 3C of the Immigration Act 1971 (continuation of leave pending variation decision), and
(c) apart from subsection (2), the period for which the licence would have been in force would have ended after the end of the leave period.

(2) The Council must specify a period in the licence as the period for which it remains in force; and that period must end at or before the end of the leave period.

(3) Subsection (4) applies if—
(a) a licence within section 11(1)(a) or (b) is to be granted to a person who has been granted leave to enter or remain in the United Kingdom for a limited period, and
(b) the person's leave has been extended by virtue of section 3C of the Immigration Act 1971 (continuation of leave pending variation decision).

(4) The Council must specify a period in the licence as the period for which it remains in force; and that period must not exceed six months.

(5) A licence within section 11(1)(a) ceases to be in force if the person to whom it was granted becomes disqualified by reason of the person's immigration status from driving a private hire vehicle.

(6) A licence within section 11(1)(b) ceases to be in force if the person to whom it was granted becomes disqualified by reason of the person's immigration status from driving a hackney carriage.

(7) If a licence granted in accordance with subsection (2) or (4) expires, the person to whom it was granted must, within the period of 7 days beginning with the day after that on which it expired, return the licence and the person's driver's badge to the Council.

(8) If subsection (5) or (6) applies to a licence, the person to whom it was granted must, within the period of 7 days beginning with the day after the day on which the person first became disqualified, return the licence and the person's driver's badge to the Council.

(9) A person who, without reasonable excuse, contravenes subsection (7) or (8) is guilty of an offence and liable on summary conviction—
(a) to a fine not exceeding level 3 on the standard scale, and
(b) in the case of a continuing offence, to a fine not exceeding ten pounds for each day during which an offence continues after conviction.

(10) The Secretary of State may by regulations made by statutory instrument amend the amount for the time being specified in subsection (9)(b).

(11) Regulations under subsection (10) may make transitional, transitory or saving provision.

(12) A statutory instrument containing regulations under subsection (10) may not be made unless a draft of the instrument has been laid before, and approved by a resolution of, each House of Parliament."

10 (1) Section 13 (licensing of operators of private hire vehicles) is amended as follows.

(2) In subsection (1)—

(a) after "satisfied" insert "—(a)", and

(b) at the end of paragraph (a) insert "; and

(b) if the applicant is an individual, that the applicant is not disqualified by reason of the applicant's immigration status from operating a private hire vehicle."

(3) After subsection (1) insert—

"(1A) In determining for the purposes of subsection (1) whether an applicant is disqualified by reason of the applicant's immigration status from operating a private hire vehicle, the Council must have regard to any guidance issued by the Secretary of State."

(4) In subsection (2) for "Every" substitute "Subject to section 13A, every".

11 After section 13 insert—

"13A Operators' licences for persons subject to immigration control

"13A Operators' licences for persons subject to immigration control

(1) Subsection (2) applies if—

(a) a licence under section 13 is to be granted to a person who has been granted leave to enter or remain in the United Kingdom for a limited period ("the leave period"),

(b) the person's leave has not been extended by virtue of section 3C of the Immigration Act 1971 (continuation of leave pending variation decision), and

(c) apart from subsection (2), the period for which the licence would have been in force would have ended after the end of the leave period.

(2) The Council must specify a period in the licence as the period for which it remains in force; and that period must end at or before the end of the leave period.

(3) Subsection (4) applies if—

(a) a licence under section 13 is to be granted to a person who has been granted leave to enter or remain in the United Kingdom for a limited period, and

(b) the person's leave has been extended by virtue of section 3C of the Immigration Act 1971 (continuation of leave pending variation decision).

(4) The Council must specify a period in the licence as the period for which it remains in force; and that period must not exceed six months.

(5) A licence under section 13 ceases to be in force if the person to whom it was granted becomes disqualified by reason of the person's immigration status from operating a private hire vehicle.

(6) If a licence granted in accordance with subsection (2) or (4) expires, the person to whom it was granted must, within the period of 7 days beginning with the day after that on which it expired, return the licence to the Council.

(7) If subsection (5) applies to a licence, the person to whom it was granted must, within the period of 7 days beginning with the day after the day on which the person first became disqualified, return it to the Council.

(8) A person who, without reasonable excuse, contravenes subsection (6) or (7) is guilty of an offence and liable on summary conviction—

(a) to a fine not exceeding level 3 on the standard scale, and

(b) in the case of a continuing offence, to a fine not exceeding ten pounds for each day during which an offence continues after conviction.

(9) The Secretary of State may by regulations made by statutory instrument amend the amount for the time being specified in subsection (8)(b).

(10) Regulations under subsection (9) may make transitional, transitory or saving provision.

(11) A statutory instrument containing regulations under subsection (9) may not be made unless a draft of the instrument has been laid before, and approved by a resolution of, each House of Parliament."

12 (1) Section 17 (qualification for drivers of hackney carriages) is amended as follows.

(2) In subsection (1)—

(a) in paragraph (a) after "satisfied" insert "—(i)", and

(b) for the "or" at the end of paragraph (a) substitute "and

(ii) that the applicant is not disqualified by reason of the applicant's immigration status from driving a hackney carriage; or".

(3) After subsection (1) insert—

"(1A) In determining for the purposes of subsection (1) whether an applicant is disqualified by reason of the applicant's immigration status from driving a hackney carriage, the Council must have regard to any guidance issued by the Secretary of State."

13 (1) Section 19 (suspension and revocation of drivers' licences) is amended as follows.

(2) In subsection (1) before the "or" at the end of paragraph (a) insert—

"(aa) that he has since the grant of the licence been convicted of an immigration offence or required to pay an immigration penalty;".

(3) After subsection (1) insert—

"(1A) Subsection (1)(aa) does not apply if—

(a) in a case where the driver has been convicted of an immigration offence, the conviction is a spent conviction within the meaning of the Rehabilitation of Offenders Act 1974, or

(b) in a case where the driver has been required to pay an immigration penalty—

(i) more than three years have elapsed since the date on which the penalty was imposed, and

(ii) the amount of the penalty has been paid in full."

(4) After subsection (2) insert—

"(2A) The requirement in subsection (2)(a) to return a driver's badge does not apply in a case where section 20A applies (but see subsection (2) of that section)."

14 (1) Section 20 (suspension and revocation of operators' licences) is amended as follows.

(2) In subsection (1) before the "or" at the end of paragraph (c) insert—

"(ca) that the operator has since the grant of the licence been convicted of an immigration offence or required to pay an immigration penalty;".

(3) After subsection (1) insert—

"(1A) Subsection (1)(ca) does not apply if—

(a) in a case where the operator has been convicted of an immigration offence, the conviction is a spent conviction within the meaning of the Rehabilitation of Offenders Act 1974, or

(b) in a case where the operator has been required to pay an immigration penalty—

(i) more than three years have elapsed since the date on which the penalty was imposed, and

(ii) the amount of the penalty has been paid in full."

15 After section 20 insert—

"20A Return of licences suspended or revoked on immigration grounds

"20A Return of licences suspended or revoked on immigration grounds

(1) Subsection (2) applies if—

(a) under section 19 the Council suspend, revoke or refuse to renew the licence of a driver of a hackney carriage or a private hire vehicle on the ground mentioned in subsection (1)(aa) of that section, or

(b) under section 20 the Council suspend, revoke or refuse to renew an operator's licence on the ground mentioned in subsection (1)(ca) of that section.

(2) The person to whom the licence was granted must, within the period of 7 days beginning with the relevant day, return to the Council—

(a) the licence, and

(b) in the case of a licence of a driver of a hackney carriage or a private hire vehicle, the person's driver's badge.

(3) In subsection (2) "the relevant day" means—

(a) where the licence is suspended or revoked, the day on which the suspension or revocation takes effect;

(b) where the Council refuse to renew the licence, the day on which the licence expires as a result of the failure to renew it.

(4) A person who, without reasonable excuse, contravenes subsection (2) is guilty of an offence and liable on summary conviction—

(a) to a fine not exceeding level 3 on the standard scale, and

(b) in the case of a continuing offence, to a fine not exceeding ten pounds for each day during which an offence continues after conviction.

(5) The Secretary of State may by regulations made by statutory instrument amend the amount for the time being specified in subsection (4)(b).

(6) Regulations under subsection (5) may make transitional, transitory or saving provision.

(7) A statutory instrument containing regulations under subsection (5) may not be made unless a draft of the instrument has been laid before, and approved by a resolution of, each House of Parliament."

16 In section 37 (appeals) after subsection (2) insert—

"(3) On an appeal under this Act or an appeal under section 302 of the Act of 1936 as applied by this section, the court is not entitled to entertain any question as to whether—

(a) a person should be, or should have been, granted leave to enter or remain in the United Kingdom, or

(b) a person has, after the date of the decision being appealed against, been granted leave to enter or remain in the United Kingdom."

Local Government (Miscellaneous Provisions) Act 1976 (c. 57)

17 The Local Government (Miscellaneous Provisions) Act 1976 is amended as follows.

18 (1) Section 51 (licensing of drivers of private hire vehicles) is amended as follows.

(2) In subsection (1)—

(a) in paragraph (a) after "satisfied" insert "—(i)", and

(b) for the "or" at the end of paragraph (a) substitute "and

(ii) that the applicant is not disqualified by reason of the applicant's immigration status from driving a private hire vehicle; or".

(3) After subsection (1) insert—

"(1ZA) In determining for the purposes of subsection (1) whether an applicant is disqualified by reason of the applicant's immigration status from driving a private hire vehicle, a district council must have regard to any guidance issued by the Secretary of State."

19 In section 53(1) (drivers' licences for hackney carriages and private hire vehicles)—

(a) in paragraph (a) for "Every" substitute "Subject to section 53A, every", and

(b) in paragraph (b) after "1889," insert "but subject to section 53A,".

20 After section 53 insert—

"53A Drivers' licences for persons subject to immigration control

"53A Drivers' licences for persons subject to immigration control

(1) Subsection (2) applies if—

(a) a licence within section 53(1)(a) or (b) is to be granted to a person who has been granted leave to enter or remain in the United Kingdom for a limited period ("the leave period");

(b) the person's leave has not been extended by virtue of section 3C of the Immigration Act 1971 (continuation of leave pending variation decision); and

(c) apart from subsection (2), the period for which the licence would have been in force would have ended after the end of the leave period.

(2) The district council which grants the licence must specify a period in the licence as the period for which it remains in force; and that period must end at or before the end of the leave period.

(3) Subsection (4) applies if—

(a) a licence within section 53(1)(a) or (b) is to be granted to a person who has been granted leave to enter or remain in the United Kingdom for a limited period; and

(b) the person's leave has been extended by virtue of section 3C of the Immigration Act 1971 (continuation of leave pending variation decision).

(4) The district council which grants the licence must specify a period in the licence as the period for which it remains in force; and that period must not exceed six months.

(5) A licence within section 53(1)(a) ceases to be in force if the person to whom it was granted becomes disqualified by reason of the person's immigration status from driving a private hire vehicle.

(6) A licence within section 53(1)(b) ceases to be in force if the person to whom it was granted becomes disqualified by reason of the person's immigration status from driving a hackney carriage.

(7) If a licence granted in accordance with subsection (2) or (4) expires, the person to whom it was granted must, within the period of 7 days beginning with the day after that on which it expired, return the licence and the person's driver's badge to the district council which granted the licence.

(8) If subsection (5) or (6) applies to a licence, the person to whom it was granted must, within the period of 7 days beginning with the day after the day on which the person first became disqualified, return the licence and the person's driver's badge to the district council which granted the licence.

(9) A person who, without reasonable excuse, contravenes subsection (7) or (8) is guilty of an offence and liable on summary conviction—

(a) to a fine not exceeding level 3 on the standard scale; and

(b) in the case of a continuing offence, to a fine not exceeding ten pounds for each day during which an offence continues after conviction.

(10) The Secretary of State may by regulations made by statutory instrument amend the amount for the time being specified in subsection (9)(b).

(11) Regulations under subsection (10) may make transitional, transitory or saving provision.

(12) A statutory instrument containing regulations under subsection (10) may not be made unless a draft of the instrument has been laid before, and approved by a resolution of, each House of Parliament."

21 (1) Section 55 (licensing of operators of private hire vehicles) is amended as follows.

(2) In subsection (1)—

(a) after "satisfied" insert "—(a)", and

(b) at the end of paragraph (a) insert "; and

(b) if the applicant is an individual, that the applicant is not disqualified by reason of the applicant's immigration status from operating a private hire vehicle."

(3) After subsection (1) insert—

"(1A) In determining for the purposes of subsection (1) whether an applicant is disqualified by reason of the applicant's immigration status from operating a private hire vehicle, a district council must have regard to any guidance issued by the Secretary of State."

(4) In subsection (2) for "Every" substitute "Subject to section 55ZA, every".

22 After section 55 insert—

"55ZA Operators' licences for persons subject to immigration control

"55ZA Operators' licences for persons subject to immigration control

(1) Subsection (2) applies if—

(a) a licence under section 55 is to be granted to a person who has been granted leave to enter or remain in the United Kingdom for a limited period ("the leave period");

(b) the person's leave has not been extended by virtue of section 3C of the Immigration Act 1971 (continuation of leave pending variation decision); and

(c) apart from subsection (2), the period for which the licence would have been in force would have ended after the end of the leave period.

(2) The district council which grants the licence must specify a period in the licence as the period for which it remains in force; and that period must end at or before the end of the leave period.

(3) Subsection (4) applies if—

(a) a licence under section 55 is to be granted to a person who has been granted leave to enter or remain in the United Kingdom for a limited period; and

(b) the person's leave has been extended by virtue of section 3C of the Immigration Act 1971 (continuation of leave pending variation decision).

(4) The district council which grants the licence must specify a period in the licence as the period for which it remains in force; and that period must not exceed six months.

(5) A licence under section 55 ceases to be in force if the person to whom it was granted becomes disqualified by reason of the person's immigration status from operating a private hire vehicle.

(6) If a licence granted in accordance with subsection (2) or (4) expires, the person to whom it was granted must, within the period of 7 days beginning with the day after that on which it expired, return the licence to the district council which granted the licence.

(7) If subsection (5) applies to a licence, the person to whom it was granted must, within the period of 7 days beginning with the day after the day on which the person first became disqualified, return it to the district council which granted the licence.

(8) A person who, without reasonable excuse, contravenes subsection (6) or (7) is guilty of an offence and liable on summary conviction—

(a) to a fine not exceeding level 3 on the standard scale; and

(b) in the case of a continuing offence, to a fine not exceeding ten pounds for each day during which an offence continues after conviction.

(9) The Secretary of State may by regulations made by statutory instrument amend the amount for the time being specified in subsection (8)(b).

(10) Regulations under subsection (9) may make transitional, transitory or saving provision.

(11) A statutory instrument containing regulations under subsection (9) may not be made unless a draft of the instrument has been laid before, and approved by a resolution of, each House of Parliament."

23 (1) Section 59 (qualification for drivers of hackney carriages) is amended as follows.

(2) In subsection (1)—

(a) in paragraph (a) after "satisfied" insert "—(i)", and

(b) for the "or" at the end of paragraph (a) substitute "and

(ii) that the applicant is not disqualified by reason of the applicant's immigration status from driving a hackney carriage; or".

(3) After subsection (1) insert—

"(1ZA) In determining for the purposes of subsection (1) whether an applicant is disqualified by reason of the applicant's immigration status from driving a hackney carriage, a district council must have regard to any guidance issued by the Secretary of State."

24 (1) Section 61 (suspension and revocation of drivers' licences) is amended as follows.

(2) In subsection (1) before the "or" at the end of paragraph (a) insert—

"(aa) that he has since the grant of the licence been convicted of an immigration offence or required to pay an immigration penalty;".

(3) After subsection (1) insert—

"(1A) Subsection (1)(aa) does not apply if—

(a) in a case where the driver has been convicted of an immigration offence, the conviction is a spent conviction within the meaning of the Rehabilitation of Offenders Act 1974, or

(b) in a case where the driver has been required to pay an immigration penalty—

(i) more than three years have elapsed since the date on which the penalty was imposed, and

(ii) the amount of the penalty has been paid in full."

(4) After subsection (2) insert—

"(2ZA) The requirement in subsection (2)(a) to return a driver's badge does not apply in a case where section 62A applies (but see subsection (2) of that section)."

25 (1) Section 62 (suspension and revocation of operators' licences) is amended as follows.

(2) In subsection (1) before the "or" at the end of paragraph (c) insert—

"(ca) that the operator has since the grant of the licence been convicted of an immigration offence or required to pay an immigration penalty;".

(3) After subsection (1) insert—

"(1A) Subsection (1)(ca) does not apply if—

(a) in a case where the operator has been convicted of an immigration offence, the conviction is a spent conviction within the meaning of the Rehabilitation of Offenders Act 1974, or

(b) in a case where the operator has been required to pay an immigration penalty—

(i) more than three years have elapsed since the date on which the penalty was imposed, and

(ii) the amount of the penalty has been paid in full."

26 After section 62 insert—

"62A Return of licences suspended or revoked on immigration grounds

"62A Return of licences suspended or revoked on immigration grounds

(1) Subsection (2) applies if—

(a) under section 61 a district council suspend, revoke or refuse to renew the licence of a driver of a hackney carriage or a private hire vehicle on the ground mentioned in subsection (1)(aa) of that section, or

(b) under section 62 a district council suspend, revoke or refuse to renew an operator's licence on the ground mentioned in subsection (1)(ca) of that section.

(2) The person to whom the licence was granted must, within the period of 7 days beginning with the relevant day, return to the district council—

(a) the licence, and

(b) in the case of a licence of a driver of a hackney carriage or a private hire vehicle, the person's driver's badge.

(3) In subsection (2) "the relevant day" means—

(a) where the licence is suspended or revoked, the day on which the suspension or revocation takes effect;

(b) where the district council refuse to renew the licence, the day on which the licence expires as a result of the failure to renew it.

(4) A person who, without reasonable excuse, contravenes subsection (2) is guilty of an offence and liable on summary conviction—

(a) to a fine not exceeding level 3 on the standard scale, and

(b) in the case of a continuing offence, to a fine not exceeding ten pounds for each day during which an offence continues after conviction.

(5) The Secretary of State may by regulations made by statutory instrument amend the amount for the time being specified in subsection (4)(b).

(6) Regulations under subsection (5) may make transitional, transitory or saving provision.

(7) A statutory instrument containing regulations under subsection (5) may not be made unless a draft of the instrument has been laid before, and approved by a resolution of, each House of Parliament."

27 In section 77 (appeals) after subsection (3) insert—

"(4) On an appeal under this Part of this Act or an appeal under section 302 of the Act of 1936 as applied by this section, the court is not entitled to entertain any question as to whether—

(a) a person should be, or should have been, granted leave to enter or remain in the United Kingdom; or

(b) a person has, after the date of the decision being appealed against, been granted leave to enter or remain in the United Kingdom."

28 After section 79 insert—

"79A Persons disqualified by reason of immigration status

"79A Persons disqualified by reason of immigration status

(1) For the purposes of this Part of this Act a person is disqualified by reason of the person's immigration status from carrying on a licensable activity if the person is subject to immigration control and—

(a) the person has not been granted leave to enter or remain in the United Kingdom; or

(b) the person's leave to enter or remain in the United Kingdom—

(i) is invalid;

(ii) has ceased to have effect (whether by reason of curtailment, revocation, cancellation, passage of time or otherwise); or

(iii) is subject to a condition preventing the person from carrying on the licensable activity.

(2) Where a person is on immigration bail within the meaning of Part 1 of Schedule 10 to the Immigration Act 2016—

(a) the person is to be treated for the purposes of this Part of this Act as if the person had been granted leave to enter the United Kingdom; but

(b) any condition as to the person's work in the United Kingdom to which the person's immigration bail is subject is to be treated for those purposes as a condition of leave.

(3) For the purposes of this section a person is subject to immigration control if under the Immigration Act 1971 the person requires leave to enter or remain in the United Kingdom.

(4) For the purposes of this section a person carries on a licensable activity if the person—

(a) drives a private hire vehicle;

(b) operates a private hire vehicle; or

(c) drives a hackney carriage.

79B Immigration offences and immigration penalties

79B Immigration offences and immigration penalties

(1) In this Part of this Act "immigration offence" means—

(a) an offence under any of the Immigration Acts;

(b) an offence under section 1 of the Criminal Attempts Act 1981 of attempting to commit an offence within paragraph (a); or

(c) an offence under section 1 of the Criminal Law Act 1977 of conspiracy to commit an offence within paragraph (a).

(2) In this Part of this Act "immigration penalty" means a penalty under—

(a) section 15 of the Immigration, Asylum and Nationality Act 2006 ("the 2006 Act"); or

(b) section 23 of the Immigration Act 2014 ("the 2014 Act").

(3) For the purposes of this Part of this Act a person to whom a penalty notice under section 15 of the 2006 Act has been given is not to be treated as having been required to pay an immigration penalty if—

(a) the person is excused payment by virtue of section 15(3) of that Act; or

(b) the penalty is cancelled by virtue of section 16 or 17 of that Act.

(4) For the purposes of this Part of this Act a person to whom a penalty notice under section 15 of the 2006 Act has been given is not to be treated as having been required to pay an immigration penalty until such time as—

(a) the period for giving a notice of objection under section 16 of that Act has expired and the Secretary of State has considered any notice given within that period; and

(b) if a notice of objection was given within that period, the period for appealing under section 17 of that Act has expired and any appeal brought within that period has been finally determined, abandoned or withdrawn.

(5) For the purposes of this Part of this Act a person to whom a penalty notice under section 23 of the 2014 Act has been given is not to be treated as having been required to pay an immigration penalty if—

(a) the person is excused payment by virtue of section 24 of that Act; or

(b) the penalty is cancelled by virtue of section 29 or 30 of that Act.

(6) For the purposes of this Part of this Act a person to whom a penalty notice under section 23 of the 2014 Act has been given is not to be treated as having been required to pay an immigration penalty until such time as—

(a) the period for giving a notice of objection under section 29 of that Act has expired and the Secretary of State has considered any notice given within that period; and

(b) if a notice of objection was given within that period, the period for appealing under section 30 of that Act has expired and any appeal brought within that period has been finally determined, abandoned or withdrawn."

Civic Government (Scotland) Act 1982 (c. 45)

29 The Civic Government (Scotland) Act 1982 is amended as follows.

30 In section 13 (taxi and private hire car driving licences) after subsection (3) insert—

"(3A) A licensing authority shall not grant a licence to any person under this section unless the authority is satisfied that the person is not disqualified by reason of the person's immigration status from driving a taxi or private hire car.

(3B) Section 13A makes provision for the purposes of subsection (3A) about the circumstances in which a person is disqualified by reason of the person's immigration status from driving a taxi or private hire car.

(3C) In determining for the purposes of subsection (3A) whether a person is disqualified by reason of the person's immigration status from driving a taxi or private hire car, a licensing authority must have regard to any guidance issued by the Secretary of State."

31 After section 13 insert—

"13A Persons disqualified by reason of immigration status

"13A Persons disqualified by reason of immigration status

(1) For the purposes of section 13(3A) a person is disqualified by reason of the person's immigration status from driving a taxi or private hire car if the person is subject to immigration control and—

(a) the person has not been granted leave to enter or remain in the United Kingdom, or

(b) the person's leave to enter or remain in the United Kingdom—
(i) is invalid,
(ii) has ceased to have effect (whether by reason of curtailment, revocation, cancellation, passage of time or otherwise), or
(iii) is subject to a condition preventing the person from driving a taxi or private hire car.

(2) Where a person is on immigration bail within the meaning of Part 1 of Schedule 10 to the Immigration Act 2016—
(a) the person is to be treated for the purposes of this section as if the person had been granted leave to enter the United Kingdom, but
(b) any condition as to the person's work in the United Kingdom to which the person's immigration bail is subject is to be treated for those purposes as a condition of leave.

(3) For the purposes of this section a person is subject to immigration control if under the Immigration Act 1971 the person requires leave to enter or remain in the United Kingdom."

32 (1) Schedule 1 (licensing - further provisions as to the general system) is amended as follows.

(2) In paragraph 8 (duration of licences) in sub-paragraph (8) after "paragraphs" insert "8A and".

(3) After paragraph 8 insert—

"8A Taxi etc driving licences for persons subject to immigration control

8A (1) Sub-paragraph (2) applies if—
(a) a taxi driver's licence or private hire car driver's licence is to be granted to a person who has been granted leave to enter or remain in the United Kingdom for a limited period ("the leave period"),
(b) the person's leave has not been extended by virtue of section 3C of the Immigration Act 1971 (continuation of leave pending variation decision), and
(c) apart from sub-paragraph (2), the period for which the licence would have had effect would have ended after the end of the leave period.

(2) The licensing authority which grants the licence must specify a period in the licence as the period for which it has effect; and that period must end at or before the end of the leave period.

(3) Sub-paragraph (4) applies if—
(a) a taxi driver's licence or private hire car driver's licence is to be granted to a person who has been granted leave to enter or remain in the United Kingdom for a limited period, and
(b) the person's leave has been extended by virtue of section 3C of the Immigration Act 1971 (continuation of leave pending variation decision).

(4) The licensing authority which grants the licence must specify a period in the licence as the period for which it has effect; and that period must not exceed six months.

(5) A taxi driver's licence or private hire car driver's licence ceases to have effect if the person to whom it was granted becomes disqualified by reason of the person's immigration status from driving a taxi or private hire car.

(6) Section 13A (persons disqualified by reason of immigration status) applies for the purposes of sub-paragraph (5) as it applies for the purposes of section 13(3A).

(7) If a licence granted in accordance with sub-paragraph (2) or (4) expires, the person to whom it was granted must, within the period of 7 days beginning with the day after that on which it expired, return the licence to the licensing authority.

(8) If sub-paragraph (5) applies to a licence, the person to whom it was granted must, within the period of 7 days beginning with the day after the day on which the person first became disqualified, return the licence to the licensing authority which granted the licence.

(9) A person who, without reasonable excuse, contravenes sub-paragraph (7) or (8) is guilty of an offence and liable on summary conviction to a fine not exceeding level 3 on the standard scale.

(10) This paragraph applies in relation to the renewal of a licence as it applies in relation to the grant of a licence."

(4) In paragraph 11 (suspension and revocation of licences) after sub-paragraph (2) insert—

"(2A) A licensing authority may order the suspension or revocation of a taxi driver's licence or a private hire car driver's licence if the holder of the licence has, since its grant, been convicted of an immigration offence or required to pay an immigration penalty (see paragraph 20).

(2B) Sub-paragraph (2A) does not apply if—

(a) in a case where the holder of the licence has been convicted of an immigration offence, the conviction is a spent conviction within the meaning of the Rehabilitation of Offenders Act 1974, or

(b) in a case where the holder of the licence has been required to pay an immigration penalty—

(i) more than three years have elapsed since the date on which the penalty was imposed, and

(ii) the amount of the penalty has been paid in full."

(5) In paragraph 18 (appeals) after sub-paragraph (8) insert—

"(8A) On an appeal under this paragraph relating to a taxi driver's licence or a private hire car driver's licence, the sheriff is not entitled to entertain any question as to whether—

(a) a person should be, or should have been, granted leave to enter or remain in the United Kingdom, or

(b) a person has, after the date of the decision being appealed against, been granted leave to enter or remain in the United Kingdom."

(6) After paragraph 19 insert—

"20 (1) In this Schedule "immigration offence" means an offence under any of the Immigration Acts.

(2) In this Schedule "immigration penalty" means a penalty under—

(a) section 15 of the Immigration, Asylum and Nationality Act 2006 ("the 2006 Act"), or

(b) section 23 of the Immigration Act 2014 ("the 2014 Act").

(3) For the purposes of this Schedule a person to whom a penalty notice under section 15 of the 2006 Act has been given is not to be treated as having been required to pay an immigration penalty if—

(a) the person is excused payment by virtue of section 15(3) of that Act, or

(b) the penalty is cancelled by virtue of section 16 or 17 of that Act.

(4) For the purposes of this Schedule a person to whom a penalty notice under section 15 of the 2006 Act has been given is not to be treated as having been required to pay an immigration penalty until such time as—

(a) the period for giving a notice of objection under section 16 of that Act has expired and the Secretary of State has considered any notice given within that period, and

(b) if a notice of objection was given within that period, the period for appealing under section 17 of that Act has expired and any appeal brought within that period has been finally determined, abandoned or withdrawn.

(5) For the purposes of this Schedule a person to whom a penalty notice under section 23 of the 2014 Act has been given is not to be treated as having been required to pay an immigration penalty if—

(a) the person is excused payment by virtue of section 24 of that Act, or

(b) the penalty is cancelled by virtue of section 29 or 30 of that Act.

(6) For the purposes of this Schedule a person to whom a penalty notice under section 23 of the 2014 Act has been given is not to be treated as having been required to pay an immigration penalty until such time as—

(a) the period for giving a notice of objection under section 29 of that Act has expired and the Secretary of State has considered any notice given within that period, and

(b) if a notice of objection was given within that period, the period for appealing under section 30 of that Act has expired and any appeal brought within that period has been finally determined, abandoned or withdrawn."

Road Traffic Offenders (Northern Ireland) Order 1996 (SI 1996/1320 (NI 10))

33 (1) Part 1 of Schedule 1 to the Road Traffic Offenders (Northern Ireland) Order 1996 (SI 1996/1320 (NI 10)) is amended as follows.

(2) After the entry relating to section 1(3) of the Taxis Act (Northern Ireland) 2008 insert—

"Section 2A(8)	Failing to return an operator's licence	Summarily	Level 3 on the standard scale".

(3) After the entry relating to section 22(6) of the Taxis Act (Northern Ireland) 2008 insert—

"Section 23A(8)	Failing to return an operator's licence	Summarily	Level 3 on the standard scale".

Private Hire Vehicles (London) Act 1998 (c. 34)

34 The Private Hire Vehicles (London) Act 1998 is amended as follows.

35 In section 1(1) (meaning of "private hire vehicle" etc)—

(a) omit the "and" at the end of paragraph (a), and

(b) at the end of paragraph (b) insert "; and

(c) operate", in relation to a private hire vehicle, means to make provision for the invitation or acceptance of, or to accept, private hire bookings in relation to the vehicle."

36 (1) Section 3 (London operator's licences) is amended as follows.

(2) In subsection (3) for the "and" at the end of paragraph (a) substitute—

"(aa) if the applicant is an individual, the applicant is not disqualified by reason of the applicant's immigration status from operating a private hire vehicle; and".

(3) After subsection (3) insert—

"(3A) In determining for the purposes of subsection (3) whether an applicant is disqualified by reason of the applicant's immigration status from operating a private hire vehicle, the licensing authority must have regard to any guidance issued by the Secretary of State."

(4) In subsection (5) for "A" substitute "Subject to section 3A, a".

37 After section 3 insert—

"3A London PHV operator's licences for persons subject to immigration control

"3A London PHV operator's licences for persons subject to immigration control

(1) Subsection (2) applies if—

(a) a London PHV operator's licence is to be granted to a person who has been granted leave to enter or remain in the United Kingdom for a limited period ("the leave period");

(b) the person's leave has not been extended by virtue of section 3C of the Immigration Act 1971 (continuation of leave pending variation decision); and

(c) apart from subsection (2), the period for which the licence would have been granted would have ended after the end of the leave period.

(2) The licence must be granted for a period which ends at or before the end of the leave period.

(3) Subsection (4) applies if—

(a) a London PHV operator's licence is to be granted to a person who has been granted leave to enter or remain in the United Kingdom for a limited period; and

(b) the person's leave has been extended by virtue of section 3C of the Immigration Act 1971 (continuation of leave pending variation decision).

(4) The licence must be granted for a period which does not exceed six months.

(5) A London PHV operator's licence ceases to be in force if the person to whom it was granted becomes disqualified by reason of the person's immigration status from operating a private hire vehicle.

(6) If subsection (5) applies to a licence, the person to whom it was granted must, within the period of 7 days beginning with the day after the day on which the person first became disqualified, return it to the licensing authority.

(7) A person who, without reasonable excuse, contravenes subsection (6) is guilty of an offence and liable on summary conviction—

(a) to a fine not exceeding level 3 on the standard scale; and

(b) in the case of a continuing offence, to a fine not exceeding ten pounds for each day during which an offence continues after conviction.

(8) The Secretary of State may by regulations amend the amount for the time being specified in subsection (7)(b)."

38 (1) Section 13 (London PHV driver's licences) is amended as follows.

(2) In subsection (2) for the "and" at the end of paragraph (a) substitute—

"(aa) the applicant is not disqualified by reason of the applicant's immigration status from driving a private hire vehicle; and".

(3) After subsection (2) insert—

"(2A) In determining for the purposes of subsection (2) whether an applicant is disqualified by reason of the applicant's immigration status from driving a private hire vehicle, the licensing authority must have regard to any guidance issued by the Secretary of State."

(4) In subsection (5) at the beginning of paragraph (c) insert "subject to section 13A,".

39 After section 13 insert—

"13A London PHV driver's licences for persons subject to immigration control

"13A London PHV driver's licences for persons subject to immigration control

(1) Subsection (2) applies if—

(a) a London PHV driver's licence is to be granted to a person who has been granted leave to enter or remain in the United Kingdom for a limited period ("the leave period");

(b) the person's leave has not been extended by virtue of section 3C of the Immigration Act 1971 (continuation of leave pending variation decision); and

(c) apart from subsection (2), the period for which the licence would have been granted would have ended after the end of the leave period.

(2) The licence must be granted for a period which ends at or before the end of the leave period.

(3) Subsection (4) applies if—

(a) a London PHV driver's licence is to be granted to a person who has been granted leave to enter or remain in the United Kingdom for a limited period; and

(b) the person's leave has been extended by virtue of section 3C of the Immigration Act 1971 (continuation of leave pending variation decision).

(4) The licence must be granted for a period which does not exceed six months.

(5) A London PHV driver's licence ceases to be in force if the person to whom it was granted becomes disqualified by reason of the person's immigration status from driving a private hire vehicle.

(6) If subsection (5) applies to a licence, the person to whom it was granted must, within the period of 7 days beginning with the day after the day on which the person first became disqualified, return the licence and the person's driver's badge to the licensing authority.

(7) A person who, without reasonable excuse, contravenes subsection (6) is guilty of an offence and liable on summary conviction—

(a) to a fine not exceeding level 3 on the standard scale; and

(b) in the casc of a continuing offence, to a fine not exceeding ten pounds for each day during which an offence continues after conviction.

(8) The Secretary of State may by regulations amend the amount for the time being specified in subsection (7)(b)."

40 (1) Section 16 (power to suspend or revoke licences) is amended as follows.

(2) In subsection (2) before the "or" at the end of paragraph (a) insert—

"(aa) the licence holder has, since the grant of the licence, been convicted of an immigration offence or required to pay an immigration penalty;".

(3) After subsection (2) insert—

"(2A) Subsection (2)(aa) does not apply if—

(a) in a case where the licence holder has been convicted of an immigration offence, the conviction is a spent conviction within the meaning of the Rehabilitation of Offenders Act 1974, or

(b) in a case where the licence holder has been required to pay an immigration penalty—

(i) more than three years have elapsed since the date on which the penalty was imposed, and

(ii) the amount of the penalty has been paid in full."

(4) In subsection (4) at the end of paragraph (a) insert—

"(aa) the licence holder has, since the grant of the licence, been convicted of an immigration offence or required to pay an immigration penalty;".

(5) After subsection (4) insert—

"(5) Subsection (4)(aa) does not apply if—

(a) in a case where the licence holder has been convicted of an immigration offence, the conviction is a spent conviction within the meaning of the Rehabilitation of Offenders Act 1974, or

(b) in a case where the licence holder has been required to pay an immigration penalty—

(i) more than three years have elapsed since the date on which the penalty was imposed, and

(ii) the amount of the penalty has been paid in full."

41 In section 25 (appeals) after subsection (7) insert—

"(8) On an appeal under this Act to the magistrates' court or the Crown Court, the court is not entitled to entertain any question as to whether—

(a) a person should be, or should have been, granted leave to enter or remain in the United Kingdom; or

(b) a person has, after the date of the decision being appealed against, been granted leave to enter or remain in the United Kingdom."

42 (1) Section 32 (regulations) is amended as follows.

(2) In subsection (1) after "other than section" in the first place those words appear insert "3A(8), 13A(8) or".

(3) After subsection (2) insert—

"(2A) The power to make regulations conferred on the Secretary of State by section 3A(8) or 13A(8) is exercisable by statutory instrument.

(2B) A statutory instrument containing regulations under either of those sections may not be made unless a draft of the instrument has been laid before, and approved by a resolution of, each House of Parliament."

(4) In subsection (4) after "made under section" insert "3A(8), 13A(8) or".

43 After section 35 insert—

"35A Persons disqualified by reason of immigration status

"35A Persons disqualified by reason of immigration status

(1) For the purposes of this Act a person is disqualified by reason of the person's immigration status from carrying on a licensable activity if the person is subject to immigration control and—

(a) the person has not been granted leave to enter or remain in the United Kingdom; or

(b) the person's leave to enter or remain in the United Kingdom—

(i) is invalid;

(ii) has ceased to have effect (whether by reason of curtailment, revocation, cancellation, passage of time or otherwise); or

(iii) is subject to a condition preventing the person from carrying on the licensable activity.

(2) Where a person is on immigration bail within the meaning of Part 1 of Schedule 10 to the Immigration Act 2016—

(a) the person is to be treated for the purposes of this Act as if the person had been granted leave to enter the United Kingdom; but

(b) any condition as to the person's work in the United Kingdom to which the person's immigration bail is subject is to be treated for those purposes as a condition of leave.

(3) For the purposes of this section a person is subject to immigration control if under the Immigration Act 1971 the person requires leave to enter or remain in the United Kingdom.

(4) For the purposes of this section a person carries on a licensable activity if the person—

(a) operates a private hire vehicle; or

(b) drives a private hire vehicle.

35B Immigration offences and immigration penalties

35B Immigration offences and immigration penalties

(1) In this Act "immigration offence" means—

(a) an offence under any of the Immigration Acts;

(b) an offence under section 1 of the Criminal Attempts Act 1981 of attempting to commit an offence within paragraph (a); or

(c) an offence under section 1 of the Criminal Law Act 1977 of conspiracy to commit an offence within paragraph (a).

(2) In this Act "immigration penalty" means a penalty under—

(a) section 15 of the Immigration, Asylum and Nationality Act 2006 ("the 2006 Act"), or

(b) section 23 of the Immigration Act 2014 ("the 2014 Act").

(3) For the purposes of this Act a person to whom a penalty notice under section 15 of the 2006 Act has been given is not to be treated as having been required to pay an immigration penalty if—

(a) the person is excused payment by virtue of section 15(3) of that Act; or

(b) the penalty is cancelled by virtue of section 16 or 17 of that Act.

(4) For the purposes of this Act a person to whom a penalty notice under section 15 of the 2006 Act has been given is not to be treated as having been required to pay an immigration penalty until such time as—

(a) the period for giving a notice of objection under section 16 of that Act has expired and the Secretary of State has considered any notice given within that period; and

(b) if a notice of objection was given within that period, the period for appealing under section 17 of that Act has expired and any appeal brought within that period has been finally determined, abandoned or withdrawn.

(5) For the purposes of this Act a person to whom a penalty notice under section 23 of the 2014 Act has been given is not to be treated as having been required to pay an immigration penalty if—

(a) the person is excused payment by virtue of section 24 of that Act; or

(b) the penalty is cancelled by virtue of section 29 or 30 of that Act.

(6) For the purposes of this Act a person to whom a penalty notice under section 23 of the 2014 Act has been given is not to be treated as having been required to pay an immigration penalty until such time as—

(a) the period for giving a notice of objection under section 29 of that Act has expired and the Secretary of State has considered any notice given within that period; and

(b) if a notice of objection was given within that period, the period for appealing under section 30 of that Act has expired and any appeal brought within that period has been finally determined, abandoned or withdrawn."

44 In section 36 (interpretation) at the appropriate place insert—

""""operate" has the meaning given in section 1(1);".

Taxis Act (Northern Ireland) 2008 (c. 4)

45 The Taxis Act (Northern Ireland) 2008 is amended as follows.

46 (1) Section 2 (operator's licences) is amended as follows.

(2) In subsection (4) for the "and" at the end of paragraph (a) substitute—

"(aa) if the applicant is an individual, the applicant is not disqualified by reason of the applicant's immigration status from operating a taxi service; and".

(3) After subsection (4) insert—

"(4A) In determining for the purposes of subsection (4) whether an applicant is disqualified by reason of the applicant's immigration status from operating a taxi service, the Department must have regard to any guidance issued by the Secretary of State."

(4) In subsection (7) for "An" substitute "Subject to section 2A, an".

47 After section 2 insert—

"2A Operator's licences for persons subject to immigration control

"2A Operator's licences for persons subject to immigration control

(1) Subsection (2) applies if—

(a) an operator's licence is to be granted to a person who has been granted leave to enter or remain in the United Kingdom for a limited period ("the leave period"),

(b) the person's leave has not been extended by virtue of section 3C of the Immigration Act 1971 (continuation of leave pending variation decision), and

(c) apart from subsection (2), the period for which the licence would have been granted would have ended after the end of the leave period.

(2) The licence must be granted for a period which ends at or before the end of the leave period.

(3) Subsection (4) applies if—

(a) an operator's licence is to be granted to a person who has been granted leave to enter or remain in the United Kingdom for a limited period, and

(b) the person's leave has been extended by virtue of section 3C of the Immigration Act 1971 (continuation of leave pending variation decision).

(4) The licence must be granted for a period which does not exceed six months.

(5) An operator's licence ceases to be in force if the person to whom it was granted becomes disqualified by reason of the person's immigration status from operating a taxi service.

(6) If a licence granted in accordance with subsection (2) or (4) expires, the person to whom it was granted must, within the period of 7 days beginning with the day after that on which it expired, return it to the Department.

(7) If subsection (5) applies to a licence, the person to whom it was granted must, within the period of 7 days beginning with the day after the day on which the person first became disqualified, return it to the Department.

(8) A person who, without reasonable excuse, contravenes subsection (6) or (7) is guilty of an offence."

48 (1) Section 23 (taxi driver's licences) is amended as follows.

(2) In subsection (2) after paragraph (a) insert—

"(aa) the applicant is not disqualified by reason of the applicant's immigration status from driving a taxi;".

(3) After subsection (2) insert—

"(2A) In determining for the purposes of subsection (2) whether an applicant is disqualified by reason of the applicant's immigration status from driving a taxi, the Department must have regard to any guidance issued by the Secretary of State."

(4) In subsection (8) for "A" substitute "Subject to section 23A, a".

49 After section 23 insert—

"23A Taxi driver's licences for persons subject to immigration control

"23A Taxi driver's licences for persons subject to immigration control

(1) Subsection (2) applies if—

(a) a taxi driver's licence is to be granted to a person who has been granted leave to enter or remain in the United Kingdom for a limited period ("the leave period"),

(b) the person's leave has not been extended by virtue of section 3C of the Immigration Act 1971 (continuation of leave pending variation decision), and

(c) apart from subsection (2), the period for which the licence would have been granted would have ended after the end of the leave period.

(2) The licence must be granted for a period which ends at or before the end of the leave period.

(3) Subsection (4) applies if—

(a) a taxi driver's licence is to be granted to a person who has been granted leave to enter or remain in the United Kingdom for a limited period, and

(b) the person's leave has been extended by virtue of section 3C of the Immigration Act 1971 (continuation of leave pending variation decision).

(4) The licence must be granted for a period which does not exceed six months.

(5) A taxi driver's licence ceases to be in force if the person to whom it was granted becomes disqualified by reason of the person's immigration status from driving a taxi.

(6) If a licence granted in accordance with subsection (2) or (4) expires, the person to whom it was granted must, within the period of 7 days beginning with the day after that on which it expired, return to the Department—

(a) the licence,

(b) the person's driver's badge, and

(c) any other evidence of identification which the Department has issued under section 24.

(7) If subsection (5) applies to a licence, the person to whom it was granted must, within the period of 7 days beginning with the day after the day on which the person first became disqualified, return to the Department—

(a) the licence,
(b) the person's driver's badge, and
(c) any other evidence of identification which the Department has issued under section 24.

(8) A person who, without reasonable excuse, contravenes subsection (6) or (7) is guilty of an offence."

50 (1) Section 26 (power to suspend, revoke or curtail licences) is amended as follows.

(2) In subsection (2) before the "or" at the end of paragraph (a) insert—

"(aa) the licence holder has, since the grant of the licence, been convicted of an immigration offence or required to pay an immigration penalty;".

(3) After subsection (2) insert—

"(2A) Subsection (2)(aa) does not apply if—

(a) in a case where the licence holder has been convicted of an immigration offence, the conviction is a spent conviction within the meaning of the Rehabilitation of Offenders (Northern Ireland) Order 1978 (SI 1978/1908 (NI 27)), or
(b) in a case where the licence holder has been required to pay an immigration penalty—
(i) more than three years have elapsed since the date on which the penalty was imposed, and
(ii) the amount of the penalty has been paid in full."

(4) In subsection (6) before the "or" at the end of paragraph (a) insert—

"(aa) the licence holder has, since the grant of the licence, been convicted of an immigration offence or required to pay an immigration penalty;".

(5) After subsection (6) insert—

"(7) Subsection (6)(aa) does not apply if—

(a) in a case where the licence holder has been convicted of an immigration offence, the conviction is a spent conviction within the meaning of the Rehabilitation of Offenders (Northern Ireland) Order 1978 (SI 1978/1908 (NI 27)), or
(b) in a case where the licence holder has been required to pay an immigration penalty—
(i) more than three years have elapsed since the date on which the penalty was imposed, and
(ii) the amount of the penalty has been paid in full."

51 In section 32 (return of licences etc) after subsection (5) insert—

"(5A) Subsection (4) does not apply if the licence was granted in accordance with section 2A(2) or (4) or 23A(2) or (4) (but see sections 2A(6) and 23A(6))."

52 In section 34 (appeals) after subsection (5) insert—

"(6) On any appeal, the court is not entitled to entertain any question as to whether—

(a) a person should be, or should have been, granted leave to enter or remain in the United Kingdom, or

(b) a person has, after the date of the decision being appealed against, been granted leave to enter or remain in the United Kingdom."

53 After section 56 insert—

"56A Persons disqualified by reason of immigration status

"56A Persons disqualified by reason of immigration status

(1) For the purposes of this Act a person is disqualified by reason of the person's immigration status from carrying on a licensable activity if the person is subject to immigration control and—

(a) the person has not been granted leave to enter or remain in the United Kingdom, or

(b) the person's leave to enter or remain in the United Kingdom—

(i) is invalid,

(ii) has ceased to have effect (whether by reason of curtailment, revocation, cancellation, passage of time or otherwise), or

(iii) is subject to a condition preventing the person from carrying on the licensable activity.

(2) Where a person is on immigration bail within the meaning of Part 1 of Schedule 10 to the Immigration Act 2016—

(a) the person is to be treated for the purposes of this Part as if the person had been granted leave to enter the United Kingdom, but

(b) any condition as to the person's work in the United Kingdom to which the person's immigration bail is subject is to be treated for those purposes as a condition of leave.

(3) For the purposes of this section a person is subject to immigration control if under the Immigration Act 1971 the person requires leave to enter or remain in the United Kingdom.

(4) For the purposes of this section a person carries on a licensable activity if the person—

(a) operates a taxi service, or

(b) drives a taxi.

56B Immigration offences and immigration penalties

56B Immigration offences and immigration penalties

(1) In this Act "immigration offence" means—

(a) an offence under any of the Immigration Acts,

(b) an offence under Article 3 of the Criminal Attempts and Conspiracy (Northern Ireland) Order 1983 (SI 1983/1120 (NI 13)) of attempting to commit an offence within paragraph (a), or

(c) an offence under Article 9 of that Order of conspiracy to commit an offence within paragraph (a).

(2) In subsection (1)(a)—

(a) "the Immigration Acts" has the meaning given by section 61(2) of the UK Borders Act 2007, and

(b) the reference to an offence under any of the Immigration Acts includes an offence under section 133(5) of the Criminal Justice and Immigration Act 2008 (breach of condition imposed on designated person).

(3) In this Act "immigration penalty" means a penalty under—

(a) section 15 of the Immigration, Asylum and Nationality Act 2006 ("the 2006 Act"), or

(b) section 23 of the Immigration Act 2014 ("the 2014 Act").

(4) For the purposes of this Act a person to whom a penalty notice under section 15 of the 2006 Act has been given is not to be treated as having been required to pay an immigration penalty if—

(a) the person is excused payment by virtue of section 15(3) of that Act, or

(b) the penalty is cancelled by virtue of section 16 or 17 of that Act.

(5) For the purposes of this Act a person to whom a penalty notice under section 15 of the 2006 Act has been given is not to be treated as having been required to pay an immigration penalty until such time as—

(a) the period for giving a notice of objection under section 16 of that Act has expired and the Secretary of State has considered any notice given within that period, and

(b) if a notice of objection was given within that period, the period for appealing under section 17 of that Act has expired and any appeal brought within that period has been finally determined, abandoned or withdrawn.

(6) For the purposes of this Act a person to whom a penalty notice under section 23 of the 2014 Act has been given is not to be treated as having been required to pay an immigration penalty if—

(a) the person is excused payment by virtue of section 24 of that Act, or

(b) the penalty is cancelled by virtue of section 29 or 30 of that Act.

(7) For the purposes of this Act a person to whom a penalty notice under section 23 of the 2014 Act has been given is not to be treated as having been required to pay an immigration penalty until such time as—

(a) the period for giving a notice of objection under section 29 of that Act has expired and the Secretary of State has considered any notice given within that period, and

(b) if a notice of objection was given within that period, the period for appealing under section 30 of that Act has expired and any appeal brought within that period has been finally determined, abandoned or withdrawn."

Transitional provision

54 (1) Subject to sub-paragraph (2), an amendment made by any of paragraphs 3, 4, 7 to 12, 18 to 23, 30, 32(2) and (3), 36 to 39 and 46 to 49 does not apply in relation to

an application for a licence made before the coming into force of that paragraph or a licence granted in response to such an application.

(2) Sub-paragraph (1) does not prevent an amendment made by any of those paragraphs from applying in relation to—

(a) an application for the renewal of a licence where that licence was granted before the coming into force of that paragraph, or

(b) a licence renewed in response to such an application.

55 (1) Subject to sub-paragraphs (2) and (3), an amendment made by any of paragraphs 13, 14, 24, 25, 32(4), 40 and 50 applies in relation to a licence granted before or after the coming into force of that paragraph.

(2) An amendment made by any of those paragraphs applies in relation to a conviction for an immigration offence only if the person in question has been convicted of that offence after the coming into force of that paragraph in respect of the person's conduct after that time.

(3) An amendment made by any of those paragraphs applies in relation to a requirement to pay an immigration penalty only if the person in question has been required to pay the penalty after the coming into force of that paragraph in respect of the person's conduct after that time.

56 (1) Section 19(1) of the Plymouth City Council Act 1975 has effect in relation to the licence of a driver of a hackney carriage or private hire vehicle granted before the coming into force of paragraph 13 as if before the "or" at the end of paragraph (a) there were inserted—

"(ab) in the case of a refusal to renew a licence, that he is disqualified by reason of his immigration status from driving a hackney carriage or a private hire vehicle;".

(2) Section 20A(1)(a) of that Act has effect in relation to such a licence as if after "subsection (1)(aa)" there were inserted "or (ab)".

(3) Section 20(1) of that Act has effect in relation to an operator's licence granted before the coming into force of paragraph 14 as if before the "or" at the end of paragraph (c) there were inserted—

"(cb) in the case of a refusal to renew a licence, that the operator is disqualified by reason of the operator's immigration status from operating a private hire vehicle;".

(4) Section 20A(1)(b) of that Act has effect in relation to such a licence as if after "subsection (1)(ca)" there were inserted "or (cb)".

(5) Section 61(1) of the Local Government (Miscellaneous Provisions) Act 1976 has effect in relation to the licence of a driver of a hackney carriage or private hire vehicle granted before the coming into force of paragraph 24 as if before the "or" at the end of paragraph (a) there were inserted—

"(ab) in the case of a refusal to renew a licence, that he is disqualified by reason of his immigration status from driving a hackney carriage or a private hire vehicle;".

(6) Section 62A(1)(a) of that Act has effect in relation to such a licence as if after "subsection (1)(aa)" there were inserted "or (ab)".

(7) Section 62(1) of that Act has effect in relation to an operator's licence granted before the coming into force of paragraph 25 as if before the "or" at the end of paragraph (c) there were inserted—

"(cb) in the case of a refusal to renew a licence, that the operator is disqualified by reason of the operator's immigration status from operating a private hire vehicle;".

(8) Section 62A(1)(b) of that Act has effect in relation to such a licence as if after "subsection (1)(ca)" there were inserted "or (cb)".

(9) Subsections (3A) to (3C) of section 13 of the Civic Government (Scotland) Act 1982 apply in relation to an application for the renewal of a taxi driver's or private hire car driver's licence granted before the coming into force of paragraph 30 as they apply in relation to an application for the grant of such a licence made after that time.

SCHEDULE 6

Section 38

ILLEGAL WORKING CLOSURE NOTICES AND ILLEGAL WORKING COMPLIANCE ORDERS

Illegal working closure notices

1 (1) An immigration officer of at least the rank of chief immigration officer may issue an illegal working closure notice in respect of premises if satisfied on reasonable grounds that the conditions in sub-paragraphs (3) and (6) are met.

(2) An illegal working closure notice is a notice which prohibits, for a period specified in the notice—

(a) access to the premises other than by a person who habitually lives on the premises, except where authorised in writing by an immigration officer;

(b) paid or voluntary work being performed on the premises, except where so authorised.

(3) The condition in this sub-paragraph is that an employer operating at the premises is employing a person over the age of 16 and subject to immigration control—

(a) who has not been granted leave to enter or remain in the United Kingdom, or

(b) whose leave to enter or remain in the United Kingdom—

(i) is invalid,

(ii) has ceased to have effect (whether by reason of curtailment, revocation, cancellation, passage of time or otherwise), or

(iii) is subject to a condition preventing the person from accepting the employment.

(4) Where a person is on immigration bail within the meaning of Part 1 of Schedule 10—

(a) the person is to be treated for the purposes of sub-paragraph (3) as if the person had been granted leave to enter the United Kingdom, but

(b) any condition as to the person's work in the United Kingdom to which the person's immigration bail is subject is to be treated for those purposes as a condition of leave.

(5) A person falling within sub-paragraph (3) is referred to in this Schedule as an "illegal worker".

(6) The condition in this sub-paragraph is that the employer, or a connected person in relation to the employer—

(a) has been convicted of an offence under section 21 of the Immigration, Asylum and Nationality Act 2006 ("the 2006 Act"),

(b) has, during the period of three years ending with the date on which the illegal working closure notice is issued, been required to pay a penalty under section 15 of the 2006 Act, or

(c) has at any time been required to pay such a penalty and failed to pay it.

(7) Sub-paragraph (6)(a) does not apply in relation to a conviction which is a spent conviction for the purposes of the Rehabilitation of Offenders Act 1974 or the Rehabilitation of Offenders (Northern Ireland) Order 1978 (S.I. 1978/1908 (N.I. 27)).

(8) For the purposes of sub-paragraph (6)(b) and (c)—

(a) a person to whom a penalty notice under section 15 of the 2006 Act has been given is not to be treated as having been required to pay the penalty if—

(i) the person is excused payment by virtue of section 15(3) of that Act, or

(ii) the penalty is cancelled by virtue of section 16 or 17 of that Act;

(b) a person to whom such a notice has been given is not to be treated as having been required to pay the penalty until such time as—

(i) the period for giving a notice of objection under section 16 of the 2006 Act has expired and the Secretary of State has considered any notice given within that period, and

(ii) if a notice of objection was given within that period, the period for appealing under section 17 of that Act has expired and any appeal brought within that period has been finally determined, abandoned or withdrawn.

(9) For the purposes of sub-paragraph (6), a person is a connected person in relation to an employer if—

(a) where the employer is a body corporate, the person is—

(i) a director, manager or secretary of the body corporate,

(ii) purporting to act as a director, manager or secretary of the body corporate, or

(iii) if the affairs of the body corporate are managed by its members, a member of the body corporate;

(b) where the employer is a partnership (whether or not a limited partnership), the person is a partner or purporting to act as a partner;

(c) where the employer is an individual, the person is—

(i) a body corporate of which the individual has at any time been a director, manager or secretary,

(ii) a body corporate in relation to which the individual has at any time purported to act as a director, manager or secretary,

(iii) a body corporate whose affairs are managed by its members and the individual has at any time been a member of the body corporate,

(iv) a partnership (whether or not a limited partnership) in which the individual has at any time been a partner or in relation to which the individual has at any time purported to act as a partner.

(10) An illegal working closure notice may not be issued if the employer shows in relation to the employment of each illegal worker that if a penalty notice were given under section 15 of the 2006 Act the employer would be excused under subsection (3) of that section from paying the penalty.

(11) An illegal working closure notice may be issued only if reasonable efforts have been made to inform—

(a) people who live on the premises (whether habitually or not), and

(b) any person who has an interest in the premises,

that the notice is going to be issued.

(12) Before issuing an illegal working closure notice the immigration officer must ensure that any person the officer thinks appropriate has been consulted.

(13) The Secretary of State may by regulations amend sub-paragraph (1) to change the rank specified in that sub-paragraph.

2 (1) An illegal working closure notice must—

(a) identify the premises;

(b) explain the effect of the notice;

(c) state that failure to comply with the notice is an offence;

(d) state that an application will be made under paragraph 5 for an illegal working compliance order;

(e) specify when and where the application will be heard;

(f) explain the effect of an illegal working compliance order.

(2) The maximum period that may be specified in an illegal working closure notice is 24 hours unless sub-paragraph (3) applies.

(3) The maximum period is 48 hours if the notice is issued by an immigration officer of at least the rank of immigration inspector.

(4) In calculating when the period of 48 hours ends, Christmas Day is to be disregarded.

(5) The period specified in an illegal working closure notice to which sub-paragraph (3) does not apply may be extended by up to 24 hours if an extension notice is issued by an officer of at least the rank of immigration inspector.

(6) An extension notice is a notice which—

(a) identifies the illegal working closure notice to which it relates, and

(b) specifies the period of the extension.

(7) The Secretary of State may by regulations amend sub-paragraph (3) or sub-paragraph (5) to change the rank specified in that sub-paragraph.

Cancellation of illegal working closure notices

3 (1) An immigration officer may by the issue of a cancellation notice cancel an illegal working closure notice if—

(a) the immigration officer considers that the condition in paragraph 1(3) or (6) is not met, or

(b) the employer shows in relation to the employment of each illegal worker that if a penalty notice were given under section 15 of the 2006 Act the employer would be excused under subsection (3) of that section from paying the penalty.

(2) A cancellation notice may be issued only—

(a) by an immigration officer of at least the rank of the immigration officer who issued the illegal working closure notice, or

(b) where the illegal working closure notice has been extended by an extension notice, by an immigration officer of at least the rank of the immigration officer who issued the extension notice.

Service of notices

4 (1) A notice under paragraph 1, 2 or 3 must be served by an immigration officer.

(2) The immigration officer must if possible—

(a) fix a copy of the notice to at least one prominent place on the premises,

(b) fix a copy of the notice to each normal means of access to the premises,

(c) fix a copy of the notice to any outbuildings that appear to the immigration officer to be used with or as part of the premises,

(d) give a copy of the notice to at least one person who appears to the immigration officer to have control of or responsibility for the premises,

(e) give a copy of the notice to the people who live on the premises and to any person who does not live there but was informed (under paragraph 1(11)) that the notice was going to be issued.

(3) If the immigration officer reasonably believes, at the time of serving the notice, that there are persons occupying another part of the building or other structure in which the premises are situated whose access to that part will be impeded if an illegal working compliance order is made under paragraph 5, the immigration officer must also if possible serve the notice on those persons.

(4) The immigration officer may enter any premises, using reasonable force if necessary, for the purposes of complying with sub-paragraph (2)(a).

Illegal working compliance orders

5 (1) Whenever an illegal working closure notice is issued an application must be made to the court for an illegal working compliance order (unless the notice has been cancelled under paragraph 3).

(2) An application for an illegal working compliance order must be made by an immigration officer.

(3) The application must be heard by the court not later than 48 hours after service of the illegal working closure notice.

(4) In calculating when the period of 48 hours ends, Christmas Day is to be disregarded.

(5) The court may make an illegal working compliance order in respect of premises if it is satisfied, on the balance of probabilities—

(a) that the conditions in paragraph 1(3) and (6) are met, and
(b) that it is necessary to make the illegal working compliance order to prevent an employer operating at the premises from employing an illegal worker.

(6) An illegal working compliance order may—
(a) prohibit or restrict access to the premises;
(b) require a person specified in the order to carry out, at such times as may be so specified, such checks relating to the right to work as may be prescribed by the Secretary of State in regulations;
(c) require a person specified in the order to produce to an immigration officer, at such times and such places as may be so specified, such documents relating to the right to work as may be prescribed by the Secretary of State in regulations;
(d) specify the times at which and the circumstances in which an immigration officer may enter the premises to carry out such investigations or inspections as may be specified in the order;
(e) make such other provision as the court considers appropriate.

(7) Different provisions in an illegal working compliance order may have effect for different periods.

(8) The maximum period for which an illegal working compliance order or any provision in it may have effect is 12 months.

(9) Provision included in an illegal working compliance order which prohibits or restricts access may make such provision—
(a) in relation to all persons, all persons except those specified, or all persons except those of a specified description;
(b) having effect at all times, or at all times except those specified;
(c) having effect in all circumstances, or in all circumstances except those specified.

(10) An illegal working compliance order, or any provision of it, may—
(a) be made in respect of the whole or any part of the premises;
(b) include provision about access to a part of the building or structure of which the premises form part.

(11) The court must notify the relevant licensing authority if it makes an illegal working compliance order in relation to premises in England and Wales in respect of which a premises licence is in force.

Illegal working compliance orders: adjournment of hearing

6 (1) This paragraph applies where an application has been made under paragraph 5 for an illegal working compliance order.

(2) The court may adjourn the hearing of the application for a period of not more than 14 days to enable any person who has an interest in the premises to show why an illegal working compliance order should not be made.

(3) If the court adjourns the hearing it may order that the illegal working closure notice continues in force until the end of the period of adjournment.

Extension of illegal working compliance orders

7 (1) An immigration officer may apply to the court for an extension (or further extension) of the period for which any provision of an illegal working compliance order is in force.

(2) The court may grant an application under this paragraph only if it is satisfied, on the balance of probabilities, that it is necessary to grant it to prevent an employer operating at the premises from employing an illegal worker.

(3) Where an application is made under this section, the court may issue a summons directed to—

(a) any person on whom the illegal working closure notice was served under paragraph 4, or

(b) any other person who appears to the court to have an interest in the premises,

requiring the person to appear before the court to respond to the application.

(4) If a summons is issued, a notice stating the date, time and place of the hearing of the application must be served on the persons to whom the summons is directed.

(5) No application may be granted under this paragraph such that an illegal working compliance order, or any provision in it—

(a) is extended for a period exceeding 6 months, or

(b) is in force for a period exceeding 24 months in total.

Variation or discharge of illegal working compliance orders

8 (1) An application may be made to the court under this paragraph—

(a) by an immigration officer for an illegal working compliance order to be varied or discharged,

(b) by a person on whom the illegal working closure notice was served under paragraph 4, or by any other person who has an interest in the premises, for an illegal working compliance order to be varied or discharged.

(2) Where an application is made under this paragraph, the court may issue a summons directed to—

(a) an immigration officer,

(b) any person on whom the illegal working closure notice was served under paragraph 4, or

(c) any other person who appears to the court to have an interest in the premises,

requiring the person to appear before the court to respond to the application.

(3) If a summons is issued, a notice stating the date, time and place of the hearing of the application must be served on the persons to whom the summons is directed.

(4) The court may not discharge an illegal working compliance order unless it is satisfied, on the balance of probabilities, that it is no longer necessary to prevent an employer operating at the premises from employing an illegal worker.

Notice and orders: appeals

9 (1) An appeal against a decision—

(a) to make, extend or vary an illegal working compliance order;

(b) not to discharge an illegal working compliance order;

(c) to order that an illegal working closure notice continues in force,

may be made by a person on whom the illegal working closure notice was served under paragraph 4, or any other person who has an interest in the premises.

(2) An appeal against a decision—

(a) not to make an illegal working compliance order;

(b) not to extend a provision of an illegal working compliance order, or not to vary such an order, made on the application of an immigration officer;

(c) to vary or discharge an illegal working compliance order;

(d) not to order that an illegal working closure notice continues in force,

may be made by an immigration officer.

(3) An appeal under this paragraph—

(a) if it is in relation to premises in England and Wales or Northern Ireland, is to the Crown Court,

(b) if it is in relation to premises in Scotland, is to the sheriff appeal court.

(4) An appeal under this paragraph must be made within the period of 21 days beginning with the date of the decision to which it relates.

(5) On an appeal under this paragraph the court may make whatever order it thinks appropriate.

(6) The court must notify the relevant licensing authority if it makes an illegal working compliance order in relation to premises in England and Wales in respect of which a premises licence is in force.

Notices and orders: enforcement

10 (1) Where access to premises is prohibited or restricted by virtue of an illegal working closure notice or an illegal working compliance order an immigration officer or a constable may enter the premises and do anything necessary to secure the premises against entry.

(2) A person acting under sub-paragraph (1) may use reasonable force.

(3) An immigration officer or a constable, together with any person acting under that person's supervision, may also enter such premises to carry out essential maintenance or repairs.

Notices and orders: offences

11 (1) A person who without reasonable excuse remains on or enters premises in contravention of an illegal working closure notice commits an offence.

(2) A person who without reasonable excuse contravenes an illegal working compliance order commits an offence.

(3) A person who without reasonable excuse obstructs a person acting under paragraph 4 or paragraph 10 commits an offence.

(4) A person guilty of an offence under this paragraph is liable on summary conviction—

(a) in England and Wales, to imprisonment for a term not exceeding 51 weeks, to a fine or to both;
(b) in Scotland, to imprisonment for a term not exceeding 12 months, to a fine not exceeding level 5 on the standard scale or to both;
(c) in Northern Ireland, to imprisonment for a term not exceeding 6 months, to a fine not exceeding level 5 on the standard scale or to both.

(5) In relation to an offence committed before section 281(5) of the Criminal Justice Act 2003 comes into force, the reference in sub-paragraph (4)(a) to 51 weeks is to be read as a reference to 6 months.

Access to other premises

12 (1) Where—
(a) access to premises is prohibited or restricted by a provision of an illegal working compliance order,
(b) those premises are part of a building or structure, and
(c) there is another part of that building or structure that is not subject to the prohibition or restriction,

an occupier or owner of that other part may apply to the court for an order under this paragraph.

(2) Notice of an application under this paragraph must be given to—
(a) whatever immigration officer the court thinks appropriate;
(b) each person on whom the illegal working closure notice was served under paragraph 4,
(c) any other person who has an interest in the premises.

(3) On an application under this paragraph the court may make whatever order it thinks appropriate in relation to access to any part of the building or structure mentioned in sub-paragraph (1).

(4) For the purposes of sub-paragraph (3), it does not matter whether provision has been made under paragraph 5(10)(b).

Reimbursement of costs

13 (1) Where the Secretary of State incurs expenditure for the purpose of clearing, securing or maintaining premises in respect of which an illegal working compliance order is in force, the Secretary of State may apply to the court for an order under this paragraph.

(2) On an application under this paragraph the court may make whatever order it thinks appropriate for the reimbursement (in full or in part) by the owner or occupier of the premises of the expenditure mentioned in sub-paragraph (1).

(3) An application for an order under this paragraph may not be heard unless it is made before the end of the period of 3 months starting with the day on which the illegal working compliance order ceases to have effect.

(4) An order under this paragraph may be made only against a person who has been served with the application for the order.

Exemption from liability

14 (1) Each of the following—

(a) the Secretary of State,

(b) an immigration officer,

(c) a police officer,

(d) the chief officer of police under whose direction or control a police officer acts,

is not liable for damages in proceedings for judicial review or the tort of negligence or misfeasance in public office, arising out of anything done or omitted to be done by the person in the exercise or purposed exercise of a power under this Schedule.

(2) Sub-paragraph (1) does not apply to an act or omission shown to have been in bad faith.

(3) Sub-paragraph (1) does not apply so as to prevent an award of damages made in respect of an act or omission on the ground that the act or omission was unlawful by virtue of section 6(1) of the Human Rights Act 1998.

(4) This paragraph does not affect any other exemption from liability (whether at common law or otherwise).

Compensation

15 (1) A person who claims to have incurred financial loss in consequence of an illegal working closure notice, other than one cancelled under paragraph 3(1)(b), may apply to the court for compensation.

(2) An application under this paragraph may not be heard unless it is made before the end of the period of 3 months starting with the day on which the notice ceases to have effect.

(3) On an application under this paragraph the court may order the payment of compensation out of money provided by Parliament if it is satisfied—

(a) that at the time the notice was issued, the condition in paragraph 1(3) or (6) was not met;

(b) that the applicant has incurred financial loss in consequence of the notice; and

(c) that having regard to all the circumstances it is appropriate to order payment of compensation in respect of that loss.

Guidance

16 (1) The Secretary of State may issue guidance about the exercise of functions under this Schedule.

(2) The Secretary of State may revise any guidance issued under this paragraph.

(3) Before issuing or revising guidance under this paragraph the Secretary of State must consult—

(a) persons whom the Secretary of State considers to represent the views of immigration officers and of chief officers of police, and

(b) such other persons as the Secretary of State considers appropriate.

(4) The Secretary of State must arrange for any guidance issued or revised under this paragraph to be published.

Interpretation

17 (1) In this Schedule—

"court", except where the context otherwise requires, means—

(a) in relation to premises in England and Wales or Northern Ireland, the magistrates' court;

(b) in relation to premises in Scotland, the sheriff court;

"owner" in relation to premises, means—

(a) a person (other than a mortgagee not in possession) entitled to dispose of the fee simple of the premises, whether in possession or in reversion;

(b) a person who holds or is entitled to the rents and profits of the premises under a lease that (when granted) was for a term of not less than 3 years;

"person who has an interest", in relation to premises, includes—

(a) the owner;

(b) any person with control of or responsibility for the premises;

(c) any person who otherwise occupies the premises;

"premises" includes—

(a) any land, vehicle, vessel or other place (whether enclosed or not);

(b) any outbuildings that are, or are used as, part of premises;

"premises licence" has the meaning given by section 11 of the Licensing Act 2003;

"relevant licensing authority" has the meaning given by section 12 of that Act.

(2) In this Schedule—

(a) a reference to employment is to employment under a contract of service or apprenticeship, whether express or implied and whether oral or written;

(b) a person is subject to immigration control if under the Immigration Act 1971 the person requires leave to enter or remain in the United Kingdom.

Amendment of Licensing Act 2003

18 After section 167(1) of the Licensing Act 2003 insert—

"(1A) This section also applies where a court has made an illegal working compliance order under Schedule 6 to the Immigration Act 2016 and the relevant licensing authority has accordingly received a notice under that Schedule."

SCHEDULE 7

Section 45

BANK ACCOUNTS

1 The Immigration Act 2014 is amended as follows.

2 After section 40 (prohibition on opening current accounts for disqualified persons) insert—

"40A Requirement to carry out immigration checks in relation to current accounts

"40A "40A Requirement to carry out immigration checks in relation to current accounts

(1) A bank or building society must, at such times or with such frequency as is specified in regulations made by the Treasury, carry out an immigration check in relation to each current account held with it that is not an excluded account.

(2) For the purposes of this section carrying out an "immigration check" in relation to a current account means checking whether, according to information supplied by the Secretary of State to a specified anti-fraud organisation or a specified data-matching authority, the account is operated by or for a disqualified person.

(3) A "disqualified person" is a person—

(a) who is in the United Kingdom,

(b) who requires leave to enter or remain in the United Kingdom but does not have it, and

(c) for whom the Secretary of State considers that a current account should not be provided by a bank or building society.

(4) A current account is an excluded account for the purposes of subsection (1) if the account is operated by or for a person or body of a description specified in regulations made by the Treasury.

(5) An account is operated by or for a person or body if the person or body is an account holder or a signatory or identified as a beneficiary in relation to the account.

(6) A bank or building society must—

(a) make arrangements with a specified anti-fraud organisation or a specified data-matching authority for the purpose of enabling the bank or building society to carry out immigration checks in relation to current accounts, and

(b) pay any reasonable fee required to be paid under those arrangements.

(7) In this section "specified anti-fraud organisation" and "specified data-matching authority" have the same meaning as in section 40(3)(a).

40B Requirement to notify existence of current accounts for disqualified persons

40B 40B Requirement to notify existence of current accounts for disqualified persons

(1) This section applies where, as a result of an immigration check carried out under section 40A, a bank or building society identifies a current account that is operated by or for a person who the bank or building society believes to be a disqualified person.

(2) Where this section applies, the bank or building society (as the case may be) must as soon as reasonably practicable—

(a) notify the Secretary of State that a current account held with it is operated by or for a person who it believes to be a disqualified person, and

(b) provide the Secretary of State with such other information as may be prescribed.

(3) A notification made, or information provided, under subsection (2) must be made or provided in the prescribed form and manner.

(4) In subsections (2) and (3) "prescribed" means prescribed in regulations made by the Treasury.

(5) Regulations under subsection (2) may (in particular) require the provision of information relating to any accounts held with the bank or building society that are operated by or for the person who is believed to be a disqualified person.

40C Action to be taken by Secretary of State following section 40B notification

40C 40C Action to be taken by Secretary of State following section 40B notification

(1) Where the Secretary of State receives a notification from a bank or building society under section 40B(2) in relation to a person, the Secretary of State must check whether the person is a disqualified person.

(2) If the Secretary of State determines that the person is a disqualified person, the Secretary of State may apply under section 40D for a freezing order in respect of one or more of the accounts held with the bank or building society that are operated by or for the disqualified person.

(3) If the Secretary of State decides not to apply for a freezing order under subsection (2), or decides to apply for a freezing order in respect of one or more but not all of the accounts held with the bank or building society that are operated by or for the disqualified person, the Secretary of State must notify the bank or building society that it is subject to the duty in section 40G(2) in relation to the disqualified person.

(4) A notification made under subsection (3) must contain the prescribed information and be made in the prescribed form and manner.

(5) In subsection (4) "prescribed" means prescribed in regulations made by the Treasury.

(6) If the Secretary of State determines that the person is not a disqualified person, the Secretary of State must notify the bank or building society accordingly.

40D Freezing orders

40D 40D Freezing orders

(1) On an application by the Secretary of State under section 40C(2), the court may make a freezing order in respect of any account specified in the application.

(2) A freezing order in respect of an account is an order that prohibits each person and body by or for whom the account is operated from making withdrawals or payments from the account.

(3) A freezing order may be made subject to exceptions.

(4) An exception may (in particular)—

(a) make provision for the disqualified person to meet his or her reasonable living expenses and reasonable legal expenses;

(b) allow another person or body by or for whom the account is operated to make withdrawals or payments from the account.

(5) An application for a freezing order may be made without notice.

(6) The court may vary or discharge a freezing order made in respect of an account (whether made under this section or on an appeal under section 40E) on an application made by—

(a) the Secretary of State, or

(b) a person or body by or for whom the account is operated.

(7) If the Secretary of State applies for a freezing order in respect of an account and the order is not made, or the order is made but subsequently discharged, the Secretary of State must notify the bank or building society that it is subject to the duty in section 40G(2) in relation to the disqualified person.

(8) A notification made under subsection (7) must contain the information and be in the form and manner prescribed in regulations made under subsection (4) of section 40C for the purposes of subsection (3) of that section.

(9) In this section—

"the court" means—

(a) in England and Wales, a magistrates' court;

(b) in Scotland, the sheriff;

(c) in Northern Ireland, a court of summary jurisdiction;

"the disqualified person" means the person who, following a check under section 40C(1), was determined to be a disqualified person, resulting in the application for the freezing order.

40E Freezing orders: appeals

40E 40E Freezing orders: appeals

(1) An appeal may be made to the relevant appeal court against a decision of a court under section 40D.

(2) The right of appeal under subsection (1) is exercisable by—

(a) the Secretary of State, and

(b) if the decision relates to a freezing order that is in force in respect of an account, a person or body by or for whom the account is operated.

(3) On an appeal under this section the relevant appeal court may make—

(a) whatever orders are necessary to give effect to its determination of the appeal;

(b) whatever incidental or consequential orders appear to it to be just.

(4) In this section "the relevant appeal court" means—

(a) the Crown Court, where the decision appealed against is a decision of a magistrates' court;

(b) the Sheriff Appeal Court, where the decision appealed against is a decision of the sheriff;

(c) a county court, where the decision appealed against is a decision of a court of summary jurisdiction.

40F Freezing orders: code of practice

40F 40F Freezing orders: code of practice

(1) The Secretary of State must issue a code of practice—

(a) specifying the factors that the Secretary of State will consider when deciding whether to apply for a freezing order under section 40C(2),

(b) outlining the arrangements for keeping a freezing order under review for the purpose of deciding whether to apply under section 40D(6) for its variation or discharge, and

(c) specifying the factors that the Secretary of State will consider when deciding whether to make such an application.

(2) The Secretary of State must from time to time review the code and may revise and re-issue it following a review.

(3) The code (or revised code)—

(a) may not be issued unless a draft has been laid before Parliament, and

(b) comes into force in accordance with provision contained in regulations made by the Secretary of State.

40G Closure of accounts not subject to freezing order

40G 40G Closure of accounts not subject to freezing order

(1) This section applies where—

(a) a bank or building society makes a notification under section 40B(2) in relation to a person,

(b) the person is determined by the Secretary of State (following a check under section 40C(1)) to be a disqualified person, and

(c) the bank or building society receives a notification under section 40C(3) or 40D(7) in relation to the disqualified person.

(2) Where this section applies the bank or building society must as soon as reasonably practicable close each account held with it that—

(a) in the case of a notification under section 40C(3), is operated by or for the disqualified person and is not the subject of an application for a freezing order;

(b) in the case of a notification under section 40D(7), is operated by or for the disqualified person and in respect of which a freezing order is not in force.

(3) The bank or building society may delay closing an account which it would otherwise be required to close under subsection (2) if at the time at which it would otherwise be required to close it—

(a) the account is overdrawn, or

(b) where the account is operated by or for the disqualified person and one or more bodies or other persons, the bank or building society considers that closing the account would significantly adversely affect the interests of any of those other bodies or persons.

(4) Where subsection (3) applies, closure of the account may be delayed for such period as is reasonable (but not indefinitely).

(5) If an account falling within subsection (2) is operated by or for the disqualified person and one or more bodies or other persons, the bank or building society is to be treated as having complied with that subsection in relation to that account if, as soon as reasonably practicable, it takes all such steps as are necessary to prevent the account from being operated by or for the disqualified person (instead of closing the account).

(6) Where the bank or building society closes an account in compliance with this section, it must tell each person or body by or for whom the account is operated, if it may lawfully do so, why it has closed the account.

(7) Where the bank or building society prevents an account from being operated by or for the disqualified person by virtue of subsection (5), it must tell each person or body by or for whom the account is operated, if it may lawfully do so, why it has prevented the account from being operated by or for the disqualified person.

(8) The bank or building society must provide the Secretary of State with information about the steps that it has taken to comply with this section.

(9) Information provided under subsection (8) must be provided in the prescribed form and manner and at the prescribed times or with the prescribed frequency.

(10) In subsection (9) "prescribed" means prescribed in regulations made by the Treasury.

40H Sections 40A to 40G: interpretation

40H 40H Sections 40A to 40G: interpretation

(1) This section applies for the purposes of sections 40A to 40G.

(2) "Account" includes a financial product by means of which a payment may be made.

(3) "Freezing order" has the meaning given by section 40D(2).

(4) "Disqualified person" has the meaning given by section 40A(3).

(5) References to an account being operated by or for a person or body are to be read in accordance with section 40A(5)."

3 (1) Section 41 (regulation by Financial Conduct Authority) is amended as follows.

(2) In subsection (1), at the end insert "and the requirements imposed on them by sections 40A, 40B and 40G".

(3) In subsection (2)(a), at the end insert "or immigration checks under section 40A".

4 In section 42 (meaning of "bank" and "building society"), in subsections (1) and (5), for "and 41" substitute "to 41".

5 (1) Section 43 (power to amend) is amended as follows.

(2) In subsection (1)(b), after "40(1)" insert "or the requirement in section 40A(1)".

(3) In subsection (1)(c), for "that section" substitute "section 40 or 40A".

6 In section 74 (orders and regulations), in subsection (2) (statutory instruments to which the affirmative resolution procedure applies), after paragraph (b) insert—

"(ba) regulations under section 40A(4);

(bb) regulations under section 40B;".

7 (1) Section 18 of the Civil Jurisdiction and Judgments Act 1982 (enforcement of UK judgments in other parts of UK) is amended as follows.

(2) In subsection (3), for "subsection (4)" substitute "subsections (4) and (4ZA)".

(3) After subsection (4) insert—

"(4ZA) This section applies to a freezing order made under section 40D of the Immigration Act 2014 by a magistrates' court in England and Wales or a court of summary jurisdiction in Northern Ireland."

SCHEDULE 8

Section 54

AMENDMENTS TO SEARCH WARRANT PROVISIONS

Immigration Act 1971 (c. 77)

1 The Immigration Act 1971 is amended as follows.

2 (1) Section 28D (entry and search of premises) is amended as follows.

(2) In subsection (1)—

(a) in paragraph (b) for "specified in the application" substitute "mentioned in subsection (1A)", and

(b) at the end of paragraph (e) insert "in relation to each set of premises specified in the application,".

(3) After subsection (1) insert—

"(1A) The premises referred to in subsection (1)(b) above are—

(a) one or more sets of premises specified in the application, or

(b) subject to subsection (2A), any premises occupied or controlled by a person specified in the application, including such sets of premises as are so specified (in which case the application is for an "all premises warrant").

(1B) If the application is for an all premises warrant, the justice of the peace must also be satisfied—

(a) that because of the particulars of the offence referred to in paragraph (a) of subsection (1), there are reasonable grounds for believing that it is necessary to search premises occupied or controlled by the person in question which are not specified in the application in order to find the material referred to in paragraph (b) of that subsection, and

(b) that it is not reasonably practicable to specify in the application all the premises which the person occupies or controls and which might need to be searched.

(1C) Subject to subsection (2A), the warrant may authorise entry to and search of premises on more than one occasion if, on the application, the justice of the peace is satisfied that it is necessary to authorise multiple entries in order to achieve the purpose for which the justice issues the warrant.

(1D) If it authorises multiple entries, the number of entries authorised may be unlimited, or limited to a maximum."

(4) In subsection (2) after "conditions" insert "referred to in subsection (1)(e)".

(5) After subsection (2) insert—

"(2A) A justice of the peace in Scotland may not issue—

(a) an all premises warrant under this section, or

(b) a warrant under this section authorising multiple entries."

(6) In subsection (7)—

(a) for "subsection (1)" substitute "this section",

(b) in paragraph (a) for "the reference" substitute "references" and for "a reference" substitute "references", and

(c) in paragraph (b) for "paragraph (d)" substitute "subsection (1)(d)".

3 (1) Section 28FB (search for personnel records with warrant) is amended as follows.

(2) In subsection (1)—

(a) after "business premises" insert "mentioned in subsection (1A)", and

(b) at the end of paragraph (c) insert "in relation to each set of premises specified in the application."

(3) After subsection (1) insert—

"(1A) The premises referred to in subsection (1) above are—

(a) one or more sets of premises specified in the application, or

(b) subject to subsection (3C), any premises occupied or controlled by a person specified in the application, including such sets of premises as are so specified (in which case the application is for an "all premises warrant").

(1B) If the application is for an all premises warrant, the justice of the peace must also be satisfied—

(a) that there are reasonable grounds for believing that it is necessary to search premises occupied or controlled by the person in question which are not specified in the application in order to find the records referred to in subsection (1)(b), and

(b) that it is not reasonably practicable to specify in the application all the premises which the person occupies or controls and which might need to be searched."

(4) In subsection (2) for "Those conditions are" substitute "The conditions referred to in subsection (1)(c) are".

(5) After subsection (3) insert—

"(3A) Subject to subsection (3C), the warrant may authorise entry to and search of premises on more than one occasion if, on the application, the justice of the peace is satisfied that it is necessary to authorise multiple entries in order to achieve the purpose for which the justice issues the warrant.

(3B) If it authorises multiple entries, the number of entries authorised may be unlimited, or limited to a maximum.

(3C) A justice of the peace in Scotland may not issue—

(a) an all premises warrant under this section, or

(b) a warrant under this section authorising multiple entries."

4 (1) Section 28J (search warrants: safeguards) is amended as follows.

(2) In subsection (2)—

(a) after paragraph (a) insert—

"(aa) if the application is for a warrant authorising entry and search on more than one occasion, state the ground on which the officer applies for such a warrant, and whether the officer seeks a warrant authorising an unlimited number of entries, or (if not) the maximum number of entries desired;", and

(b) for paragraph (b) substitute—

"(b) specify the matters set out in subsection (2A) below; and".

(3) After subsection (2) insert—

"(2A) The matters which must be specified pursuant to subsection (2)(b) above are—

(a) if the application relates to one or more sets of premises specified in the application, each set of premises which it is desired to enter and search;

(b) if the application relates to any premises occupied or controlled by a person specified in the application—

(i) as many sets of premises which it is desired to enter and search as it is reasonably practicable to specify;

(ii) the person who is in occupation or control of those premises and any others which it is desired to enter and search;

(iii) why it is necessary to search more premises than those specified under sub-paragraph (i);

(iv) why it is not reasonably practicable to specify all the premises which it is desired to enter and search."

(4) In subsection (6) at the end insert "unless it specifies that it authorises multiple entries".

(5) After subsection (6) insert—

"(6A) If it specifies that it authorises multiple entries, it must also specify whether the number of entries authorised is unlimited, or limited to a specified maximum."

(6) In subsection (7) for paragraph (c) substitute—

"(c) each set of premises to be searched, or (in the case of an all premises warrant) the person who is in occupation or control of premises to be searched, together with any premises under the person's occupation or control which can be specified and which are to be searched; and".

(7) For subsection (9) substitute—

"(9) Two copies must be made of a warrant which specifies only one set of premises and does not authorise multiple entries; and as many copies as are reasonably required may be made of any other kind of warrant."

(8) After subsection (10) insert—

"(10A) All premises warrant" means a warrant issued in response to an application of the kind mentioned in section 24E(6)(b), 28D(1A)(b) or 28FB(1A)(b) or paragraph 25A(6AA)(b) of Schedule 2.

(10B) References in this section to a warrant authorising multiple entries is to a warrant of the kind mentioned in section 24E(8), 28D(1C) or 28FB(3A) or paragraph 25A(6AC) of Schedule 2."

5 (1) Section 28K (execution of warrants) is amended as follows.

(2) After subsection (2) insert—

"(2A) A person so authorised has the same powers as the officer whom the person accompanies in respect of—

(a) the execution of the warrant, and

(b) the seizure or detention of anything to which the warrant relates.

(2B) But the person may exercise those powers only in the company, and under the supervision, of an immigration officer."

(3) In subsection (3) for "one month" substitute "three months".

(4) After subsection (3) insert—

"(3A) If the warrant is an all premises warrant, no premises which are not specified in it may be entered or searched unless an immigration officer of at least the rank of chief immigration officer has in writing authorised them to be entered.

(3B) No premises may be entered or searched for the second or any subsequent time under a warrant which authorises multiple entries unless an immigration officer of at least the rank of chief immigration officer has in writing authorised that entry to those premises."

(5) In subsection (4)(a) after "and" insert ", if not in uniform,".

(6) After subsection (8) insert—

"(8A) Unless the warrant is a warrant specifying one set of premises only, the officer must comply with subsection (8) separately in respect of each set of premises entered and searched.

(8B) Subject to subsection (8C), a warrant must be returned in accordance with subsection (9)—

(a) when it has been executed, or

(b) in the case of a specific premises warrant which has not been executed, an all premises warrant or any warrant authorising multiple entries, on the expiry of the period of three months referred to in subsection (3) or sooner.

(8C) Subsection (8B) does not apply to a warrant issued by a justice of the peace in Scotland or by the sheriff if the warrant has been executed."

(7) In subsection (9) for the words from "A warrant" to "its execution," substitute "The warrant".

(8) After subsection (13) insert—

"(13A) In subsection (8B)—

"specific premises warrant" means a warrant which is not an all premises warrant;

"all premises warrant" means a warrant issued in response to an application of the kind mentioned in section 24E(6)(b), 28D(1A)(b) or 28FB(1A)(b) or paragraph 25A(6AA)(b) of Schedule 2.

(13B) The reference in subsection (8B) to a warrant authorising multiple entries is to a warrant of the kind mentioned in section 24E(8), 28D(1C) or 28FB(3A) or paragraph 25A(6AC) of Schedule 2."

6 (1) Paragraph 25A of Schedule 2 (search of premises for nationality documents) is amended as follows.

(2) In sub-paragraph (6A)—

(a) for "specified in the application" substitute "mentioned in sub-paragraph (6AA)", and

(b) at the end of paragraph (b) insert "in relation to each set of premises specified in the application,".

(3) After sub-paragraph (6A) insert—

"(6AA) The premises referred to in sub-paragraph (6A) above are—

(a) one or more sets of premises specified in the application, or

(b) subject to sub-paragraph (6BA), any premises occupied or controlled by a person specified in the application, including such sets of premises as are so specified (in which case the application is for an "all premises warrant").

(6AB) If the application is for an all premises warrant, the justice of the peace must also be satisfied—

(a) that there are reasonable grounds for believing that it is necessary to search premises occupied or controlled by the person in question which are not specified in the application in order to find the relevant documents, and

(b) that it is not reasonably practicable to specify in the application all the premises which the person occupies or controls and which might need to be searched.

(6AC) Subject to sub-paragraph (6BA), the warrant may authorise entry to and search of premises on more than one occasion if, on the application, the justice of the peace is satisfied that it is necessary to authorise multiple entries in order to achieve the purpose for which the justice issues the warrant.

(6AD) If it authorises multiple entries, the number of entries authorised may be unlimited, or limited to a maximum."

(4) In sub-paragraph (6B) after "conditions" insert "mentioned in sub-paragraph (6A)(b)".

(5) After sub-paragraph (6B) insert—

"(6BA) A justice of the peace in Scotland may not issue—

(a) an all premises warrant under this paragraph, or

(b) a warrant under this paragraph authorising multiple entries."

(6) In sub-paragraph (6C) for "sub-paragraph (6A)" substitute "sub-paragraphs (6A) to (6BA)".

UK Borders Act 2007 (c. 30)

7 (1) Section 45 of the UK Borders Act 2007 (search of premises for nationality documents) is amended as follows.

(2) In subsection (2)—

(a) in paragraph (b) for "specified in the application" substitute "mentioned in subsection (2A)", and

(b) at the end of paragraph (d) insert "in relation to each set of premises specified in the application,".

(3) After subsection (2) insert—

"(2A) The premises referred to in subsection (2)(b) above are—

(a) one or more sets of premises specified in the application, or

(b) subject to subsection (3A), any premises occupied or controlled by a person specified in the application, including such sets of premises as are so specified (in which case the application is for an "all premises warrant").

(2B) If the application is for an all premises warrant, the justice of the peace must also be satisfied—

(a) that there are reasonable grounds for believing that it is necessary to search premises occupied or controlled by the person in question which are not specified in the application in order to find the nationality documents, and

(b) that it is not reasonably practicable to specify in the application all the premises which the person occupies or controls and which might need to be searched.

(2C) Subject to subsection (3A), the warrant may authorise entry to and search of premises on more than one occasion if, on the application, the justice of the peace is satisfied that it is necessary to authorise multiple entries in order to achieve the purpose for which the justice issues the warrant.

(2D) If it authorises multiple entries, the number of entries authorised may be unlimited, or limited to a maximum."

(4) In subsection (3) after "conditions" insert "mentioned in subsection (2)(d)".

(5) After subsection (3) insert—

"(3A) A justice of the peace in Scotland may not issue—

(a) an all premises warrant under this section, or

(b) a warrant under this section authorising multiple entries."

SCHEDULE 9

Section 55

DUTY TO SUPPLY NATIONALITY DOCUMENTS TO SECRETARY OF STATE: PERSONS TO WHOM DUTY APPLIES

This is the new Schedule A1 to the Immigration and Asylum Act 1999 referred to in section 55—

"SCHEDULE A1

Section 20A

PERSONS TO WHOM SECTION 20A APPLIES

1 Law enforcement

1 The chief officer of police for a police area in England and Wales.

2 The chief constable of the Police Service of Scotland.

3 The Chief Constable of the Police Service of Northern Ireland.

4 The Chief Constable of the British Transport Police Force.

5 A Port Police Force established under an order made under section 14 of the Harbours Act 1964.

6 The Port Police Force established under Part 10 of the Port of London Act 1968.

7 A Port Police Force established under section 79 of the Harbours, Docks and Piers Clauses Act 1847.

8 The National Crime Agency.

9 Local government

9 A county council or district council in England.

10 A London borough council.

11 The Greater London Authority.

12 The Common Council of the City of London in its capacity as a local authority.

13 The Council of the Isles of Scilly.

14 A county council or a county borough council in Wales.

15 A council constituted under section 2 of the Local Government etc (Scotland) Act 1994.

16 A district council in Northern Ireland.

17 Regulatory bodies

17 The Gangmasters and Labour Abuse Authority.

18 The Security Industry Authority.

19 Health bodies

19 An NHS trust established under section 25 of the National Health Service Act 2006 or under section 18 of the National Health Service (Wales) Act 2006.

20 An NHS foundation trust within the meaning given by section 30 of the National Health Service Act 2006.

21 A Local Health Board established under section 11 of the National Health Service (Wales) Act 2006.

22 A National Health Service Trust established under section 12A of the National Health Service (Scotland) Act 1978.

23 A Health and Social Care trust established under Article 10 of the Health and Personal Social Services (Northern Ireland) Order 1991 (SI 1991/194 (NI 1)).

24 Education bodies

24 The proprietor of a school or 16 to 19 Academy within the meaning of the Education Act 1996 (see sections 4 and 579(1) of that Act).

25 The governing body of an institution within the further education sector within the meaning of the Further and Higher Education Act 1992 (see sections 90 and 91 of that Act).

26 The governing body of a qualifying institution within the meaning of Part 2 of the Higher Education Act 2004 (see sections 11 and 21 of that Act).

27 The proprietor or governing body of a school within the meaning of the Education (Scotland) Act 1980 (see section 135(1) of that Act).

28 The proprietor or governing body of a post-16 education body within the meaning of the Further and Higher Education (Scotland) Act 2005 (see section 35 of that Act).

29 The proprietor of a school within the meaning of the Education and Libraries (Northern Ireland) Order 1986 (SI 1986/594 (NI 3)) (see Article 2(2) of that Order).

30 The governing body of an institution of further education within the meaning of the Further Education (Northern Ireland) Order 1997 (SI 1997/1772 (NI 15)) (see Article 2(2) of that Order).

31 The governing body of a higher education institution as defined by Article 30(3) of the Education and Libraries (Northern Ireland) Order 1993 (SI 1993/2810 (NI 12)).

32 Registration officials

32 The Registrar General for England and Wales.

33 A superintendent registrar of births, deaths and marriages.

34 A registrar of births, deaths and marriages.

35 A civil partnership registrar within the meaning of Chapter 1 of Part 2 of the Civil Partnership Act 2004 (see section 29 of that Act).

36 The Registrar General for Scotland.

37 A district registrar within the meaning of section 7 of the Registration of Births, Deaths and Marriages (Scotland) Act 1965.

38 A senior registrar within the meaning of that section.

39 An assistant registrar within the meaning of that section.

40 The Registrar General for Northern Ireland.

41 A person appointed under Article 31(1) or (3) of the Marriage (Northern Ireland) Order 2003 (SI 2003/413 (NI 3)).

42 A person appointed under section 152(1) or (3) of the Civil Partnership Act 2004.

43 Other bodies: Northern Ireland

43 The Northern Ireland Housing Executive."

SCHEDULE 10

Section 61

IMMIGRATION BAIL

PART 1

MAIN PROVISIONS

Power to grant immigration bail

1 (1) The Secretary of State may grant a person bail if—
(a) the person is being detained under paragraph 16(1), (1A) or (2) of Schedule 2 to the Immigration Act 1971 (detention of persons liable to examination or removal),
(b) the person is being detained under paragraph 2(1), (2) or (3) of Schedule 3 to that Act (detention pending deportation),
(c) the person is being detained under section 62 of the Nationality, Immigration and Asylum Act 2002 (detention of persons liable to examination or removal), or
(d) the person is being detained under section 36(1) of the UK Borders Act 2007 (detention pending deportation).

(2) The Secretary of State may grant a person bail if the person is liable to detention under a provision mentioned in sub-paragraph (1).

(3) The First-tier Tribunal may, on an application made to the Tribunal for the grant of bail to a person, grant that person bail if—
(a) the person is being detained under paragraph 16(1), (1A) or (2) of Schedule 2 to the Immigration Act 1971,
(b) the person is being detained under paragraph 2(1), (2) or (3) of Schedule 3 to that Act,
(c) the person is being detained under section 62 of the Nationality, Immigration and Asylum Act 2002, or
(d) the person is being detained under section 36(1) of the UK Borders Act 2007.

(4) In this Schedule references to the grant of immigration bail, in relation to a person, are to the grant of bail to that person under any of sub-paragraphs (1) to (3) or under paragraph 10(12) or (13) (release following arrest for breach of bail conditions).

(5) A person may be granted and remain on immigration bail even if the person can no longer be detained, if—
(a) the person is liable to detention under a provision mentioned in sub-paragraph (1), or
(b) the Secretary of State is considering whether to make a deportation order against the person under section 5(1) of the Immigration Act 1971.

(6) A grant of immigration bail to a person does not prevent the person's subsequent detention under a provision mentioned in sub-paragraph (1).

(7) For the purposes of this Schedule a person is on immigration bail from when a grant of immigration bail to the person commences to when it ends.

(8) A grant of immigration bail to a person ends when—

(a) in a case where sub-paragraph (5) applied to the person, that sub-paragraph no longer applies to the person,

(b) the person is granted leave to enter or remain in the United Kingdom,

(c) the person is detained under a provision mentioned in sub-paragraph (1), or

(d) the person is removed from or otherwise leaves the United Kingdom.

(9) This paragraph is subject to paragraph 3 (exercise of power to grant immigration bail).

Conditions of immigration bail

2 (1) Subject to sub-paragraph (2), if immigration bail is granted to a person, it must be granted subject to one or more of the following conditions—

(a) a condition requiring the person to appear before the Secretary of State or the First-tier Tribunal at a specified time and place;

(b) a condition restricting the person's work, occupation or studies in the United Kingdom;

(c) a condition about the person's residence;

(d) a condition requiring the person to report to the Secretary of State or such other person as may be specified;

(e) an electronic monitoring condition (see paragraph 4);

(f) such other conditions as the person granting the immigration bail thinks fit.

(2) Sub-paragraph (3) applies in place of sub-paragraph (1) in relation to a person who is being detained under a provision mentioned in paragraph 1(1)(b) or (d) or who is liable to detention under such a provision.

(3) If immigration bail is granted to such a person—

(a) subject to sub-paragraphs (5) to (9), it must be granted subject to an electronic monitoring condition,

(b) if, by virtue of sub-paragraph (5) or (7), it is not granted subject to an electronic monitoring condition, it must be granted subject to one or more of the other conditions mentioned in sub-paragraph (1), and

(c) if it is granted subject to an electronic monitoring condition, it may be granted subject to one or more of those other conditions.

(4) Immigration bail granted in accordance with sub-paragraph (1) or (3) may also be granted subject to a financial condition (see paragraph 5).

(5) Sub-paragraph (3)(a) does not apply to a person who is granted immigration bail by the Secretary of State if the Secretary of State considers that to impose an electronic monitoring condition on the person would be—

(a) impractical, or

(b) contrary to the person's Convention rights.

(6) Where sub-paragraph (5) applies, the Secretary of State must not grant immigration bail to the person subject to an electronic monitoring condition.

(7) Sub-paragraph (3)(a) does not apply to a person who is granted immigration bail by the First-tier Tribunal if the Secretary of State informs the Tribunal that the Secretary

of State considers that to impose an electronic monitoring condition on the person would be—

(a) impractical, or

(b) contrary to the person's Convention rights.

(8) Where sub-paragraph (7) applies, the First-tier Tribunal must not grant immigration bail to the person subject to an electronic monitoring condition.

(9) In considering for the purposes of this Schedule whether it would be impractical to impose an electronic monitoring condition on a person, or would be impractical for a person to continue to be subject to such a condition, the Secretary of State may in particular have regard to—

(a) any obstacles to making arrangements of the kind mentioned in paragraph 4 in relation to the person,

(b) the resources that are available for imposing electronic monitoring conditions on persons to whom sub-paragraph (2) applies and for managing the operation of such conditions in relation to such persons,

(c) the need to give priority to the use of those resources in relation to particular categories of persons to whom that sub-paragraph applies, and

(d) the matters listed in paragraph 3(2) as they apply to the person.

(10) In this Schedule "Convention rights" is to be construed in accordance with section 1 of the Human Rights Act 1998.

(11) In this Schedule "bail condition", in relation to a person on immigration bail, means a condition to which the person's bail is subject.

Exercise of power to grant immigration bail

3 (1) The Secretary of State or the First-tier Tribunal must have regard to the matters listed in sub-paragraph (2) in determining—

(a) whether to grant immigration bail to a person, and

(b) the conditions to which a person's immigration bail is to be subject.

(2) Those matters are—

(a) the likelihood of the person failing to comply with a bail condition,

(b) whether the person has been convicted of an offence (whether in or outside the United Kingdom or before or after the coming into force of this paragraph),

(c) the likelihood of a person committing an offence while on immigration bail,

(d) the likelihood of the person's presence in the United Kingdom, while on immigration bail, causing a danger to public health or being a threat to the maintenance of public order,

(e) whether the person's detention is necessary in that person's interests or for the protection of any other person, and

(f) such other matters as the Secretary of State or the First-tier Tribunal thinks relevant.

(3) A person who is being detained under paragraph 16(1) of Schedule 2 to the Immigration Act 1971 must not be granted immigration bail by the First-tier Tribunal until after the end of the period of 8 days beginning with the date of the person's arrival in the United Kingdom.

(4) A person must not be granted immigration bail by the First-tier Tribunal without the consent of the Secretary of State if—

(a) directions for the removal of the person from the United Kingdom are for the time being in force, and

(b) the directions require the person to be removed from the United Kingdom within the period of 14 days beginning with the date of the decision on whether the person should be granted immigration bail.

(5) If the Secretary of State or the First-tier Tribunal decides to grant, or to refuse to grant, immigration bail to a person, the Secretary of State or the Tribunal must give the person notice of the decision.

(6) Where the First-tier Tribunal is required under sub-paragraph (5) to a give a person notice of a decision, it must also give the Secretary of State notice of the decision.

(7) Where the decision is to grant immigration bail, a notice under sub-paragraph (5) or (6) must state—

(a) when the grant of immigration bail commences, and

(b) the bail conditions.

(8) The commencement of a grant of immigration bail may be specified to be conditional on arrangements specified in the notice being in place to ensure that the person is able to comply with the bail conditions.

Electronic monitoring condition

4 (1) In this Schedule an "electronic monitoring condition" means a condition requiring the person on whom it is imposed ("P") to co-operate with such arrangements as the Secretary of State may specify for detecting and recording by electronic means one or more of the following—

(a) P's location at specified times, during specified periods of time or while the arrangements are in place;

(b) P's presence in a location at specified times, during specified periods of time or while the arrangements are in place;

(c) P's absence from a location at specified times, during specified periods of time or while the arrangements are in place.

(2) The arrangements may in particular—

(a) require P to wear a device;

(b) require P to make specified use of a device;

(c) require P to communicate in a specified manner and at specified times or during specified periods;

(d) involve the exercise of functions by persons other than the Secretary of State or the First-tier Tribunal.

(3) If the arrangements require P to wear, or make specified use of, a device they must—

(a) prohibit P from causing or permitting damage to, or interference with the device, and

(b) prohibit P from taking or permitting action that would or might prevent the effective operation of the device.

(4) In this paragraph "specified" means specified in the arrangements.

(5) An electronic monitoring condition may not be imposed on a person unless the person is at least 18 years old.

Financial condition

5 (1) In this Schedule a "financial condition" means a condition requiring the payment of a sum of money by the person to whom immigration bail is granted ("P") or another person, in a case where P fails to comply with another condition to which P's immigration bail is subject.

(2) A financial condition may be imposed on P only if the person imposing the condition thinks that it would be appropriate to do so with a view to ensuring that P complies with the other bail conditions.

(3) The financial condition must specify—

(a) the sum of money required to be paid,

(b) when it is to be paid, and

(c) the form and manner in which it is to be paid.

(4) A sum to be paid under a financial condition is to be paid to the person who granted the immigration bail, subject to sub-paragraph (5).

(5) If the First-tier Tribunal has directed that the power in paragraph 6(1) (power to vary bail conditions) is to be exercisable by the Secretary of State in relation to P, the sum is to be paid to the Secretary of State.

(6) No sum is required to be paid under a financial condition unless the person who is liable to make a payment under it has been given an opportunity to make representations to the person to whom it is to be paid.

(7) In England and Wales a sum payable under a financial condition is recoverable as if it were payable under an order of the county court in England and Wales.

(8) In Scotland a sum payable under a financial condition may be enforced in the same manner as an extract registered decree arbitral bearing a warrant for execution issued by the sheriff court of any sheriffdom in Scotland.

(9) In Northern Ireland a sum payable under a financial condition is recoverable as if it were payable under an order of a county court in Northern Ireland.

(10) Where action is taken under this paragraph for the recovery of a sum payable under a financial condition, the requirement to pay the sum is—

(a) in relation to England and Wales, to be treated for the purposes of section 98 of the Courts Act 2003 (register of judgments and orders etc) as if it were a judgment entered in the county court;

(b) in relation to Northern Ireland, to be treated for the purposes of Article 116 of the Judgments Enforcement (Northern Ireland) Order 1981 (S.I. 1981/226 (N.I. 6)) (register of judgments) as if it were a judgment in respect of which an application has been accepted under Article 22 or 23(1) of that Order.

Power to vary bail conditions

6 (1) Subject to this paragraph and to paragraphs 7 and 8, where a person is on immigration bail—

(a) any of the conditions to which it is subject may be amended or removed, or
(b) one or more new conditions of the kind mentioned in paragraph 2(1) or (4) may be imposed on the person.

(2) The power in sub-paragraph (1) is exercisable by the person who granted the immigration bail, subject to sub-paragraphs (3) and (4).

(3) The Secretary of State may exercise the power in sub-paragraph (1) in relation to a person to whom immigration bail was granted by the First-tier Tribunal if the Tribunal so directs.

(4) If the First-tier Tribunal gives a direction under sub-paragraph (3), the Tribunal may not exercise the power in sub-paragraph (1) in relation to the person.

(5) The First-tier Tribunal may not exercise the power in sub-paragraph (1)(a) so as to amend an electronic monitoring condition.

(6) If the Secretary of State or the First-tier Tribunal exercises, or refuses to exercise, the power in sub-paragraph (1), the Secretary of State or the Tribunal must give notice to the person who is on immigration bail.

(7) Where the First-tier Tribunal is required under sub-paragraph (6) to give notice to a person, it must also give notice to the Secretary of State.

Removal etc of electronic monitoring condition: bail managed by Secretary of State

7 (1) This paragraph applies to a person who—
(a) is on immigration bail—
(i) pursuant to a grant by the Secretary of State, or
(ii) pursuant to a grant by the First-tier Tribunal in a case where the Tribunal has directed that the power in paragraph 6(1) is exercisable by the Secretary of State, and
(b) before the grant of immigration bail, was detained or liable to detention under a provision mentioned in paragraph 1(1)(b) or (d).

(2) Where the person is subject to an electronic monitoring condition, the Secretary of State—
(a) must not exercise the power in paragraph 6(1) so as to remove the condition unless sub-paragraph (3) applies, but
(b) if that sub-paragraph applies, must exercise that power so as to remove the condition.

(3) This sub-paragraph applies if the Secretary of State considers that—
(a) it would be impractical for the person to continue to be subject to the condition, or
(b) it would be contrary to that person's Convention rights for the person to continue to be subject to the condition.

(4) If, by virtue of paragraph 2(5) or (7) or this paragraph, the person is not subject to an electronic monitoring condition, the Secretary of State—
(a) must not exercise the power in paragraph 6(1) so as to impose such a condition on the person unless sub-paragraph (5) applies, but
(b) if that sub-paragraph applies, must exercise that power so as to impose such a condition on the person.

(5) This sub-paragraph applies if, having considered whether it would be impractical or contrary to the person's Convention rights to impose such a condition on the person, the Secretary of State—

(a) does not consider that it would be impractical to do so, and

(b) does not consider that it would be contrary to the person's Convention rights to do so.

Amendment etc of electronic monitoring condition: bail managed by First-tier Tribunal

8 (1) This paragraph applies to a person who—

(a) is on immigration bail pursuant to a grant by the First-tier Tribunal in a case where the Tribunal has not directed that the power in paragraph 6(1) is exercisable by the Secretary of State, and

(b) before the person was granted immigration bail, was detained or liable to detention under a provision mentioned in paragraph 1(1)(b) or (d).

(2) Where the person is subject to an electronic monitoring condition, the First-tier Tribunal—

(a) must not exercise the power in paragraph 6(1) so as to remove the condition unless sub-paragraph (3) applies, but

(b) if that sub-paragraph applies, must exercise that power so as to remove the condition.

(3) This sub-paragraph applies if the Secretary of State notifies the First-tier Tribunal that the Secretary of State considers that—

(a) it would be impractical for the person to continue to be subject to the condition, or

(b) it would be contrary to that person's Convention rights for the person to continue to be subject to the condition.

(4) If, by virtue of paragraph 2(7) or this paragraph, the person is not subject to an electronic monitoring condition, the First-tier Tribunal—

(a) must not exercise the power in paragraph 6(1) so as to impose such a condition on the person unless sub-paragraph (5) applies, but

(b) if that sub-paragraph applies, must exercise that power so as to impose such a condition on the person.

(5) This sub-paragraph applies if the Secretary of State notifies the First-tier Tribunal that the Secretary of State—

(a) does not consider that it would be impractical to impose such a condition on thc pcrson, and

(b) does not consider that it would be contrary to the person's Convention rights to impose such a condition on the person.

Powers of Secretary of State to enable person to meet bail conditions

9 (1) Sub-paragraph (2) applies where—

(a) a person is on immigration bail subject to a condition requiring the person to reside at an address specified in the condition, and

(b) the person would not be able to support himself or herself at the address unless the power in sub-paragraph (2) were exercised.

(2) The Secretary of State may provide, or arrange for the provision of, facilities for the accommodation of that person at that address.

(3) But the power in sub-paragraph (2) applies only to the extent that the Secretary of State thinks that there are exceptional circumstances which justify the exercise of the power.

(4) The Secretary of State may make a payment to a person on immigration bail in respect of travelling expenses which the person has incurred or will incur for the purpose of complying with a bail condition.

(5) But the power in sub-paragraph (4) applies only to the extent that the Secretary of State thinks that there are exceptional circumstances which justify the making of the payment.

Arrest for breach of immigration bail

10 (1) An immigration officer or a constable may arrest without warrant a person on immigration bail if the immigration officer or constable—

(a) has reasonable grounds for believing that the person is likely to fail to comply with a bail condition, or

(b) has reasonable grounds for suspecting that the person is failing, or has failed, to comply with a bail condition.

(2) Sub-paragraph (3) applies if an appropriate judicial officer is satisfied that there are reasonable grounds for believing that a person liable to be arrested under this paragraph is to be found on any premises.

(3) The appropriate judicial officer may issue a warrant authorising any immigration officer or constable to enter, by reasonable force if necessary, the premises named in the warrant for the purposes of searching for and arresting that person.

(4) Sections 28J and 28K of the Immigration Act 1971 (warrants: application and execution) apply, with any necessary modifications, to warrants under sub-paragraph (3).

(5) Sub-paragraph (6) applies where—

(a) a warrant under this paragraph is issued for the purposes of the arrest of a person under this paragraph, and

(b) an immigration officer or a constable enters premises in reliance on the warrant and detains a person on the premises.

(6) A detainee custody officer may enter the premises, if need be by reasonable force, for the purpose of carrying out a search.

(7) In sub-paragraph (6)—

"detainee custody officer" means a person in respect of whom a certificate of authorisation is in force under section 154 of the Immigration and Asylum Act 1999 (detained persons: escort and custody), and

"search" means a search under paragraph 2(1)(a) of Schedule 13 to that Act (escort arrangements: power to search detained person).

(8) Paragraphs 25A to 25C of Schedule 2 to the Immigration Act 1971 (entry and search of persons and premises) apply in relation to a person arrested under this paragraph as they apply in relation to a person arrested under that Schedule.

(9) A person arrested under this paragraph—

(a) must, as soon as is practicable after the person's arrest, be brought before the relevant authority, and

(b) may be detained under the authority of the Secretary of State in the meantime.

(10) The relevant authority is—

(a) the Secretary of State, if the Secretary of State granted immigration bail to the arrested person or the First-tier Tribunal has directed that the power in paragraph 6(1) is exercisable by the Secretary of State in relation to that person, or

(b) otherwise, the First-tier Tribunal.

(11) Where an arrested person is brought before the relevant authority, the relevant authority must decide whether the arrested person has broken or is likely to break any of the bail conditions.

(12) If the relevant authority decides the arrested person has broken or is likely to break any of the bail conditions, the relevant authority must—

(a) direct that the person is to be detained under the provision mentioned in paragraph 1(1) under which the person is liable to be detained, or

(b) grant the person bail subject to the same or different conditions, subject to sub-paragraph (14).

(13) If the relevant authority decides the person has not broken and is not likely to break any of the bail conditions, the relevant authority must grant the person bail subject to the same conditions (but this is subject to sub-paragraph (14), and does not prevent the subsequent exercise of the powers in paragraph 6).

(14) The power in sub-paragraph (12) to grant bail subject to the same conditions and the duty in sub-paragraph (13) to do so do not affect the requirement for the grant of bail to comply with paragraph 2.

(15) In this paragraph—

"appropriate judicial officer" means—

(a) in relation to England and Wales, a justice of the peace;

(b) in relation to Scotland, the sheriff or a justice of the peace;

(c) in relation to Northern Ireland, a lay magistrate;

"premises"—

(a) in relation to England and Wales, has the same meaning as in the Police and Criminal Evidence Act 1984;

(b) in relation to Scotland, has the same meaning as in section 412 of the Proceeds of Crime Act 2002;

(c) in relation to Northern Ireland, has the same meaning as in the Police and Criminal Evidence (Northern Ireland) Order 1989 (SI 1989/1341 (NI 12)).

Duty to arrange consideration of bail

11 (1) Subject as follows, the Secretary of State must arrange a reference to the First-tier Tribunal for the Tribunal to decide whether to grant bail to a person if—

(a) the person is being detained under a provision mentioned in paragraph 1(1)(a) or (c), and

(b) the period of four months beginning with the relevant date has elapsed.

(2) In sub-paragraph (1)(b) "the relevant date" means—

(a) the date on which the person's detention began, or

(b) if a relevant event has occurred in relation to the person since that date, the last date on which such an event has occurred in relation to the person.

(3) The following are relevant events in relation to a person for the purposes of sub-paragraph (2)(b)—

(a) consideration by the First-tier Tribunal of whether to grant immigration bail to the person;

(b) withdrawal by the person of an application for immigration bail treated as made by the person as the result of a reference under this paragraph;

(c) withdrawal by the person of a notice given under sub-paragraph (6)(b).

(4) The reference in sub-paragraph (3)(a) to consideration of whether to grant immigration bail to a person—

(a) includes such consideration regardless of whether there is a hearing or the First-tier Tribunal makes a determination in the case in question;

(b) includes the dismissal of an application by virtue of provision made under paragraph 12(2).

(5) The reference in sub-paragraph (3)(a) to consideration of whether to grant immigration bail to a person does not include such consideration in a case where—

(a) the person has made an application for bail, other than one treated as made by the person as the result of a reference under this paragraph, and

(b) the First-tier Tribunal is prevented from granting bail to the person by paragraph 3(4) (requirement for Secretary of State's consent to bail).

(6) The duty in sub-paragraph (1) to arrange a reference does not apply if—

(a) section 3(2) of the Special Immigration Appeals Commission Act 1997 (persons detained in interests of national security etc) applies to the person, or

(b) the person has given to the Secretary of State, and has not withdrawn, written notice that the person does not wish the person's case to be referred to the First-tier Tribunal under this paragraph.

(7) A reference to the First-tier Tribunal under this paragraph in relation to a person is to be treated for all purposes as an application by that person for the grant of bail under paragraph 1(3).

Tribunal Procedure Rules

12 (1) Tribunal Procedure Rules must make provision with respect to applications to the First-tier Tribunal under this Schedule and matters arising out of such applications.

(2) Tribunal Procedure Rules must secure that, where the First-tier Tribunal has decided not to grant a person immigration bail, the Tribunal must dismiss without a hearing any further application for the person to be granted immigration bail which—

(a) is an application to which sub-paragraph (3) applies, but

(b) is not an application to which sub-paragraph (4) applies.

(3) This sub-paragraph applies to an application made during the period of 28 days beginning with the date of the decision mentioned in sub-paragraph (2).

(4) This sub-paragraph applies to an application on which the person demonstrates there has been a material change in the person's circumstances.

Transitional provision

13 (1) Regulations under section 92(1) may, in particular, provide for a person to whom this sub-paragraph applies to be treated, for such purposes as may be specified, as having been granted immigration bail in such circumstances and subject to such conditions as may be specified.

(2) Sub-paragraph (1) applies to a person who, at the specified time, was not in detention on the basis that—

(a) the person had been temporarily admitted to the United Kingdom under paragraph 21 of Schedule 2 to the Immigration Act 1971,

(b) the person had been released from detention under that paragraph,

(c) the person was liable to be detained under paragraph 2(1) of Schedule 3 to the Immigration Act 1971 but, by virtue of a direction of the Secretary of State or the court, was not so detained,

(d) the person was liable to be detained under paragraph 2(2) or (3) of that Schedule but was not so detained,

(e) the person had been released from detention under section 36(3) of the UK Borders Act 2007, or

(f) the person had been released on bail from detention under any provision of the Immigration Acts.

(3) Regulations under section 92(1) may, in particular—

(a) make provision about the circumstances in which the power in paragraph 6(1) may or must be exercised so as to impose an electronic monitoring condition on a person to whom this sub-paragraph applies;

(b) enable the Secretary of State to exercise a discretion in determining whether an electronic monitoring condition should be imposed on such a person,

and may, in particular, do so by providing for paragraph 7 or 8 to have effect with modifications in relation to such a person.

(4) Sub-paragraph (3) applies to a person who—

(a) by virtue of regulations under section 92(1) is treated as having been granted immigration bail as a result of falling within—

(i) sub-paragraph (2)(c), (d) or (e), or

(ii) sub-paragraph (2)(f) on the basis that the person had been released on bail from detention under paragraph 2 of Schedule 3 to the Immigration Act 1971,

(b) is not treated as being subject to an electronic monitoring condition, and

(c) is not otherwise subject to an electronic monitoring condition.

(5) Sub-paragraph (3) applies to a person who—

(a) is on immigration bail pursuant to a grant before the coming into force of paragraph 2(2) and (3), or the coming into force of those provisions in relation to grants of that kind,

(b) before the grant of immigration bail, was detained or liable to detention under a provision mentioned in paragraph 1(1)(b) or (d), and

(c) is not subject to an electronic monitoring condition.

(6) In this paragraph "specified" means specified in regulations under section 92(1).

PART 2

AMENDMENTS TO OTHER ACTS

Immigration Act 1971 (c. 77)

14 The Immigration Act 1971 is amended as follows.

15 In section 11(1) (construction of references to entry)—

(a) omit ", or temporarily admitted or released while liable to detention,",

(b) omit "or by Part III of the Immigration and Asylum Act 1999", and

(c) for "or by section 68 of the Nationality, Immigration and Asylum Act 2002" substitute "or on immigration bail within the meaning of Schedule 10 to the Immigration Act 2016".

16 (1) Section 24 (illegal entry and other similar offences) is amended as follows.

(2) In subsection (1)—

(a) omit paragraph (e), and

(b) at the end of paragraph (g) insert ";

(h) if the person is on immigration bail within the meaning of Schedule 10 to the Immigration Act 2016 and, without reasonable excuse, the person breaches a bail condition within the meaning of that Schedule."

(3) In subsection (3) for "28" substitute "28(1)".

(4) After that subsection insert—

"(3A) The extended time limit for prosecutions which is provided for by section 28(1A) below shall apply to offences under subsection (1)(h) above."

17 (1) Section 28 (proceedings for offences) is amended as follows.

(2) In subsection (1) for "24" substitute "24(3)".

(3) After that subsection insert—

"(1A) Where the offence is one to which, under section 24(3A), an extended time limit for prosecutions is to apply, then—

(a) an information relating to the offence may in England and Wales be tried by a magistrates' court if it is laid—

(i) within the period of six months beginning with the date of the commission of the offence, or

(ii) within the period of three months beginning with the date when the person is first arrested for the offence or under paragraph 10 of Schedule 10 to the Immigration Act 2016 (arrest for breach of bail condition), if that period expires after the end of the period mentioned in sub-paragraph (i),

(b) summary proceedings for the offence may in Scotland be commenced—

(i) within the period of six months beginning with the date of the commission of the offence, or

(ii) within the period of three months beginning with the date when the person is first arrested for the offence or under paragraph 10 of Schedule 10 to the Immigration Act 2016 (arrest for breach of bail condition), if that period expires after the end of the period mentioned in sub-paragraph (i), and

(c) a complaint charging the commission of an offence under this paragraph may in Northern Ireland be heard and determined by a magistrates' court if it is made—

(i) within the period of six months beginning with the date of the commission of the offence, or

(ii) within the period of three months beginning with the date when the person is first arrested for the offence or under paragraph 10 of Schedule 10 to the Immigration Act 2016 (arrest for breach of bail condition), if that period expires after the end of the period mentioned in sub-paragraph (i)."

(4) In subsection (2) for "subsection (1)(b)" substitute "subsections (1)(b) and (1A)(b)".

18 In section 28B(5) (meaning of "relevant offence") for "(e) or (f)" substitute "(f) or (h)".

19 In section 28D(4) (meaning of "relevant offence") for "(e) or (f)" substitute "(f) or (h)".

20 In Schedule 2 (administrative provisions as to control on entry etc) omit paragraphs 21 to 25 and 29 to 34.

21 (1) Schedule 3 (supplementary provisions as to deportation) is amended as follows.

(2) In paragraph 2—

(a) in sub-paragraph (1)—

(i) omit the words from ", unless" in the first place it appears to "below,", and

(ii) for the words from "unless" in the second place it appears to the end of the sub-paragraph substitute "unless—

(a) the court by which the recommendation is made grants bail to the person, or

(b) the person is released on immigration bail under Schedule 10 to the Immigration Act 2016.",",

(b) in sub-paragraph (1A) for the words from "direct" to the end of the sub-paragraph substitute "release the person on bail without setting aside the recommendation.",

(c) in sub-paragraph (3) for the words from "unless" to the end of the sub-paragraph substitute "unless he is released on immigration bail under Schedule 10 to the Immigration Act 2016.", and

(d) for sub-paragraphs (4A) to (6) substitute—

"(5) The provisions of Schedule 10 to the Immigration Act 2016 that apply in relation to the grant of immigration bail by the First-tier Tribunal apply in relation to the grant of bail by the court under sub-paragraph (1) or (1A).

(6) If the court grants bail to a person under sub-paragraph (1) or (1A), Schedule 10 to the Immigration Act 2016 applies in relation to that person as if the person had been granted immigration bail by the First-tier Tribunal under that Schedule.

(7) A reference in any provision of, or made under, an enactment other than this paragraph to immigration bail granted, or a condition imposed, under Schedule 10 to the Immigration Act 2016 includes bail granted by the court under sub-paragraph (1) or (1A) or (as the case may be) a condition imposed by the court on the grant of such bail."

(3) Omit paragraphs 3 to 10.

Special Immigration Appeals Commission Act 1997 (c. 68)

22 The Special Immigration Appeals Commission Act 1997 is amended as follows.

23 In section 3(1) (jurisdiction: bail) for "Schedule 2 to the Immigration Act 1971" substitute "Schedule 10 to the Immigration Act 2016".

24 (1) Section 5 (procedure in relation to jurisdiction under sections 2 and 3) is amended as follows.

(2) In subsection (4)(a) for "Part II of Schedule 2 to the Immigration Act 1971" substitute "Schedule 10 to the Immigration Act 2016".

(3) In subsection (5) for "paragraphs 22 to 24 of Schedule 2 to the Immigration Act 1971" substitute "Schedule 10 to the Immigration Act 2016".

(4) In subsection (5A)—

(a) for "bail under paragraph 22 or 29 of Schedule 2 to the Immigration Act 1971" substitute "immigration bail under Schedule 10 to the Immigration Act 2016", and

(b) for "bail" in the second place it appears substitute "immigration bail".

25 For Schedule 3 substitute—

"SCHEDULE 3 Section 3

BAIL: MODIFICATIONS OF SCHEDULE 10 TO THE IMMIGRATION ACT 2016

1 Paragraph 1(3) (power to grant bail) has effect as if—

(a) for "The First-tier Tribunal" there were substituted "The Special Immigration Appeals Commission", and
(b) for "the Tribunal" there were substituted "the Commission".

2 Paragraph 2 (conditions of immigration bail) has effect as if—
(a) in sub-paragraphs (1)(a), (7) and (8) for "the First-tier Tribunal" there were substituted "the Special Immigration Appeals Commission", and
(b) in sub-paragraph (7) for "the Tribunal" there were substituted "the Commission".

3 Paragraph 3 (exercise of power to grant immigration bail) has effect as if—
(a) in sub-paragraphs (1), (2)(f), (3), (4), (5) and (6) for "the First-tier Tribunal" there were substituted "the Special Immigration Appeals Commission", and
(b) in sub-paragraph (5) for "the Tribunal" there were substituted "the Commission".

4 Paragraph 4(2)(d) (arrangements under electronic monitoring condition) has effect as if for "the First-tier Tribunal" there were substituted "the Special Immigration Appeals Commission".

5 Paragraph 5(5) (payment of sum under financial condition) has effect as if for "the First-tier Tribunal" there were substituted "the Special Immigration Appeals Commission".

6 Paragraph 6 (power to vary bail conditions) has effect as if—
(a) in sub-paragraphs (3), (4), (6) and (7) for "the First-tier Tribunal" there were substituted "the Special Immigration Appeals Commission",
(b) in sub-paragraph (5) for "The First-tier Tribunal" there were substituted "The Special Immigration Appeals Commission,", and
(c) in sub-paragraphs (3), (4) and (6) for "the Tribunal" there were substituted "the Commission".

7 Paragraph 7(1)(a)(ii) (removal etc of electronic monitoring condition: bail managed by Secretary of State) has effect as if—
(a) for "the First-tier Tribunal" there were substituted "the Special Immigration Appeals Commission", and
(b) for "the Tribunal" there were substituted "the Commission".

8 Paragraph 8 (amendment etc of electronic monitoring condition: bail managed by First-tier Tribunal) has effect as if—
(a) in sub-paragraphs (1)(a), (2), (3), (4) and (5) for "the First-tier Tribunal" there were substituted "the Special Immigration Appeals Commission", and
(b) in sub-paragraph (1)(a) for "the Tribunal" there were substituted "the Commission".

9 Paragraph 10(10) (meaning of "relevant authority") has effect as if for "the First-tier Tribunal" in both places there were substituted "the Special Immigration Appeals Commission"."

Immigration and Asylum Act 1999 (c. 33)

26 The Immigration and Asylum Act 1999 is amended as follows.

27 In section 10(9) (removal of persons unlawfully in the United Kingdom: application of Schedule 2 to the Immigration Act 1971) omit paragraphs (h) and (i).

28 In section 53 (applications for bail in immigration cases) omit subsection (4).

29 In section 95(9A) (support for asylum seekers etc: matters to which conditions may relate) in paragraph (b) for the words from "restriction" to the end of the paragraph substitute "condition imposed under Schedule 10 to the Immigration Act 2016 (immigration bail)."

30 (1) Section 141 (fingerprinting: persons temporarily admitted to the United Kingdom) is amended as follows.

(2) In subsection (7)(b) for "temporarily admitted under paragraph 21 of Schedule 2 to the 1971 Act" substitute "granted immigration bail under Schedule 10 to the Immigration Act 2016".

(3) In subsection (8)(b) for "admit him temporarily" substitute "grant him bail".

Nationality, Immigration and Asylum Act 2002 (c. 41)

31 The Nationality, Immigration and Asylum Act 2002 is amended as follows.

32 (1) Section 23 (power for residence restriction to include requirement to reside at accommodation centre) is amended as follows.

(2) In subsection (1) for "restriction" substitute "condition".

(3) For subsection (2) substitute—

"(2) In subsection (1) "residence condition" means a condition imposed under Schedule 10 to the Immigration Act 2016."

(4) In subsection (4) for "restriction" substitute "condition".

33 In section 30 (conditions of residence at accommodation centres) in subsection (7) for the words from "restriction" to the end of the subsection substitute "condition imposed under Schedule 10 to the Immigration Act 2016."

34 (1) Section 62 (detention by the Secretary of State) is amended as follows.

(2) In subsection (3) omit paragraph (b) (but not the "and" at the end of it).

(3) Omit subsection (4).

35 Omit sections 68 (bail) and 69 (reporting restriction: travel expenses).

36 (1) Section 70 (power for residence restriction to take account of induction programmes for asylum seekers) is amended as follows.

(2) In subsection (1) for "restriction" in both places substitute "condition".

(3) For subsection (2) substitute—

"(2) In subsection (1) "residence condition" means a condition imposed under Schedule 10 to the Immigration Act 2016."

(4) In subsection (5) for "restrictions" substitute "conditions".

37 (1) Section 71 (asylum seeker: residence etc restriction) is amended as follows.

(2) In subsection (2)—

(a) for the words from "restriction" to "restrictions)" substitute "condition which may be imposed under Schedule 10 to the Immigration Act 2016", and

(b) for "that Schedule" substitute "Schedule 2 to the Immigration Act 1971".

(3) In subsection (3)—

(a) for "restriction" in each place substitute "condition",

(b) for "paragraph 21 of that Schedule" substitute "Schedule 10 to the Immigration Act 2016", and

(c) for "that Schedule" substitute "Schedule 2 to the Immigration Act 1971".

(4) In subsection (4) for "restriction" substitute "condition".

Asylum and Immigration (Treatment of Claimants, etc) Act 2004 (c. 19)

38 In the Asylum and Immigration (Treatment of Claimants, etc) Act 2004 omit section 36 (electronic monitoring).

Immigration, Asylum and Nationality Act 2006 (c. 13)

39 In section 24 of the Immigration, Asylum and Nationality Act 2006 (temporary admission)—

(a) in the heading, for "Temporary admission, &c" substitute "Immigration bail",

(b) for "paragraph 21(1) of Schedule 2 to the Immigration Act 1971 (c 77) (temporary admission or release from detention)" substitute "a grant of immigration bail to the person under Schedule 10 to the Immigration Act 2016", and

(c) in paragraph (b) for "paragraph 21(2)" substitute "that Schedule as a condition of that person's immigration bail".

UK Borders Act 2007 (c. 30)

40 (1) Section 36 of the UK Borders Act 2007 (detention) is amended as follows.

(2) In subsection (2) for the words from "unless" to the end of the subsection substitute "unless the person is granted immigration bail under Schedule 10 to the Immigration Act 2016."

(3) In subsection (3) for "direct release" substitute "release a person on bail".

(4) After subsection (3) insert—

"(3A) The provisions of Schedule 10 to the Immigration Act 2016 that apply in relation to the grant of immigration bail by the First-tier Tribunal apply in relation to the grant of bail by the court under subsection (3).

(3B) If the court grants bail to a person under subsection (3), Schedule 10 to the Immigration Act 2016 applies in relation to that person as if the person had been granted immigration bail by the First-tier Tribunal under that Schedule.

(3C) A reference in any provision of, or made under, an enactment other than this section to immigration bail granted, or a condition imposed, under Schedule 10 to the Immigration Act 2016 includes bail granted by the court under subsection (3) or (as the case may be) a condition imposed by the court on the grant of such bail."

(5) In subsection (4) omit "(including provisions about bail)".

(6) Omit subsection (5).

Criminal Justice and Immigration Act 2008 (c. 4)

41 The Criminal Justice and Immigration Act 2008 is amended as follows.

42 In section 132(4) (special immigration status: effect of designation) in paragraph (b) for the words from "temporary admission" to the end of the paragraph substitute "immigration bail under Schedule 10 to the Immigration Act 2016."

43 In section 133 (special immigration status: conditions) for subsections (3) and (4) substitute—

"(3) If a condition is imposed under this section on a designated person, the person imposing the condition may also impose an electronic monitoring condition within the meaning of Schedule 10 to the Immigration Act 2016 on the designated person.

(3A) Paragraph 4 (electronic monitoring conditions) of that Schedule applies in relation to a condition imposed under subsection (3) as it applies to an electronic monitoring condition imposed under that Schedule.

(4) Paragraph 9(4) and (5) (bail conditions: travelling expenses) of that Schedule applies in relation to conditions imposed under subsection (2)(c) as it applies to conditions imposed under that Schedule."

SCHEDULE 11

Section 66

Support for certain categories of migrant

PART 1

Amendments of the Immigration Acts

Abolition of power to support certain categories of migrant

1 Section 4 of the Immigration and Asylum Act 1999 (provision of accommodation for failed asylum-seekers, etc) is repealed.

2 In consequence of the repeal made by paragraph 1—

(a) in section 26A of the Immigration Act 1971, omit subsection (1)(b)(ii);

(b) in the following provisions, omit "section 4 or"—

(i) section 3A(7A) of the Protection from Eviction Act 1977;

(ii) paragraph 3A(1) of Schedule 2 to the Housing (Northern Ireland) Order 1983 (S.I. 1983/1118 (N.I. 15));
(iii) section 23A(5A) of the Rent (Scotland) Act 1984;
(iv) paragraph 4A(1) of Schedule 1 to the Housing Act 1985;
(v) paragraph 11B of Schedule 4 to the Housing (Scotland) Act 1988;
(vi) paragraph 12A(1) of Schedule 1 to the Housing Act 1988;

(c) in section 99 of the Immigration and Asylum Act 1999, in subsections (1) and (4), omit "4,";

(d) in section 103 of that Act—
(i) omit subsection (2A), and
(ii) in subsections (6) and (7), for "section 4 or 95" substitute "section 95";

(e) in section 118(1)(b) of that Act, omit "4,";

(f) in section 166(5) of that Act, omit paragraph (za);

(g) in the Nationality, Immigration and Asylum Act 2002—
(i) in section 23, omit subsection (5),
(ii) in section 26, in subsection (3), omit "4,",
(iii) omit section 49,
(iv) in section 51, in subsection (2), omit paragraph (b), and
(v) in section 55, in subsection (2)(a), omit "4,";

(h) in the Asylum and Immigration (Treatment of Claimants, etc.) Act 2004, omit section 10;

(i) in the Immigration, Asylum and Nationality Act 2006, omit section 43(1)(b), (2), (5), (6) and (7);

(j) in the UK Borders Act 2007—
(i) in section 17, in subsection (1)(a), omit "(and section 4)", and
(ii) in section 40, in subsection (1), omit paragraph (e);

(k) in section 134 of the Criminal Justice and Immigration Act 2008, omit subsection (5);

(l) in Schedule 1 to the Legal Aid, Sentencing and Punishment of Offenders Act 2012, in paragraph 31(1)(a), omit "4 or" and "persons temporarily admitted and";

(m) in paragraph 8 of Schedule 3 to the Immigration Act 2014, omit paragraph (a).

Power to support people making further submissions in relation to protection claims

3 (1) Section 94 of the Immigration and Asylum Act 1999 (interpretation of Part 6) is amended as follows.

(2) In subsection (1)—

(a) for the definition of "asylum-seeker" substitute—
""asylum-seeker" means a person falling within subsection (2A) or (2B) (but see also subsection (3C));";

(b) omit the definition of "claim for asylum";

(c) before the definition of "housing accommodation" insert—
""further qualifying submissions" has the meaning given by subsection (2C);";

(d) after the definition of "Northern Ireland authority" insert—

""protection claim" has the meaning given by section 82(2) of the Nationality, Immigration and Asylum Act 2002;".

(3) After subsection (2) insert—

"(2A) A person is an asylum-seeker for the purposes of this Part if—

(a) the person is at least 18 years old,

(b) the person has made a protection claim, and

(c) the person's claim—

(i) has been recorded by the Secretary of State, but

(ii) has not been determined.

(2B) A person is also an asylum-seeker for the purposes of this Part if—

(a) the person is at least 18 years old,

(b) the person has made further qualifying submissions (see subsection (2C)), and

(c) the person's submissions—

(i) have been recorded by the Secretary of State, but

(ii) have not been determined before the end of such period as may be prescribed.

(2C) A person makes "further qualifying submissions" if—

(a) the person makes submissions to the Secretary of State that the person's removal from the United Kingdom would breach any of the obligations mentioned in section 82(2)(a)(i) or (ii) of the Nationality, Immigration and Asylum Act 2002 (protection claims), and

(b) the submissions fall to be considered by the Secretary of State under paragraph 353 of the immigration rules."

(4) In subsection (3), for "claim for asylum" substitute "protection claim".

(5) After subsection (3) insert—

"(3A) For the purposes of this Part, further qualifying submissions made by a person are determined—

(a) at the end of a prescribed period beginning with the relevant day (see subsection (3B)), or

(b) in a case where no period is prescribed for the purposes of paragraph (a), at the end of the relevant day.

(3B) In subsection (3A) "the relevant day" means the day on which the Secretary of State notifies the person that the submissions made by the person are to be—

(a) accepted,

(b) rejected without being treated as a fresh protection claim, or

(c) treated as a fresh protection claim.

(3C) If—

(a) further qualifying submissions made by a person are rejected without being treated as a fresh protection claim, and

(b) the person is granted permission to apply for judicial review of that rejection,

the person is to be treated as an asylum-seeker for the purposes of this Part during the review period (see subsection (3D)).

(3D) In subsection (3C) "the review period" means the period—

(a) beginning with the day on which permission to apply for judicial review is granted, and

(b) ending with—

(i) a prescribed period beginning with the day on which the judicial review is disposed of, or

(ii) in a case where no period is prescribed for the purposes of sub-paragraph (i), that day."

(6) In subsection (8), after "subsection (3)" insert "or (3B)".

4 In consequence of the repeal made by paragraph 3(2)(b)—

(a) in section 96 of the Immigration and Asylum Act 1999 (ways in which support may be provided), in subsection (1)(c), for "claim for asylum" substitute "protection claim";

(b) in section 141 of that Act (fingerprinting)—

(i) in subsections (7)(e), (8)(e) and (9)(e), for "claim for asylum" substitute "protection claim", and

(ii) in subsection (15), for ""Claim for asylum"" substitute ""Protection claim"";

(c) in section 167 of that Act (interpretation), in subsection (1), in the definition of "claim for asylum", for "Parts V and VI and section 141" substitute "Part 5";

(d) in Schedule 8 to that Act (provision of support: regulations), in paragraph 9(2)(b), for "claim for asylum" substitute "protection claim";

(e) in section 135 of the Criminal Justice and Immigration Act 2008 (support: supplemental), in subsection (5), for "claim for asylum" substitute "protection claim".

Power to support failed asylum-seekers

5 Part 6 of the Immigration and Asylum Act 1999 (support for asylum-seekers) is amended as follows.

6 The heading of the Part becomes "SUPPORT FOR ASYLUM-SEEKERS, ETC".

7 (1) Section 94 (interpretation of Part 6) is amended as follows.

(2) In subsection (1)—

(a) in the definition of "dependant", after "asylum-seeker" insert ", a failed asylum-seeker";

(b) after the definition of "the Executive" insert—

""failed asylum-seeker" has the meaning given by subsection (2D);";

(c) for the definition of "supported person" substitute—

""supported person" means—

(a) in relation to support under section 95, an asylum-seeker, or a dependant of an asylum-seeker, who has applied for support and for whom support is provided under that section, and

(b) in relation to support under section 95A, a failed asylum-seeker, or a dependant of a failed asylum-seeker, who has applied for support and for whom support is provided under that section."

(3) In subsection (2), after "section 95" insert "or 95A".

(4) After subsection (2C) (inserted by paragraph 3(3) above) insert—

"(2D) A person is a failed asylum-seeker for the purposes of this Part if—

(a) the person is at least 18 years old,

(b) the person—

(i) was an asylum-seeker, or

(ii) would have been an asylum-seeker at any time if the person had been at least 18 years old at that time,

(c) the person's protection claim has been rejected, and

(d) the person is not an asylum-seeker."

(5) Omit subsections (5) and (6).

8 In section 95 (persons for whom support may be provided), the heading becomes "**Support for asylum-seekers, etc**".

9 After section 95 insert—

"95A Support for failed asylum-seekers, etc who are unable to leave UK

"95A Support for failed asylum-seekers, etc who are unable to leave UK

(1) The Secretary of State may provide, or arrange for the provision of, support for a person, for such period or periods as may be prescribed, if—

(a) the person is a failed asylum-seeker, or a dependant of a failed asylum-seeker,

(b) an application for support under this section is made in respect of the person which meets such requirements as may be prescribed,

(c) it appears to the Secretary of State that the person is destitute, or is likely to become destitute within such period as may be prescribed, and

(d) the person faces a genuine obstacle to leaving the United Kingdom.

(2) Subsections (3) to (8) of section 95 (meaning of "destitute") apply for the purposes of this section as they apply for the purposes of that section.

(3) Regulations made by the Secretary of State may make provision for determining what is, or is not, to be regarded as a genuine obstacle to leaving the United Kingdom for the purposes of this section.

(4) The Secretary of State may make regulations prescribing other criteria to be used in determining—

(a) whether or not to provide support, or arrange for the provision of support, for a person under this section;

(b) whether or not to continue to provide support, or arrange for the provision of support, for a person under this section.

(5) Regulations under subsection (4) may, in particular—

(a) provide for the provision of support (or the continuation of the provision of support) to be subject to conditions;

(b) provide for the provision of support (or the continuation of the provision of support) to be a matter for the Secretary of State's discretion to a prescribed extent or in cases of a prescribed description.

(6) A condition imposed by regulations under subsection (5)(a) may, in particular, relate to any of the following—

(a) any matter relating to the use of the support provided;

(b) compliance with a condition imposed under Schedule 10 to the Immigration Act 2016 (immigration bail);

(c) the person's performance of, or participation in, community activities in accordance with arrangements made by the Secretary of State.

(7) A copy of any conditions imposed by regulations under subsection (5)(a) must be given to the supported person.

(8) For the purposes of subsection (6)(c)—

(a) "community activities" means activities that appear to the Secretary of State to be beneficial to the public or a section of the public, and

(b) the Secretary of State may, in particular—

(i) appoint one person to supervise or manage the performance of, or participation in, activities by another person;

(ii) enter into a contract (with a local authority or any other person) for the provision of services by way of making arrangements for community activities in accordance with this section;

(iii) pay, or arrange for the payment of, allowances to a person performing or participating in community activities in accordance with arrangements under this section.

(9) Regulations by virtue of subsection (6)(c) may, in particular, provide for a condition requiring the performance of, or participation in, community activities to apply to a person only if—

(a) accommodation is to be, or is being, provided for the person under this section, and

(b) the Secretary of State has made arrangements for community activities in an area that includes the place where the accommodation is to be, or is being, provided.

(10) A local authority or other person may undertake to manage or participate in arrangements for community activities in accordance with this section.

(11) The powers conferred by Schedule 8 (supplementary regulation-making powers) are exercisable with respect to the powers conferred by this section as they are exercisable with respect to the powers conferred by section 95, but with the modification in subsection (12).

(12) Paragraph 9 of Schedule 8 (notice to quit) has effect with respect to the powers conferred by this section as if sub-paragraph (2)(b) were omitted."

10 (1) Section 96 (ways in which support may be provided) is amended as follows.

(2) In subsection (1)—

(a) after "section 95" insert "or 95A";

(b) in paragraph (c), for "the asylum-seeker" substitute "an asylum-seeker";

(c) in paragraph (d)—

(i) for "the asylum-seeker" substitute "an asylum-seeker", and

(ii) after "dependants" insert ", or a failed asylum-seeker and his dependants,";

(d) in paragraph (e)—

(i) for "the asylum-seeker" substitute "an asylum-seeker", and

(ii) after "dependants" insert ", or a failed asylum-seeker and his dependants,".

(3) After subsection (1) insert—

"(1A) Support under section 95A may, in particular, be provided in the form of vouchers which may be exchanged for goods or services (as well as in the form of cash)."

(4) In subsection (2), after "section 95" insert "or 95A".

11 (1) Section 97 (supplemental) is amended as follows.

(2) In subsection (1)—

(a) after "section 95" insert "or 95A";

(b) after "regard to" insert "the following";

(c) in paragraph (a), at the beginning insert "in the case of the provision of accommodation under section 95,".

(3) In subsections (4), (5) and (7), after "section 95" insert "or 95A".

(4) After subsection (7) insert—

"(8) A tenancy is not a Scottish secure tenancy (within the meaning of the Housing (Scotland) Act 2001 (asp 10)) if it is granted in order to provide accommodation under section 95A.

(9) A tenancy which would be a Scottish secure tenancy but for subsection (8) becomes a Scottish secure tenancy if the landlord notifies the tenant that it is to be regarded as such."

12 In section 98, the heading becomes "**Temporary support for asylum-seekers, etc**".

13 After section 98 insert—

"98A Temporary support for failed asylum seekers, etc

"98A Temporary support for failed asylum-seekers, etc

(1) The Secretary of State may provide, or arrange for the provision of, support for persons within subsection (2) who it appears to the Secretary of State—

(a) may be destitute, and
(b) may face a genuine obstacle to leaving the United Kingdom.

(2) The persons referred to in subsection (1) are—
(a) failed asylum-seekers, and
(b) dependants of failed asylum-seekers.

(3) Support may be provided under this section only until the Secretary of State is able to determine whether support may be provided under section 95A.

(4) Subsections (3) to (12) of section 95A apply for the purposes of this section as they apply for the purposes of that section."

14 (1) Section 99 (provision of support by local authorities) is amended as follows.

(2) In subsection (1), for "or 98" substitute "95A, 98 or 98A".

(3) In subsection (3)—
(a) after "section 95" insert "or 95A";
(b) for "section 96(1) and (2)" substitute "section 96(1) to (2)".

(4) In subsection (4), for "or 98" substitute "95A, 98 or 98A".

15 In section 100 (local authority and other assistance for Secretary of State), in subsection (1), after "section 95" insert "or 95A".

16 In section 101 (reception zones), in subsection (3), after "section 95" (in both places where it occurs) insert "or 95A".

17 In section 112 (recovery of expenditure on support: misrepresentation etc), in subsections (1)(b) and (3), for "section 95 or 98" substitute "section 95, 95A, 98 or 98A".

18 In section 113 (recovery of expenditure on support from sponsor), in subsections (1)(b), (4) and (5)(a), after "section 95" insert "or 95A".

19 (1) Section 114 (overpayments) is amended as follows.

(2) In subsection (1), for "section 95 or 98" substitute "section 95, 95A, 98 or 98A".

(3) In subsection (4), for "section 95" substitute "section 95, 95A or 98A".

20 In section 118 (housing authority accommodation), in subsection (1)(b), for "or 98" substitute "95A, 98 or 98A".

21 (1) Section 122 (support for children) is amended as follows.

(2) In subsection (1), after "section 95" insert "or 95A".

(3) In subsection (2), after "section 95" insert "or (as the case may be) 95A".

(4) In subsections (3) and (4), after "section 95" insert "or 95A".

(5) In subsection (5)—
(a) in paragraph (b)(i), after "section 95" insert "or 95A", and
(b) in paragraph (b)(ii), after "section 95" insert "or (as the case may be) 95A".

22 (1) Section 125 (entry of premises) is amended as follows.

(2) In subsection (1), for "section 95 or 98" substitute "section 95, 95A, 98 or 98A".

(3) In subsection (2)—

(a) in paragraph (b), at the beginning insert "in the case of accommodation provided under section 95 or 98,";

(b) after that paragraph insert—

"(ba) in the case of accommodation provided under section 95A or 98A, the accommodation is being used for any purpose other than the accommodation of the failed asylum-seeker or any dependant of his,".

23 In section 127 (requirement to supply information about redirection of post), in subsection (1)(c), after "asylum-seekers" insert "or failed asylum-seekers".

24 (1) Section 166 (regulations and orders) is amended as follows.

(2) In subsection (5) (regulations subject to the affirmative procedure) for the "or" at the end of paragraph (c) substitute—

"(ca) section 95A, or".

(3) After subsection (5) insert—

"(5A) No regulations under paragraph 1 of Schedule 8 which make provision with respect to the powers conferred by section 95A are to be made unless a draft of the regulations has been laid before Parliament and approved by a resolution of each House.

(5B) Subsection (5A) does not apply to regulations under paragraph 1 of that Schedule which make provision of the kind mentioned in paragraph 3(a) of that Schedule."

(4) In subsection (6) (regulations subject to the negative procedure) for the "or" at the end of paragraph (a) substitute—

"(aa) under the provision mentioned in subsection (5A) and containing regulations to which that subsection applies, or".

25 In section 26A of the Immigration Act 1971 (registration card), in subsection (1)(b), after sub-paragraph (i) insert—

"(ia) a claim for support under section 95A of the Immigration and Asylum Act 1999 (whether or not made by that person)."

26 (1) The Nationality, Immigration and Asylum Act 2002 is amended as follows.

(2) In section 18 (definition of asylum-seeker for purposes of Part 2), omit subsection (2).

(3) In section 26 (withdrawal of support), in subsection (3)—

(a) for "95 or 98" substitute "95, 95A, 98 or 98A";

(b) omit "(asylum-seeker)".

(4) In section 35—

(a) in subsection (2), for "section 95 or 98" substitute "section 95, 95A, 98 or 98A";

(b) in subsection (3), after "section 95" insert "or 95A".

(5) In section 43—

(a) in subsection (1), for "asylum-seeker" substitute "asylum-seekers and failed asylum-seekers, etc";

(b) the heading of that section becomes "**Form of support under Part 6 of the Immigration and Asylum Act 1999**".

(6) In section 51 (choice of form of support), in subsection (2), omit the "and" after paragraph (b) and after paragraph (c) insert ", and

(d) sections 95A and 98A of that Act (support for destitute failed asylum-seekers)."

(7) In section 55 (late claim for asylum: refusal of support), in subsection (2), after paragraph (a) insert—

"(aa) sections 95A and 98A of that Act (support for failed asylum-seeker, &c),".

(8) In Schedule 3 (withholding and withdrawal of support)—

(a) omit paragraph 7A;

(b) in paragraph 14(1) and (2), for ", 7 or 7A" substitute "or 7".

27 In section 9 of the Asylum and Immigration (Treatment of Claimants, etc.) Act 2004 (failed asylum-seekers: withdrawal of support)—

(a) omit subsections (1) and (4);

(b) in subsection (3)(a) and (b), omit "other than paragraph 7A".

28 In the Immigration, Asylum and Nationality Act 2006, omit section 44 (power to repeal paragraph 7A of Schedule 3 to the Nationality, Immigration and Asylum Act 2002).

29 In section 40 of the UK Borders Act 2007 (supply of Revenue and Customs information), in subsection (1)(f), for "asylum-seekers and their dependants" substitute "persons".

30 In Schedule 3 to the Immigration Act 2014 (excluded residential tenancy agreements), in paragraph 8 (accommodation provided by virtue of immigration provisions)—

(a) in paragraph (b) after "95" insert "or 95A", and

(b) in paragraph (c) after "98" insert "or 98A".

Accommodation centres: definition of "asylum-seeker" etc

31 (1) Section 18 of the Nationality, Immigration and Asylum Act 2002 (definition of asylum-seeker for purposes of Part 2) is amended as follows.

(2) For subsection (1) substitute—

"(1) For the purposes of this Part a person is an "asylum-seeker" if—

(a) the person is at least 18 years old,

(b) the person has made a protection claim, and

(c) the person's claim—

(i) has been recorded by the Secretary of State, but

(ii) has not been determined.

(1A) A person is also an "asylum-seeker" for the purposes of this Part if the person is an asylum-seeker for the purposes of Part 6 of the Immigration and Asylum Act 1999 by virtue of section 94(2B) or (3C) of that Act."

(3) For subsection (3) substitute—

"(3) Protection claim" has the meaning given by section 82(2)."

32 (1) In consequence of the amendment made by paragraph 31(3), section 26A of the Immigration Act 1971 (registration card) is amended as follows.

(2) In subsection (1)(b)(i), for "claim for asylum" substitute "protection claim".

(3) In subsection (2), for ""claim for asylum"" substitute ""protection claim"".

33 In consequence of the amendments made by paragraph 31, the Nationality, Immigration and Asylum Act 2002 is amended as follows.

34 In section 16 (establishment of accommodation centres), in subsection (3)(b), for "claims for asylum" substitute "protection claims".

35 In section 21(3), for "claim for asylum" substitute "protection claim".

36 In section 29 (facilities), in subsection (1)(c), for "claim for asylum" substitute "protection claim".

37 (1) Section 55 (late claim for asylum: refusal of support) is amended as follows.

(2) In subsections (1)(a), (3)(a) and (6)(a), for "claim for asylum" substitute "protection claim".

(3) In subsection (9), for ""claim for asylum"" substitute ""protection claim"".

(4) The heading of the section becomes "**Late protection claim: refusal of support**".

38 In section 70 (induction), in the definition of "asylum-seeker" in subsection (3), after "section 18(1)(a)" insert "of this Act and section 94(2B)(a) of the Immigration and Asylum Act 1999".

39 (1) Section 71 (asylum-seeker: residence, etc restriction) is amended as follows.

(2) In subsection (1)(a), for "claim for asylum" substitute "protection claim".

(3) In subsection (5), for ""claim for asylum"" substitute ""protection claim"".

40 In Schedule 3 (withholding and withdrawal of support), in paragraph 17(1), for the definition of "asylum-seeker" substitute—

""asylum-seeker" has the meaning given by section 18,".

Repeal of uncommenced provisions

41 The following provisions of the Nationality, Immigration and Asylum Act 2002, which contain amendments that have never been brought into force, are repealed—

(a) section 44 (which amends sections 94 and 95 of the Immigration and Asylum Act 1999);
(b) sections 45 and 46;
(c) section 47 (which inserts a new section 122 into that Act);
(d) section 53 (which inserts new sections 103, 103A and 103B into that Act).

42 In Schedule 15 to the National Health Service (Wales) Act 2006, in paragraph 2, for sub-paragraph (7) substitute—

"(7) Subsections (3) and (5) to (8) of section 95 of the Immigration and Asylum Act 1999, and paragraph 2 of Schedule 8 to that Act, apply for the purposes of sub-paragraph (6) as they apply for the purposes of that section, but with references in section 95(5) and (7) and that paragraph to the Secretary of State being read as references to a local social services authority."

43 In Schedule 3 to the National Health Service (Consequential Provisions) Act 2006, omit paragraph 9.

44 In section 21 of the Care Act 2014, for subsections (2) and (3) substitute—

"(2) For the purposes of subsection (1), section 95(3) and (5) to (8) of, and paragraph 2 of Schedule 8 to, the 1999 Act apply but with references in section 95(5) and (7) and that paragraph to the Secretary of State being read as references to the local authority in question."

45 In section 46 of the Social Services and Well-being (Wales) Act 2014, for subsections (2) and (3) substitute—

"(2) For the purposes of subsection (1), section 95(3) and (5) to (8) of, and paragraph 2 of Schedule 8 to, the 1999 Act apply but with references in section 95(5) and (7) and that paragraph to the Secretary of State being read as references to the local authority in question."

PART 2

TRANSITIONAL AND SAVING PROVISION

46 (1) The repeals made by paragraphs 1 and 2 do not apply in relation to—

(a) any person for whom accommodation is being provided under section 4 of the Immigration and Asylum Act 1999 immediately before the day on which those paragraphs come into force,

(b) any person who has made an application before that day for accommodation to be provided under that section and whose application has not been determined or withdrawn before that day,

(c) any person who has appealed before that day against a decision not to provide accommodation for the person under that section, or a decision not to continue to provide accommodation for the person under that section, and whose appeal has not been determined or withdrawn before that day, and

(d) any dependant of a person within paragraph (a), (b) or (c).

This is subject to sub-paragraph (2).

(2) The repeals made by paragraph 2(d) (which remove the right to appeal against a decision not to continue to provide accommodation for a person under section 4 of the Immigration and Asylum Act 1999) apply in relation to any decision not to continue to provide accommodation under that section for any person within sub-paragraph (1) which is made on or after the day on which paragraph 2(d) comes into force.

(3) On and after the day on which paragraphs 1 and 2 come into force, section 4 of the Immigration and Asylum Act 1999 has effect in relation to persons within sub-paragraph (1) as if in subsection (11)(b) the word "not" were omitted.

(4) In this paragraph "dependant" has the same meaning as in Part 6 of the Immigration and Asylum Act 1999 (see section 94 of that Act).

47 (1) The repeal made by paragraph 7(5) does not apply in relation to—

(a) any person for whom support is being provided under section 95 of the Immigration and Asylum Act 1999 by virtue of section 94(5) of that Act immediately before the day on which paragraph 7(5) comes into force,

(b) any person who has made an application before that day for support to be provided under section 95 of that Act and whose application has not been determined or withdrawn before that day,

(c) any person who has appealed before that day against a decision not to provide support for the person under that section, or a decision not to continue to provide support for the person under that section, and whose appeal has not been determined or withdrawn before that day, and

(d) any dependant of a person within paragraph (a), (b) or (c).

(2) Where by virtue of sub-paragraph (1) a person is provided with support under section 95 of the Immigration and Asylum Act 1999 by virtue of section 94(5) of that Act on or after the day on which paragraph 7(5) comes into force, section 103 of that Act (appeals) does not apply in relation to any decision not to continue to provide that support for that person which is made on or after that day.

(3) In this paragraph "dependant" has the same meaning as in Part 6 of the Immigration and Asylum Act 1999 (see section 94 of that Act).

48 Schedule 3 to the Nationality, Immigration and Asylum Act 2002 (withholding and withdrawal of support) has effect as if—

(a) after paragraph 7C there were inserted—

"7D Eighth class of ineligible person: transitional cases

7D (1) Paragraph 1 applies to a person if—

(a) the person is a transitionally-supported person (see sub-paragraph (3)),

(b) the Secretary of State has certified that, in the Secretary of State's opinion, the person has failed without reasonable excuse to take reasonable steps—

(i) to leave the United Kingdom voluntarily, or

(ii) to place himself in a position in which he is able to leave the United Kingdom voluntarily,

(c) the person has received a copy of the Secretary of State's certificate, and

(d) the period of 14 days, beginning with the date on which the person receives the copy of the certificate, has elapsed.

(2) Paragraph 1 also applies to a dependant of a person to whom that paragraph applies by virtue of sub-paragraph (1).

(3) A person is a "transitionally-supported person" if—

(a) accommodation is provided for the person by virtue of section 4 of the Immigration and Asylum Act 1999 as that section has effect by virtue of paragraph 46 of Schedule 11 to the Immigration Act 2016, or

(b) support is provided for the person under section 95 of the Immigration and Asylum Act 1999 by virtue of section 94(5) of that Act, as that provision has effect by virtue of paragraph 47 of that Schedule.

(4) For the purpose of sub-paragraph (1)(d), if the Secretary of State sends a copy of a certificate by first class post to a person's last known address, the person is treated as receiving the copy on the second day after the day on which it was posted.

(5) The Secretary of State may by regulations vary the period specified in sub-paragraph (1)(d).", and

(b) in paragraph 14 (information), references to paragraph 7 included a reference to the paragraph 7D treated as inserted by this Schedule.

SCHEDULE 12

Section 68

AVAILABILITY OF LOCAL AUTHORITY SUPPORT

1 Schedule 3 to the Nationality, Immigration and Asylum Act 2002 (withholding and withdrawal of support) is amended as follows.

2 (1) Paragraph 1 (ineligibility for support) is amended as follows.

(2) In sub-paragraph (1) (excluded support or assistance) after paragraph (g) insert—

"(ga) in relation only to a person in England to whom this paragraph applies by virtue of paragraph 4, 5 or 7B—

(i) section 23CZA of that Act (arrangements for certain former relevant children to continue to live with former foster parents), or

(ii) regulations under section 23D of that Act (personal advisers),".

(3) In that sub-paragraph, in paragraph (h) for "or 36" substitute ", 35A or 35B".

(4) After sub-paragraph (2) insert—

"(2A) In the case of the provisions referred to in sub-paragraph (1)(ga), sub-paragraph (2) applies only in relation to a person in England to whom this paragraph applies by virtue of paragraph 4, 5 or 7B."

3 After paragraph 1 insert—

"1A (1) A person to whom this paragraph applies is not eligible for assistance under section 23C(4)(b), 23CA(4) or 24B(2)(b) of the Children Act 1989 (grants to meet expenses connected with education or training) which consists of a grant to enable the person to meet all or part of the person's tuition fees.

(2) The duty in section 23C(4)(b) or 23CA(4) of that Act and the power in section 24B(2)(b) of that Act may not be exercised or performed in respect of a person to whom this paragraph applies so as to make a grant to enable the person to meet all or part of the person's tuition fees.

(3) This paragraph applies to a person in England who is aged 18 or over and who—

(a) has leave to enter or remain in the United Kingdom which has been granted for a limited period,

(b) is an asylum-seeker, or

(c) has made an application for leave to enter or remain in the United Kingdom which has not been withdrawn or determined.

(4) In this paragraph "tuition fees" means fees payable for a course of a description mentioned in Schedule 6 to the Education Reform Act 1988."

4 (1) Paragraph 2(1) (exceptions) is amended as follows.

(2) In paragraph (c) for "or 10" substitute ", 10, 10A or 10B".

(3) After the "or" at the end of paragraph (c) insert—

"(ca) under section 95A or 98A of the Immigration and Asylum Act 1999 (support for failed asylum-seekers etc), or".

5 After paragraph 2 insert—

"2A (1) Paragraph 1(1)(g) or (ga) does not prevent the provision of support or assistance under a relevant provision to a person to whom paragraph 1 would otherwise apply by virtue of paragraph 7B if—

(a) conditions A and B are satisfied in relation to that person, and

(b) condition C, D or E is satisfied in relation to that person.

(2) In sub-paragraph (1) "relevant provision" means—

(a) section 23C, 23CZA or 23CA of the Children Act 1989,

(b) regulations under section 23D of that Act, or

(c) section 24A or 24B of that Act.

(3) Condition A is that—

(a) the person has made an application for leave to enter or remain in the United Kingdom, and

(b) where regulations made by the Secretary of State require that the application must be of a kind specified in the regulations for this condition to be satisfied, the application is of that kind.

(4) Condition B is that—

(a) the application is the first application for leave to enter or remain in the United Kingdom that the person has made, or

(b) where regulations under sub-paragraph (3)(b) require that the application must be of a kind specified in the regulations for condition A to be satisfied, the application is the first application of that kind that the person has made.

(5) Condition C is that the application has not been determined or withdrawn.

(6) Condition D is that—

(a) the application has been refused,

(b) the person could bring an appeal under section 82(1) against the refusal (ignoring any possibility of an appeal out of time with permission), and

(c) if the person brought such an appeal, it would not be one that, by virtue of section 92(6), would have to be continued from outside the United Kingdom.

(7) Condition E is that—

(a) the application has been refused,

(b) the person has appealed under section 82(1) against the refusal,

(c) the appeal is not one that, by virtue of section 92(6), must be continued from outside the United Kingdom, and

(d) the appeal is pending within the meaning of section 104.

(8) For the purposes of sub-paragraph (3) the Secretary of State may by regulations provide for circumstances in which—

(a) a person is to be treated as having made an application for leave to enter or remain in the United Kingdom (despite not having made one), or

(b) a person is to be treated as not having made such an application where the Secretary of State is satisfied that the application made is vexatious or wholly without merit."

6 After paragraph 3 insert—

"3A Notwithstanding paragraph 3, paragraph 1(1)(g) prevents a local authority in England from providing support or assistance under section 17 of the Children Act 1989 to a person in respect of a child if—

(a) the support or assistance is of a type that could be provided to the person by virtue of paragraph 10A (see paragraph 10A(11)), and

(b) support is being provided to the person by virtue of paragraph 10A or there are reasonable grounds for believing that support will be provided to the person by virtue of that paragraph.

3B Notwithstanding paragraph 3, paragraph 1(1)(g) prevents a local authority in England from providing support or assistance under section 23C, 23CA, 24A or 24B of the Children Act 1989 to a person if—

(a) support is being provided to the person by virtue of paragraph 10B or section 95A of the Immigration and Asylum Act 1999, or

(b) there are reasonable grounds for believing that support will be provided to the person by virtue of that paragraph or section.

3C Notwithstanding paragraph 3, paragraph 1(1)(ga) prevents a local authority in England from providing support or assistance under a provision mentioned in paragraph (ga) to a person if—

(a) support is being provided to the person by virtue of paragraph 10B or section 95A of the Immigration and Asylum Act 1999, or

(b) there are reasonable grounds for believing that support will be provided to the person by virtue of that paragraph or section."

7 In paragraph 6 (third class of ineligible person: failed asylum-seeker), in sub-paragraph (1), in the words before sub-paragraph (a), after "person" insert "in Wales, Scotland or Northern Ireland".

8 In paragraph 7 (fourth class of ineligible person: person unlawfully in United Kingdom), in the words before sub-paragraph (a), after "person" insert "in Wales, Scotland or Northern Ireland".

9 Before paragraph 8 insert—

"7B Sixth class of ineligible person: person in England without leave to enter or remain

7B (1) Paragraph 1 applies to a person in England if—

(a) under the Immigration Act 1971, he requires leave to enter or remain in the United Kingdom but does not have it, and

(b) he is not an asylum-seeker.

(2) Paragraph 1 also applies to a dependant of a person to whom that paragraph applies by virtue of sub-paragraph (1).

7C Seventh class of ineligible person: primary carer without leave to enter or remain

7C (1) Paragraph 1 applies to a person in England ("P") if—

(a) P is the primary carer of a British citizen ("the relevant British citizen"),

(b) the relevant British citizen is residing in the United Kingdom,

(c) the relevant British citizen would be unable to reside in the United Kingdom or in another EEA State if P were required to leave the United Kingdom,

(d) if circumstances were not as mentioned in paragraphs (a) to (c), under the Immigration Act 1971 P would require leave to enter or remain in the United Kingdom but would not have such leave, and

(e) P is not an asylum-seeker.

(2) Paragraph 1 also applies to the dependant of a person to whom that paragraph applies by virtue of sub-paragraph (1).

(3) In making for the purposes of this Schedule or regulations made under it a determination as to whether sub-paragraph (1)(c) applies in relation to P, a person may rely on—

(a) a document of a kind specified in regulations made by the Secretary of State, or

(b) information or guidance provided by the Secretary of State for the purposes of such a determination."

10 After paragraph 10 insert—

"10A Accommodation and subsistence etc: England

10A (1) The Secretary of State may make regulations providing for arrangements to be made for support to be provided to a person to whom paragraph 1 applies by virtue of paragraph 7B(1) or 7C(1) and—

(a) who is destitute,

(b) who has with him a dependent child,

(c) who is not a relevant failed asylum seeker, and

(d) in relation to whom condition A, B, C, D or E is satisfied.

(2) A person is a "relevant failed asylum seeker" for the purposes of sub-paragraph (1)(c) if the person is a failed asylum seeker within the meaning of Part 6 of the Immigration and Asylum Act 1999 and—

(a) the person is receiving support under section 95A of that Act,

(b) the person has made an application for such support which has not been refused, or

(c) there are reasonable grounds for believing such support would be provided to the person if an application by the person for such support were made.

(3) Condition A is that—

(a) the person has made an application for leave to enter or remain in the United Kingdom and has not withdrawn the application,

(b) where regulations under this paragraph require that the application must be of a kind specified in the regulations for this condition to be satisfied, the application is of that kind, and

(c) the application has not been determined.

(4) Condition B is that—

(a) the person could bring an appeal under section 82(1) (ignoring any possibility of an appeal out of time with permission), and

(b) if the person brought such an appeal, it would not be one that, by virtue of section 92(6), would have to be continued from outside the United Kingdom.

(5) Condition C is that—

(a) the person has appealed under section 82(1),

(b) the appeal is not one that, by virtue of section 92(6), must be continued from outside the United Kingdom, and

(c) the appeal is pending within the meaning of section 104.

(6) Condition D is that—

(a) the person's appeal rights are exhausted, and

(b) he has not failed to cooperate with arrangements that would enable him to leave the United Kingdom.

(7) Condition E is that a person specified in regulations under this paragraph is satisfied that the provision of support is necessary to safeguard and promote the welfare of a dependent child.

(8) Regulations under this paragraph may specify—

(a) factors which a person specified by virtue of sub-paragraph (7) may or must take into account in making a determination under that sub-paragraph;

(b) factors which such a person must not take into account in making such a determination.

(9) The Secretary of State may make regulations providing for arrangements to be made for support to be provided to a person ("P")—

(a) to whom paragraph 1 applies by virtue of paragraph 7B(1) or 7C(1), and

(b) who it appears to a person specified in the regulations may be destitute,

until a person by whom support may be provided under arrangements by virtue of sub-paragraph (1) is able to determine whether such support should be provided to P.

(10) Arrangements for a person by virtue of this paragraph may include arrangements for a dependant.

(11) The support that may be provided under arrangements by virtue of this paragraph may take the form of—

(a) accommodation;

(b) subsistence in kind, or cash or vouchers to pay for subsistence.

(12) Subsections (3) to (8) of section 95 of the Immigration and Asylum Act 1999 (meaning of "destitute") apply for the purposes of this paragraph as they apply for the purposes of that section.

(13) For the purposes of sub-paragraph (3) regulations under this paragraph may provide for circumstances in which—

(a) a person is to be treated as having made an application for leave to enter or remain in the United Kingdom (despite not having made one);

(b) a person is to be treated as not having made such an application where the Secretary of State is satisfied that the application made is vexatious or wholly without merit.

(14) For the purposes of sub-paragraph (6) a person's appeal rights are exhausted at the time when—

(a) he could not bring an appeal under section 82 (ignoring any possibility of an appeal out of time with permission), and

(b) no appeal brought by him is pending within the meaning of section 104.

10B (1) The Secretary of State may make regulations providing for arrangements to be made for support to be provided to a person to whom paragraph 1 applies by virtue of paragraph 7B(1) and—

(a) who would otherwise be eligible for support or assistance under section 23C, 23CZA or 23CA of the Children Act 1989, under regulations under section 23D of that Act or under section 24A or 24B of that Act, and

(b) in relation to whom condition A, B, C or D is satisfied.

(2) Condition A is that—

(a) the person is destitute,

(b) the person has made an application for leave to enter or remain in the United Kingdom and has not withdrawn the application,

(c) where regulations under this paragraph require that the application must be of a kind specified in the regulations for this condition to be satisfied, the application is of that kind, and

(d) the application has not been determined.

(3) Condition B is that—

(a) the person is destitute,

(b) the person could bring an appeal under section 82(1) (ignoring any possibility of an appeal out of time with permission), and

(c) if the person brought an appeal under section 82(1), it would not be one that, by virtue of section 92(6), would have to be continued from outside the United Kingdom.

(4) Condition C is that—

(a) the person is destitute,

(b) the person has appealed under section 82(1),

(c) the appeal is not one that, by virtue of section 92(6), must be continued from outside the United Kingdom, and

(d) the appeal is pending within the meaning of section 104.

(5) Condition D is that—

(a) the person's appeal rights are exhausted, and

(b) a person specified in regulations under this paragraph is satisfied that support needs to be provided to the person.

(6) Regulations under this paragraph may specify—

(a) factors which a person specified by virtue of paragraph (b) of sub-paragraph (5) may or must take into account in making a determination under that paragraph;

(b) factors which such a person must not take into account in making such a determination.

(7) The Secretary of State may make regulations providing for arrangements to be made for support to be provided to a person ("P")—

(a) to whom paragraph 1 applies by virtue of paragraph 7B(1), and

(b) who it appears to a person specified in the regulations may be destitute,

until a person by whom support may be provided under arrangements by virtue of sub-paragraph (1) is able to determine whether such support should be provided to P.

(8) The support that may be provided under arrangements by virtue of this paragraph may, in particular, take the form of—

(a) accommodation;

(b) subsistence in kind, or cash or vouchers to pay for subsistence.

(9) Subsections (3) to (8) of section 95 of the Immigration and Asylum Act 1999 (meaning of "destitute") apply for the purposes of this paragraph as they apply for the purposes of that section.

(10) For the purposes of sub-paragraph (2) regulations under this paragraph may provide for circumstances in which—

(a) a person is to be treated as having made an application for leave to enter or remain in the United Kingdom (despite not having made one);

(b) a person is to be treated as not having made such an application where the Secretary of State is satisfied that the application made is vexatious or wholly without merit.

(11) For the purposes of sub-paragraph (5) a person's appeal rights are exhausted at the time when—

(a) he could not bring an appeal under section 82 (ignoring any possibility of an appeal out of time with permission), and

(b) no appeal brought by him is pending within the meaning of section 104."

11 In paragraph 11 (assistance and accommodation: general), in the words before sub-paragraph (a), for "or 10" substitute ", 10, 10A or 10B".

12 In paragraph 13 (offences), in sub-paragraphs (1)(b) and (2)(a), for "or 10" substitute ", 10, 10A or 10B".

13 In paragraph 14 (information), in sub-paragraphs (1) and (2), for "or 7" (as substituted by paragraph 26(8)(b) of Schedule 11) substitute ", 7, 7B or 7C".

14 (1) Paragraph 15 (power to amend Schedule 3) is amended as follows.

(2) After paragraph (a) insert—

"(aa) to modify any of the classes of person to whom paragraph 1 applies;".

(3) In paragraph (c) after "remove" insert ", or modify the application of,".

(4) After paragraph (c) insert—

"(d) to enable regulations to be made by the Secretary of State providing for arrangements to be made for support to be provided to a class of person to whom paragraph 1 applies;

(e) to apply paragraph 1A in relation to Wales;

(f) to make provision which has a similar effect to paragraph 1A and which applies in relation to Scotland or Northern Ireland."

15 (1) Paragraph 16 (orders and regulations) is amended as follows.

(2) In sub-paragraph (2)(d) after "amending" insert ", repealing or revoking".

(3) In sub-paragraph (3) after "2(1)(d) or (e)" insert ", 2A(3)(b), 10A or 10B".

16 In Schedule 3 to the Immigration Act 2014 (excluded residential tenancy agreements) after paragraph 8 insert—

"8A An agreement under which accommodation is provided to a person under arrangements made by virtue of paragraph 10A or 10B of Schedule 3 to the Nationality, Immigration and Asylum Act 2002 (support for certain persons who are otherwise ineligible for support by virtue of that Schedule)."

SCHEDULE 13

Section 74

PENALTIES RELATING TO AIRPORT CONTROL AREAS

This is the Part 1A of Schedule 2 to the Immigration Act 1971 referred to in section 74(2)—

"PART 1A

PENALTY FOR BREACH OF PARAGRAPH 26(2) OR (3)

28 Penalty for breach of paragraph 26(2) or (3)

28 (1) Sub-paragraph (2) applies where the Secretary of State has given written notice under paragraph 26(2) to the owner or agent of an aircraft—

(a) designating a control area for the embarkation or disembarkation of passengers in an airport in the United Kingdom, and

(b) specifying conditions or restrictions to be observed in the control area.

(2) The Secretary of State may impose a penalty on the owner or agent if the owner or agent fails to take all reasonable steps to secure that—

(a) passengers embarking on or disembarking from the aircraft at the airport do not embark or disembark at the airport outside the control area, or

(b) the conditions or restrictions specified in the notice are observed.

(3) Sub-paragraph (4) applies where the Secretary of State has given written notice under paragraph 26(3) to a person concerned with the management of an airport in the United Kingdom—

(a) designating a control area in the airport, and

(b) specifying conditions or restrictions to be observed in the control area.

(4) The Secretary of State may impose a penalty on the person if the person fails to take all reasonable steps to secure that the conditions or restrictions specified in the notice are observed.

(5) The Secretary of State may impose a separate penalty under sub-paragraph (2) or (4) in respect of each failure of the kind mentioned in that sub-paragraph.

(6) The amount of a penalty imposed under sub-paragraph (2) or (4) may be such an amount as the Secretary of State considers appropriate; but the amount of each penalty must not exceed the prescribed maximum.

28A Codes of practice

28A (1) The Secretary of State must issue a code of practice to be followed by—

(a) agents and operators of aircraft to whom notices under paragraph 26(2) have been given, and

(b) persons concerned with the management of airports in the United Kingdom to whom notices under paragraph 26(3) have been given.

(2) The Secretary of State must have regard to the code (in addition to any other matters the Secretary of State thinks relevant)—

(a) when deciding whether to impose a penalty under paragraph 28, and

(b) when considering a notice of objection under paragraph 28C.

(3) The Secretary of State must issue a code of practice specifying matters to be considered in determining the amount of a penalty under paragraph 28.

(4) The Secretary of State must have regard to the code (in addition to any other matters the Secretary of State thinks relevant)—

(a) when imposing a penalty under paragraph 28, and

(b) when considering a notice of objection under paragraph 28C.

(5) Before issuing a code under this paragraph the Secretary of State must lay the code before Parliament.

(6) A code under this paragraph comes into force in accordance with provision made by regulations made by the Secretary of State.

(7) The Secretary of State may from time to time review a code under this paragraph and may revise and re-issue it following a review.

(8) References in sub-paragraphs (5) and (6) to a code include a revised code.

28B Penalty notices

28B (1) If the Secretary of State decides that a person is liable to a penalty under paragraph 28, the Secretary of State must notify the person of that decision.

(2) A notice under sub-paragraph (1) (a "penalty notice") must—

(a) be in writing,

(b) state why the Secretary of State thinks the recipient is liable to the penalty,

(c) state the amount of the penalty,

(d) specify the date on which the penalty notice is given,

(e) specify the date, at least 28 days after the date specified in the notice as the date on which it is given, before which the penalty must be paid,

(f) specify how the penalty must be paid,

(g) include an explanation of the steps that the person may take if the person objects to the penalty (including specifying the manner and form in which any notice of objection must be given to the Secretary of State), and

(h) include an explanation of the steps the Secretary of State may take to recover any unpaid penalty.

28C Objections

28C (1) The recipient of a penalty notice ("the recipient") may object to the penalty notice by giving a notice of objection to the Secretary of State.

(2) A notice of objection must—

(a) be in writing,

(b) give the reasons for the objection,

(c) be given in the manner and form specified in the penalty notice, and

(d) be given before the end of the period of 28 days beginning with the date specified in the penalty notice as the date on which it is given.

(3) Where the Secretary of State receives a notice of objection, the Secretary of State must consider it and—

(a) cancel the penalty,

(b) reduce the penalty,

(c) increase the penalty, or

(d) determine not to alter the penalty.

(4) After reaching a decision as to how to proceed under sub-paragraph (3), the Secretary of State must notify the recipient of the decision in writing.

(5) A notification under sub-paragraph (4) must be given before the end of the period of 70 days beginning with the date specified in the penalty notice as the date on which it is given, or such longer period as the Secretary of State may agree with the recipient.

(6) A notification under sub-paragraph (4), other than one notifying the recipient that the Secretary of State has decided to cancel the penalty, must—

(a) state the amount of the penalty following the Secretary of State's consideration of the notice of objection,

(b) state the Secretary of State's reasons for the decision under sub-paragraph (3),

(c) specify the date, at least 28 days after the date on which the notification is given, before which the penalty must be paid,

(d) specify how the penalty must be paid,

(e) include an explanation of the recipient's rights of appeal, and

(f) include an explanation of the steps the Secretary of State may take to recover any unpaid penalty.

28D Appeals

28D (1) A person ("the appellant") may appeal to the court against a decision to require the person to pay a penalty under paragraph 28.

(2) An appeal may be brought only if the appellant has given a notice of objection and the Secretary of State has—

(a) reduced the penalty under paragraph 28C(3)(b),

(b) increased the penalty under paragraph 28C(3)(c), or

(c) determined not to alter the penalty under paragraph 28C(3)(d).

(3) An appeal must be brought within the period of 28 days beginning with the date on which the appellant is notified of the Secretary of State's decision on the notice of objection under paragraph 28C(4).

(4) On appeal, the court may—

(a) allow the appeal and cancel the penalty,

(b) allow the appeal and reduce the penalty, or

(c) dismiss the appeal.

(5) An appeal is to be a re-hearing of the Secretary of State's decision to impose a penalty and is to be determined having regard to—

(a) any code of practice under paragraph 28A(1) which had effect at the time of the events to which the penalty relates,

(b) any code of practice under paragraph 28A(3) which has effect at the time of the appeal, and

(c) any other matters which the court thinks relevant (which may include matters of which the Secretary of State was unaware).

(6) Sub-paragraph (5) has effect despite any provision of rules of court.

(7) In this paragraph "the court" means—

(a) the county court, if the appeal relates to a penalty imposed under paragraph 28 in relation to an airport in England and Wales;

(b) the sheriff, if the appeal relates to a penalty imposed under paragraph 28 in relation to an airport in Scotland;

(c) a county court in Northern Ireland, if the appeal relates to a penalty imposed under paragraph 28 in relation to an airport in Northern Ireland.

(8) But—

(a) the county court in England and Wales, or a county court in Northern Ireland, may transfer proceedings under this paragraph to the High Court, and

(b) the sheriff may transfer proceedings under this paragraph to the Court of Session.

28E Enforcement

28E (1) This section applies where a sum is payable to the Secretary of State as a penalty under paragraph 28.

(2) In England and Wales the penalty is recoverable as if it were payable under an order of the county court in England and Wales.

(3) In Scotland the penalty may be enforced in the same manner as an extract registered decree arbitral bearing a warrant for execution issued by the sheriff court of any sheriffdom in Scotland.

(4) In Northern Ireland the penalty is recoverable as if it were payable under an order of a county court in Northern Ireland.

(5) Where action is taken under this paragraph for the recovery of a sum payable as a penalty under this Chapter, the penalty is—

(a) in relation to England and Wales, to be treated for the purposes of section 98 of the Courts Act 2003 (register of judgments and orders etc) as if it were a judgment entered in the county court;

(b) in relation to Northern Ireland, to be treated for the purposes of Article 116 of the Judgments Enforcement (Northern Ireland) Order 1981 (S.I. 1981/226 (N.I. 6)) (register of judgments) as if it were a judgment in respect of which an application has been accepted under Article 22 or 23(1) of that Order.

(6) Money paid to the Secretary of State by way of a penalty under paragraph 28 must be paid into the Consolidated Fund.

28F Service of documents

28F (1) A document which is to be issued or served on a person outside the United Kingdom for the purposes of paragraph 28B or 28C or in the course of proceedings under paragraph 28E may be issued or served—

(a) in person,

(b) by post,

(c) by facsimile transmission,

(d) by e-mail, or

(e) in any other prescribed manner.

(2) The Secretary of State may by regulations provide that a document issued or served in a manner listed in sub-paragraph (1) in accordance with the regulations is to be taken to have been received at a time specified by or determined in accordance with the regulations.

28G Interpretation of this Part of this Schedule

28G In this Part of this Schedule—

"penalty notice" has the meaning given by paragraph 28B(2);

"prescribed" means prescribed by regulations made by the Secretary of State.

28H Regulations under this Part of this Schedule

28H (1) Regulations under this Part of this Schedule are to be made by statutory instrument.

(2) A statutory instrument containing (whether alone or with other provision) regulations under paragraph 28(6) may not be made unless a draft of the instrument has been laid before, and approved by a resolution of, each House of Parliament.

(3) A statutory instrument containing any other regulations under this Part of this Schedule and to which sub-paragraph (2) does not apply is subject to annulment in pursuance of a resolution of either House of Parliament.

(4) Regulations under this Part of this Schedule—

(a) may make different provision for different purposes;

(b) may make incidental, supplementary, consequential, transitional, transitory or saving provision."

SCHEDULE 14 Section 75

MARITIME ENFORCEMENT

1 The Immigration Act 1971 is amended as follows.

2 In section 25(1) (offence of assisting unlawful immigration to member State), in paragraphs (a) and (b) after "breach" insert "or attempted breach".

3 In section 25A (helping an asylum-seeker to enter United Kingdom) in subsection (1)(a)—

(a) after "arrival" insert "or attempted arrival", and

(b) after "entry" insert "or attempted entry".

4 In section 25B (assisting entry to United Kingdom in breach of deportation or exclusion order)—

(a) in subsection (1), in paragraphs (a) and (b) after "breach" insert "or attempted breach",

(b) for subsection (2) substitute—

"(2) Subsection (3) applies where the Secretary of State has made an order excluding an individual from the United Kingdom on the grounds of public policy, public security or public health, other than a temporary exclusion order.",

(c) in subsection (3)—

(i) in paragraphs (a) and (b) after "remain" insert ", or attempt to arrive in, enter or remain,", and

(ii) in paragraph (c) for the words from "personally" to the end substitute "made an order excluding the individual from the United Kingdom on the grounds of public policy, public security or public health", and

(d) after subsection (4) insert—

"(5) In this section a "temporary exclusion order" means an order under section 2 of the Counter-Terrorism and Security Act 2015."

5 In section 28 (proceedings) after subsection (2) insert—

"(2A) Section 3 of the Territorial Waters Jurisdiction Act 1878 (consent of Secretary of State for certain prosecutions) does not apply to proceedings for an offence under section 25, 25A or 25B."

6 In section 28A(3) (arrest without warrant) in paragraphs (a) and (b) after "committed" insert "or attempted to commit".

7 After Part 3 insert—

"PART 3A

MARITIME ENFORCEMENT

28M Enforcement powers in relation to ships: England and Wales

28M 28M Enforcement powers in relation to ships: England and Wales

(1) An immigration officer, an English and Welsh constable or an enforcement officer may exercise the powers set out in Part 1 of Schedule 4A ("Part 1 powers") in relation to any of the following in England and Wales waters—

(a) a United Kingdom ship;

(b) a ship without nationality;

(c) a foreign ship;

(d) a ship registered under the law of a relevant territory.

(2) But Part 1 powers may be exercised only—

(a) for the purpose of preventing, detecting, investigating or prosecuting an offence under section 25, 25A or 25B, and

(b) in accordance with the rest of this section.

(3) The authority of the Secretary of State is required before an immigration officer, an English and Welsh constable or an enforcement officer may exercise Part 1 powers in relation to a foreign ship, or a ship registered under the law of a relevant territory, within the territorial sea adjacent to the United Kingdom.

(4) Authority for the purposes of subsection (3) may be given in relation to a foreign ship only if the Convention permits the exercise of Part 1 powers in relation to the ship.

28N Enforcement powers in relation to ships: Scotland

28N 28N Enforcement powers in relation to ships: Scotland

(1) An immigration officer, a Scottish constable or an enforcement officer may exercise the powers set out in Part 2 of Schedule 4A ("Part 2 powers") in relation to any of the following in Scotland waters—

(a) a United Kingdom ship;

(b) a ship without nationality;

(c) a foreign ship;

(d) a ship registered under the law of a relevant territory.

(2) But Part 2 powers may be exercised only—

(a) for the purpose of preventing, detecting, investigating or prosecuting an offence under section 25, 25A or 25B, and

(b) in accordance with the rest of this section.

(3) The authority of the Secretary of State is required before an immigration officer, a Scottish constable or an enforcement officer may exercise Part 2 powers in relation to a foreign ship, or a ship registered under the law of a relevant territory, within the territorial sea adjacent to the United Kingdom.

(4) Authority for the purposes of subsection (3) may be given in relation to a foreign ship only if the Convention permits the exercise of Part 2 powers in relation to the ship.

28O Enforcement powers in relation to ships: Northern Ireland

28O 28O Enforcement powers in relation to ships: Northern Ireland

(1) An immigration officer, a Northern Ireland constable or an enforcement officer may exercise the powers set out in Part 3 of Schedule 4A ("Part 3 powers") in relation to any of the following in Northern Ireland waters—

(a) a United Kingdom ship;

(b) a ship without nationality;

(c) a foreign ship;

(d) a ship registered under the law of a relevant territory.

(2) But Part 3 powers may be exercised only—

(a) for the purpose of preventing, detecting, investigating or prosecuting an offence under section 25, 25A or 25B, and

(b) in accordance with the rest of this section.

(3) The authority of the Secretary of State is required before an immigration officer, a Northern Ireland constable or an enforcement officer may exercise Part 3 powers in relation to a foreign ship, or a ship registered under the law of a relevant territory, within the territorial sea adjacent to the United Kingdom.

(4) Authority for the purposes of subsection (3) may be given in relation to a foreign ship only if the Convention permits the exercise of Part 3 powers in relation to the ship.

28P Hot pursuit of ships in United Kingdom waters

28P 28P Hot pursuit of ships in United Kingdom waters

(1) An immigration officer, an English and Welsh constable or an enforcement officer may exercise Part 1 powers in relation to a ship in Scotland waters or in Northern Ireland waters if—

(a) the ship is pursued there,

(b) immediately before the pursuit of the ship, the ship was in England and Wales waters, and

(c) the condition in subsection (7) is met.

(2) Part 1 powers may be exercised under subsection (1) only—

(a) for the purpose mentioned in subsection (2)(a) of section 28M, and

(b) (if relevant) in accordance with subsections (3) and (4) of that section.

(3) An immigration officer, a Scottish constable or an enforcement officer may exercise Part 2 powers in relation to a ship in England and Wales waters or in Northern Ireland waters if—

(a) the ship is pursued there,

(b) immediately before the pursuit of the ship, the ship was in Scotland waters, and

(c) the condition in subsection (7) is met.

(4) Part 2 powers may be exercised under subsection (3) only—

(a) for the purpose mentioned in subsection (2)(a) of section 28N, and

(b) (if relevant) in accordance with subsections (3) and (4) of that section.

(5) An immigration officer, a Northern Ireland constable or an enforcement officer may exercise Part 3 powers in relation to a ship in England and Wales waters or in Scotland waters if—

(a) the ship is pursued there,

(b) immediately before the pursuit of the ship, the ship was in Northern Ireland waters, and

(c) the condition in subsection (7) is met.

(6) Part 3 powers may be exercised under subsection (5) only—

(a) for the purpose mentioned in subsection (2)(a) of section 28O, and

(b) (if relevant) in accordance with subsections (3) and (4) of that section.

(7) The condition referred to in subsection (1)(c), (3)(c) and (5)(c) is that—

(a) before the pursuit of the ship, a signal is given for it to stop, and

(b) the pursuit of the ship is not interrupted.

(8) The signal referred to in subsection (7)(a) must be given in such a way as to be audible or visible from the ship.

(9) For the purposes of subsection (7)(b), pursuit is not interrupted by reason only of the fact that—

(a) the method of carrying out the pursuit, or

(b) the identity of the ship or aircraft carrying out the pursuit,

changes during the course of the pursuit.

(10) Nothing in this Part affects any other legal right of hot pursuit that a constable or an enforcement officer may have.

28Q Interpretation of Part 3A

28Q 28Q Interpretation of Part 3A

(1) In this Part—

"the Convention" means the United Nations Convention on the Law of the Sea 1982 (Cmnd 8941) and any modifications of that Convention agreed after the passing of this Act that have entered into force in relation to the United Kingdom;

"enforcement officer" means—

(a) a person who is a commissioned officer of any of Her Majesty's ships, or

(b) a person in command or charge of any aircraft or hovercraft of the Royal Navy, the Army or the Royal Air Force;

"England and Wales waters" means the sea and other waters within the seaward limits of the territorial sea adjacent to England and Wales;

"English and Welsh constable" means only a person who is—

(a) a member of a police force in England and Wales,

(b) a member of the British Transport Police Force, or

(c) a port constable, within the meaning of section 7 of the Marine Navigation Act 2013, or a person appointed to act as a constable under provision made by virtue of section 16 of the Harbours Act 1964;

"foreign ship" means a ship which—

(a) is registered in a State other than the United Kingdom, or

(b) is not so registered but is entitled to fly the flag of a State other than the United Kingdom;

"Northern Ireland constable" means only a person who is—

(a) a member of the Police Service of Northern Ireland,
(b) a member of the Police Service of Northern Ireland Reserve, or
(c) a person appointed as a special constable in Northern Ireland by virtue of provision incorporating section 79 of the Harbours, Docks, and Piers Clauses Act 1847;

"Northern Ireland waters" means the sea and other waters within the seaward limits of the territorial sea adjacent to Northern Ireland;

"Part 1 powers" means the powers set out in Part 1 of Schedule 4A;

"Part 2 powers" means the powers set out in Part 2 of that Schedule;

"Part 3 powers" means the powers set out in Part 3 of that Schedule;

"relevant territory" means—

(a) the Isle of Man;
(b) any of the Channel Islands;
(c) a British overseas territory;

"Scottish constable" means only a person who is a constable, within the meaning of section 99 of the Police and Fire Reform (Scotland) Act 2012 (asp 8);

"Scotland waters" means the sea and other waters within the seaward limits of the territorial sea adjacent to Scotland;

"ship" includes every description of vessel (including a hovercraft) used in navigation;

"ship without nationality" means a ship which—

(a) is not registered in, or otherwise entitled to fly the flag of, any State or relevant territory, or
(b) sails under the flags of two or more States or relevant territories, or under the flags of a State and relevant territory, using them according to convenience;

"United Kingdom ship" means a ship which—

(a) is registered under Part 2 of the Merchant Shipping Act 1995,
(b) is a Government ship within the meaning of that Act,
(c) is not registered in any State or relevant territory but is wholly owned by persons each of whom has a United Kingdom connection, or
(d) is registered under an Order in Council under section 1 of the Hovercraft Act 1968.

(2) For the purposes of paragraph (c) of the definition of "United Kingdom ship" in subsection (1), a person has a "United Kingdom connection" if the person is—

(a) a British citizen, a British overseas territories citizen or a British Overseas citizen,
(b) an individual who is habitually resident in the United Kingdom, or
(c) a body corporate which is established under the law of a part of the United Kingdom and has its principal place of business in the United Kingdom."

8 After Schedule 4 insert—

"SCHEDULE 4A

Sections 28M, 28N and 28O

ENFORCEMENT POWERS IN RELATION TO SHIPS

PART 1

ENGLAND AND WALES

1 Introductory

1 (1) This Part of this Schedule sets out the powers exercisable by immigration officers, English and Welsh constables and enforcement officers (referred to in this Part of this Schedule as "relevant officers") under sections 28M and 28P(1).

(2) In this Part of this Schedule—

"items subject to legal privilege" has the same meaning as in the Police and Criminal Evidence Act 1984 (see section 10 of that Act);

"the ship" means the ship in relation to which the powers set out in this Part of this Schedule are exercised.

2 Power to stop, board, divert and detain

2 (1) This paragraph applies if a relevant officer has reasonable grounds to suspect that—

(a) an offence under section 25, 25A or 25B is being, or has been, committed on the ship, or

(b) the ship is otherwise being used in connection with the commission of an offence under any of those sections.

(2) The relevant officer may—

(a) stop the ship;

(b) board the ship;

(c) require the ship to be taken to a port in the United Kingdom and detained there.

(3) The relevant officer may require the master of the ship, or any member of its crew, to take such action as is necessary for the purposes of sub-paragraph (2)(c).

(4) A relevant officer must give notice in writing to the master of any ship detained under this paragraph.

(5) The notice must state that the ship is to be detained until the notice is withdrawn by the giving of a further notice in writing signed by a relevant officer.

3 Power to search and obtain information

3 (1) This paragraph applies if a relevant officer has reasonable grounds to suspect that there is evidence on the ship (other than items subject to legal privilege) relating—

(a) to an offence under section 25, 25A and 25B, or

(b) to an offence that is connected with an offence under any of those sections.

(2) The relevant officer may search—

(a) the ship;

(b) anyone on the ship;

(c) anything on the ship (including cargo).

(3) The relevant officer may require a person on the ship to give information about himself or herself or about anything on the ship.

(4) The power to search conferred by sub-paragraph (2)—

(a) is only a power to search to the extent that it is reasonably required for the purpose of discovering evidence of the kind mentioned in sub-paragraph (1), and

(b) in the case of a search of a person, does not authorise a relevant officer to require the person to remove any clothing in public other than an outer coat, jacket or gloves.

(5) In exercising a power conferred by sub-paragraph (2) or (3) a relevant officer may—

(a) open any containers;

(b) require the production of documents, books or records relating to the ship or anything on it (but not including anything the relevant officer has reasonable grounds to believe to be an item subject to legal privilege);

(c) make photographs or copies of anything the production of which the relevant officer has power to require.

(6) The power in sub-paragraph (5)(b) to require the production of documents, books or records includes, in relation to documents, books or records kept in electronic form, power to require the provision of the documents, books or records in a form in which they are legible and can be taken away.

(7) Sub-paragraph (5) is without prejudice to the generality of the powers conferred by sub-paragraphs (2) and (3).

(8) A power conferred by this paragraph may be exercised on the ship or elsewhere.

4 Power of arrest and seizure

4 (1) This paragraph applies if a relevant officer has reasonable grounds to suspect that an offence under section 25, 25A or 25B has been, or is being, committed on the ship.

(2) The relevant officer may arrest without warrant anyone whom the constable or officer has reasonable grounds for suspecting to be guilty of the offence.

(3) The relevant officer may seize and retain anything found on the ship which appears to the officer to be evidence of the offence (but not including anything that the constable or officer has reasonable grounds to believe to be an item subject to legal privilege).

(4) A power conferred by this paragraph may be exercised on the ship or elsewhere.

5 Protective searches of persons

5 (1) A relevant officer may search a person found on the ship for anything which the officer has reasonable grounds to believe the person might use to—

- (a) cause physical injury,
- (b) cause damage to property, or
- (c) endanger the safety of any ship.

(2) The power conferred by sub-paragraph (1) may be exercised—

- (a) only if the officer has reasonable grounds to believe that anything of a kind mentioned in that sub-paragraph is concealed on the person; and
- (b) only to the extent that it is reasonably required for the purpose of discovering any such thing.

(3) The relevant officer may seize and retain anything which the officer has reasonable grounds to believe might—

- (a) cause physical injury,
- (b) cause damage to property, or
- (c) endanger the safety of any ship.

(4) If the person is detained, nothing seized under sub-paragraph (3) may be retained when the person is released from detention.

(5) A power conferred by this paragraph to search a person does not authorise a relevant officer to require the person to remove any clothing in public other than an outer coat, jacket or gloves, but it does authorise the search of a person's mouth.

(6) A power conferred by this paragraph may be exercised on the ship or elsewhere.

6 Search for nationality documents

6 (1) A relevant officer may require a person found on the ship to produce a nationality document.

(2) The relevant officer may search a person found on the ship where the officer has reasonable grounds to believe that a nationality document is concealed on the person.

(3) The power conferred by sub-paragraph (2) may be exercised—

(a) only if the officer has reasonable grounds to believe that a nationality document is concealed on the person; and

(b) only to the extent that it is reasonably required for the purpose of discovering any such document.

(4) Subject as follows, the officer may seize and retain a nationality document for as long as the officer believes the person to whom it relates will arrive in the United Kingdom by virtue of the exercise of the power in paragraph 2.

(5) The power to retain a nationality document in sub-paragraph (4) does not affect any other power of an immigration officer to retain a document.

(6) Where the nationality document has been seized and retained by a relevant officer who is not an immigration officer, the document must be passed to an immigration officer as soon as is practicable after the ship has arrived in the United Kingdom.

(7) The power conferred by this paragraph to search a person does not authorise a relevant officer to—

(a) require the person to remove any clothing in public other than an outer coat, jacket or gloves, or

(b) seize and retain any document the officer has reasonable grounds to believe to be an item subject to legal privilege.

(8) In this paragraph a "nationality document", in relation to a person, means any document which might—

(a) establish the person's identity, nationality or citizenship, or

(b) indicate the place from which the person has travelled to the United Kingdom or to which the person is proposing to go.

(9) A power conferred by this paragraph may be exercised on the ship or elsewhere.

7 Assistants

7 (1) A relevant officer may—

(a) be accompanied by other persons, and

(b) take equipment or materials,

to assist the officer in the exercise of powers under this Part of this Schedule.

(2) A person accompanying a relevant officer under sub-paragraph (1) may perform any of the officer's functions under this Part of this Schedule, but only under the officer's supervision.

8 Reasonable force

8 A relevant officer may use reasonable force, if necessary, in the performance of functions under this Part of this Schedule.

9 Evidence of authority

9 A relevant officer must produce evidence of the officer's authority if asked to do so.

10 Protection of relevant officers

10 A relevant officer is not liable in any criminal or civil proceedings for anything done in the purported performance of functions under this Part of this Schedule if the court is satisfied that—

(a) the act was done in good faith, and

(b) there were reasonable grounds for doing it.

11 Offences

11 (1) A person commits an offence under the law of England and Wales if the person—

(a) intentionally obstructs a relevant officer in the performance of functions under this Part of this Schedule, or

(b) fails without reasonable excuse to comply with a requirement made by a relevant officer in the performance of those functions.

(2) A person who provides information in response to a requirement made by a relevant officer in the performance of functions under this Part of this Schedule commits an offence under the law of England and Wales if—

(a) the information is false in a material particular, and the person either knows it is or is reckless as to whether it is, or

(b) the person intentionally fails to disclose any material particular.

(3) A relevant officer may arrest without warrant anyone whom the officer has reasonable grounds for suspecting to be guilty of an offence under this paragraph.

(4) A person guilty of an offence under this paragraph is liable on summary conviction to imprisonment for a term not exceeding 51 weeks, to a fine or to both.

(5) In the application of sub-paragraph (4) in relation to an offence committed before the coming into force of section 281(5) of the Criminal Justice Act 2003 the reference to 51 weeks is to be read as a reference to 6 months.

PART 2

SCOTLAND

12 Introductory

12 (1) This Part of this Schedule sets out the powers exercisable by immigration officers, Scottish constables and enforcement officers (referred to in this

Part of this Schedule as "relevant officers") under sections 28N and 28P(3).

(2) In this Part of this Schedule—

"items subject to legal privilege" has the same meaning as in Chapter 3 of Part 8 of the Proceeds of Crime Act 2002 (see section 412 of that Act);

"the ship" means the ship in relation to which the powers set out in this Part of this Schedule are exercised.

13 Power to stop, board, divert and detain

13 (1) This paragraph applies if a relevant officer has reasonable grounds to suspect that—

(a) an offence under section 25, 25A or 25B is being, or has been, committed on the ship, or

(b) the ship is otherwise being used in connection with the commission of an offence under any of those sections.

(2) The relevant officer may—

(a) stop the ship;

(b) board the ship;

(c) require the ship to be taken to a port in the United Kingdom and detained there.

(3) The relevant officer may require the master of the ship, or any member of its crew, to take such action as is necessary for the purposes of sub-paragraph (2)(c).

(4) A relevant officer must give notice in writing to the master of any ship detained under this paragraph.

(5) The notice must state that the ship is to be detained until the notice is withdrawn by the giving of a further notice in writing signed by a relevant officer.

14 Power to search and obtain information

14 (1) This paragraph applies if a relevant officer has reasonable grounds to suspect that there is evidence on the ship (other than items subject to legal privilege) relating—

(a) to an offence under section 25, 25A or 25B, or

(b) to an offence that is connected with an offence under any of those sections.

(2) The relevant officer may search—

(a) the ship;

(b) anyone on the ship;

(c) anything on the ship (including cargo).

(3) The relevant officer may require a person on the ship to give information about himself or herself or about anything on the ship.

(4) The power to search conferred by sub-paragraph (2)—

(a) is only a power to search to the extent that it is reasonably required for the purpose of discovering evidence of the kind mentioned in sub-paragraph (1), and

(b) in the case of a search of a person, does not authorise a relevant officer to require the person to remove any clothing in public other than an outer coat, jacket or gloves.

(5) In exercising a power conferred by sub-paragraph (2) or (3) a relevant officer may—

(a) open any containers;

(b) require the production of documents, books or records relating to the ship or anything on it (but not including anything the relevant officer has reasonable grounds to believe to be an item subject to legal privilege);

(c) make photographs or copies of anything the production of which the relevant officer has power to require.

(6) The power in sub-paragraph (5)(b) to require the production of documents, books or records includes, in relation to documents, books or records kept in electronic form, power to require the provision of the documents, books or records in a form in which they are legible and can be taken away.

(7) Sub-paragraph (5) is without prejudice to the generality of the powers conferred by sub-paragraphs (2) and (3).

(8) A power conferred by this paragraph may be exercised on the ship or elsewhere.

15 Power of arrest and seizure

15 (1) This paragraph applies if a relevant officer has reasonable grounds to suspect that an offence under section 25, 25A or 25B has been, or is being, committed on the ship.

(2) The relevant officer may arrest without warrant anyone whom the officer has reasonable grounds for suspecting to be guilty of the offence.

(3) The relevant officer may seize and retain anything found on the ship which appears to the officer to be evidence of the offence (but not including anything that the officer has reasonable grounds to believe to be an item subject to legal privilege).

(4) A power conferred by this paragraph may be exercised on the ship or elsewhere.

16 Protective searches of persons

16 (1) The relevant officer may search a person found on the ship for anything which the officer has reasonable grounds to believe the person might use to—

(a) cause physical injury,

(b) cause damage to property, or

(c) endanger the safety of any ship.

(2) The power conferred by sub-paragraph (1) may be exercised—

(a) only if the officer has reasonable grounds to believe that anything of a kind mentioned in that sub-paragraph is concealed on the person; and

(b) only to the extent that it is reasonably required for the purpose of discovering any such thing.

(3) The relevant officer may seize and retain anything which the officer has reasonable grounds to believe might—

(a) cause physical injury,

(b) cause damage to property, or

(c) endanger the safety of any ship.

(4) If the person is detained, nothing seized under sub-paragraph (3) may be retained when the person is released from detention.

(5) A power conferred by this paragraph to search a person does not authorise a relevant officer to require the person to remove any clothing in public other than an outer coat, jacket or gloves, but it does authorise the search of a person's mouth.

(6) A power conferred by this paragraph may be exercised on the ship or elsewhere.

17 Search for nationality documents

17 (1) The relevant officer may require a person found on the ship to produce a nationality document.

(2) The relevant officer may search a person found on the ship where the officer has reasonable grounds to believe that a nationality document is concealed on the person.

(3) The power conferred by sub-paragraph (2) may be exercised—

(a) only if the officer has reasonable grounds to believe that a nationality document is concealed on the person; and

(b) only to the extent that it is reasonably required for the purpose of discovering any such document.

(4) Subject as follows, the officer may seize and retain a nationality document for as long as the officer believes the person to whom it relates will arrive in the United Kingdom by virtue of the exercise of the power in paragraph 13.

(5) The power to retain a nationality document in sub-paragraph (4) does not affect any other power of an immigration officer to retain a document.

(6) Where the nationality document has been seized and retained by a relevant officer who is not an immigration officer, the document must be passed to an immigration officer as soon as is practicable after the ship has arrived in the United Kingdom.

(7) The power conferred by this paragraph to search a person does not authorise a relevant officer to—

(a) require the person to remove any clothing in public other than an outer coat, jacket or gloves, or

(b) seize and retain any document the officer has reasonable grounds to believe to be an item subject to legal privilege.

(8) In this paragraph a "nationality document", in relation to a person, means any document which might—

(a) establish the person's identity, nationality or citizenship, or

(b) indicate the place from which the person has travelled to the United Kingdom or to which the person is proposing to go.

(9) A power conferred by this paragraph may be exercised on the ship or elsewhere.

18 Assistants

18 (1) A relevant officer may—

(a) be accompanied by other persons, and

(b) take equipment or materials,

to assist the officer in the exercise of powers under this Part of this Schedule.

(2) A person accompanying a relevant officer under sub-paragraph (1) may perform any of the officer's functions under this Part of this Schedule, but only under the officer's supervision.

19 Reasonable force

19 A relevant officer may use reasonable force, if necessary, in the performance of functions under this Part of this Schedule.

20 Evidence of authority

20 A relevant officer must produce evidence of the officer's authority if asked to do so.

21 Protection of relevant officers

21 A relevant officer is not liable in any criminal or civil proceedings for anything done in the purported performance of functions under this Part of this Schedule if the court is satisfied that—

(a) the act was done in good faith, and

(b) there were reasonable grounds for doing it.

22 Offences

22 (1) A person commits an offence under the law of Scotland if the person—

(a) intentionally obstructs a relevant officer in the performance of functions under this Part of this Schedule, or

(b) fails without reasonable excuse to comply with a requirement made by a relevant officer in the performance of those functions.

(2) A person who provides information in response to a requirement made by a relevant officer in the performance of functions under this Part of this Schedule commits an offence under the law of Scotland if—

(a) the information is false in a material particular, and the person either knows it is or is reckless as to whether it is, or

(b) the person intentionally fails to disclose any material particular.

(3) A relevant officer may arrest without warrant anyone whom the officer has reasonable grounds for suspecting to be guilty of an offence under this paragraph.

(4) A person guilty of an offence under this paragraph is liable on summary conviction to imprisonment for a term not exceeding 12 months, to a fine not exceeding level 5 on the standard scale or to both.

PART 3

NORTHERN IRELAND

23 Introductory

23 (1) This Part of this Schedule sets out the powers exercisable by immigration officers, Northern Ireland constables and enforcement officers (referred to in this Part of this Schedule as "relevant officers") under sections 28O and 28P(5).

(2) In this Part of this Schedule—

"items subject to legal privilege" has the same meaning as in the Police and Criminal Evidence (Northern Ireland) Order 1989 (SI 1989/1341 (NI 12)) (see Article 12 of that Order);

"the ship" means the ship in relation to which the powers set out in this Part of this Schedule are exercised.

24 Power to stop, board, divert and detain

24 (1) This paragraph applies if a relevant officer has reasonable grounds to suspect that—

(a) an offence under section 25, 25A or 25B is being, or has been, committed on the ship, or

(b) the ship is otherwise being used in connection with the commission of an offence under any of those sections.

(2) The relevant officer may—

(a) stop the ship;

(b) board the ship;

(c) require the ship to be taken to a port in the United Kingdom and detained there.

(3) The relevant officer may require the master of the ship, or any member of its crew, to take such action as is necessary for the purposes of sub-paragraph (2)(c).

(4) A relevant officer must give notice in writing to the master of any ship detained under this paragraph.

(5) The notice must state that the ship is to be detained until the notice is withdrawn by the giving of a further notice in writing signed by a relevant officer.

25 Power to search and obtain information

25 (1) This paragraph applies if a relevant officer has reasonable grounds to suspect that there is evidence on the ship (other than items subject to legal privilege) relating—

(a) to an offence under section 25, 25A or 25B, or

(b) to an offence that is connected with an offence under any of those sections.

(2) The relevant officer may search—

(a) the ship;

(b) anyone on the ship;

(c) anything on the ship (including cargo).

(3) The relevant officer may require a person on the ship to give information about himself or herself or about anything on the ship.

(4) The power to search conferred by sub-paragraph (2)—

(a) is only a power to search to the extent that it is reasonably required for the purpose of discovering evidence of the kind mentioned in sub-paragraph (1), and

(b) in the case of a search of a person, does not authorise a relevant officer to require the person to remove any clothing in public other than an outer coat, jacket or gloves.

(5) In exercising a power conferred by sub-paragraph (2) or (3) a relevant officer may—

(a) open any containers;

(b) require the production of documents, books or records relating to the ship or anything on it (but not including anything the officer has reasonable grounds to believe to be an item subject to legal privilege);

(c) make photographs or copies of anything the production of which the officer has power to require.

(6) The power in sub-paragraph (5)(b) to require the production of documents, books or records includes, in relation to documents, books or records kept in electronic form, power to require the provision of the documents, books or records in a form in which they are legible and can be taken away.

(7) Sub-paragraph (5) is without prejudice to the generality of the powers conferred by sub-paragraphs (2) and (3).

(8) A power conferred by this paragraph may be exercised on the ship or elsewhere.

26 Power of arrest and seizure

26 (1) This paragraph applies if a relevant officer has reasonable grounds to suspect that an offence under section 25, 25A or 25B has been, or is being, committed on the ship.

(2) The relevant officer may arrest without warrant anyone whom the officer has reasonable grounds for suspecting to be guilty of the offence.

(3) The relevant officer may seize and retain anything found on the ship which appears to the officer to be evidence of the offence (but not including anything that the constable or officer has reasonable grounds to believe to be an item subject to legal privilege).

(4) A power conferred by this paragraph may be exercised on the ship or elsewhere.

27 Protective searches of persons

27 (1) The relevant officer may search a person found on the ship for anything which the officer has reasonable grounds to believe the person might use to—

(a) cause physical injury,

(b) cause damage to property, or

(c) endanger the safety of any ship.

(2) The power conferred by sub-paragraph (1) may be exercised—

(a) only if the officer has reasonable grounds to believe that anything of a kind mentioned in that sub-paragraph is concealed on the person; and

(b) only to the extent that it is reasonably required for the purpose of discovering any such thing.

(3) The relevant officer may seize and retain anything which the officer has reasonable grounds to believe might—

(a) cause physical injury,

(b) cause damage to property, or

(c) endanger the safety of any ship

(4) If the person is detained, nothing seized under sub-paragraph (3) may be retained when the person is released from detention.

(5) A power conferred by this paragraph to search a person does not authorise a relevant officer to require the person to remove any clothing in public other than an outer coat, jacket or gloves, but it does authorise the search of a person's mouth.

(6) A power conferred by this paragraph may be exercised on the ship or elsewhere.

28 Search for nationality documents

28 (1) The relevant officer may require a person found on the ship to produce a nationality document.

(2) The relevant officer may search a person found on the ship where the officer has reasonable grounds to believe that a nationality document is concealed on the person.

(3) The power conferred by sub-paragraph (2) may be exercised—

(a) only if the officer has reasonable grounds to believe that a nationality document is concealed on the person; and

(b) only to the extent that it is reasonably required for the purpose of discovering any such document.

(4) Subject as follows, the officer may seize and retain a nationality document for as long as the officer believes the person to whom it relates will arrive in the United Kingdom by virtue of the exercise of the power in paragraph 24.

(5) The power to retain a nationality document in sub-paragraph (4) does not affect any other power of an immigration officer to retain a document.

(6) Where the nationality document has been seized and retained by a relevant officer who is not an immigration officer, the document must be passed to an immigration officer as soon as is practicable after the ship has arrived in the United Kingdom.

(7) The power conferred by this paragraph to search a person does not authorise a relevant officer to—

(a) require the person to remove any clothing in public other than an outer coat, jacket or gloves, or

(b) seize and retain any document the officer has reasonable grounds to believe to be an item subject to legal privilege.

(8) In this paragraph a "nationality document", in relation to a person, means any document which might—

(a) establish the person's identity, nationality or citizenship, or

(b) indicate the place from which the person has travelled to the United Kingdom or to which the person is proposing to go.

(9) A power conferred by this paragraph may be exercised on the ship or elsewhere.

29 Assistants

29 (1) A relevant officer may—

(a) be accompanied by other persons, and

(b) take equipment or materials,

to assist the officer in the exercise of powers under this Part of this Schedule.

(2) A person accompanying a relevant officer under sub-paragraph (1) may perform any of the officer's functions under this Part of this Schedule, but only under the officer's supervision.

30 Reasonable force

30 A relevant officer may use reasonable force, if necessary, in the performance of functions under this Part of this Schedule.

31 Evidence of authority

31 A relevant officer must produce evidence of the officer's authority if asked to do so.

32 Protection of relevant officers

32 A relevant officer is not liable in any criminal or civil proceedings for anything done in the purported performance of functions under this Part of this Schedule if the court is satisfied that—

(a) the act was done in good faith, and

(b) there were reasonable grounds for doing it.

33 Offences

33 (1) A person commits an offence under the law of Northern Ireland if the person—

(a) intentionally obstructs a relevant officer in the performance of functions under this Part of this Schedule, or

(b) fails without reasonable excuse to comply with a requirement made by a relevant officer in the performance of those functions.

(2) A person who provides information in response to a requirement made by a relevant officer in the performance of functions under this Part of this Schedule commits an offence under the law of Northern Ireland if—

(a) the information is false in a material particular, and the person either knows it is or is reckless as to whether it is, or

(b) the person intentionally fails to disclose any material particular.

(3) A relevant officer may arrest without warrant anyone whom the officer has reasonable grounds for suspecting to be guilty of an offence under this paragraph.

(4) A person guilty of an offence under this paragraph is liable on summary conviction to imprisonment for a term not exceeding 6 months, to a fine not exceeding level 5 on the standard scale or to both."

SCHEDULE 15

Section 89

CIVIL REGISTRATION FEES

PART 1

POWERS TO MAKE REGULATIONS FOR THE CHARGING OF FEES

Marriage Act 1949 (c. 76)

1 Before section 72 of the Marriage Act 1949 (but after the heading of Part 6 of that Act) insert—

"71A Fees

"71A Fees

(1) The Secretary of State may by regulations provide for fees to be payable to such persons as may be prescribed in respect of—

(a) the giving of notice of a marriage to a superintendent registrar;

(b) an application for the reduction of the waiting period in relation to a notice of marriage (see section 31(5A));

(c) the registration for the solemnization of marriages of a building certified as required by law as a place of religious worship, or the cancellation of such a registration;

(d) the authorisation of a person to be present at the solemnization of marriages in such a building;

(e) the presence of a superintendent registrar or registrar at a marriage (except in a case falling within section 51(1A));

(f) the delivery under section 57(1) of a certified copy of entries in a marriage register book;

(g) the carrying out of a search of—

(i) any marriage register book,

(ii) any index kept in relation to such a book, or

(iii) certified copies of entries in such a book;

(h) the provision of a certified copy, or other record of information, relating to an entry in a marriage register book;

(i) the issue of the Registrar General's licence under section 7 of the Marriage (Registrar General's Licence) Act 1970;

(j) such other marriage services as may be prescribed.

(2) Regulations under this section may—

(a) specify the amount of any fee payable under the regulations, or

(b) set out how such a fee is to be determined.

(3) Subsection (4) applies where the regulations provide for a fee to be payable to a superintendent registrar or registrar.

(4) The regulations may provide for such part of the fee as may be specified by or determined in accordance with the regulations to be payable by the

superintendent registrar or registrar to the Registrar General in prescribed circumstances.

(5) The regulations may provide for the reimbursement, reduction, waiver or refund of part or all of a fee whether by conferring a discretion or otherwise.

(6) Regulations under this section must be made by statutory instrument.

(7) Regulations under this section may—

(a) provide for exemptions from any of the provisions of the regulations;

(b) contain such consequential, incidental, supplemental and transitional provision as the Secretary of State considers appropriate.

(8) A statutory instrument containing regulations under this section is subject to annulment in pursuance of a resolution of either House of Parliament.

(9) In this section—

"marriage services" means services in connection with marriages which are provided by or on behalf of the Registrar General, a superintendent registrar or registrar;

"prescribed" means prescribed in regulations made under this section."

Births and Deaths Registration Act 1953 (c. 20)

2 Before section 39 of the Births and Deaths Registration Act 1953 (but after the cross-heading above that section) insert—

"38A Fees

"38A Fees

(1) The Minister may by regulations provide for fees to be payable to such persons as may be prescribed in respect of—

(a) the issue of a certificate under section 13(2);

(b) the carrying out of a search of—

(i) any register of births or register of deaths,

(ii) any index kept in relation to such a register, or

(iii) certified copies of entries in such a register;

(c) the provision of a certified copy, or other record of information, relating to an entry in a register of births or a register of deaths;

(d) the provision of a short certificate of birth or a short certificate of death (see sections 33 and 33A);

(e) such other birth or death registration services as may be prescribed.

(2) Regulations under this section may—

(a) specify the amount of any fee payable under the regulations, or

(b) set out how such a fee is to be determined.

(3) Subsection (4) applies where the regulations provide for a fee to be payable to a superintendent registrar or registrar.

(4) The regulations may provide for such part of the fee as may be specified by or determined in accordance with the regulations to be payable by the superintendent registrar or registrar to the Registrar General in prescribed circumstances.

(5) The regulations may provide for the reduction, waiver or refund of part or all of a fee whether by conferring a discretion or otherwise.

(6) In this section—

"birth or death registration services" means services in connection with the registration of births or deaths which are provided—

(a) by or on behalf of the Registrar General, a superintendent registrar or registrar, or

(b) by any other person;

"prescribed" means prescribed in regulations made under this section."

Registration Service Act 1953 (c. 37)

3 After section 19A of the Registration Service Act 1953 insert—

"19B Fees in respect of provision of copies of records etc

"19B Fees in respect of provision of copies of records etc

(1) The Minister may by regulations provide for fees to be payable to the Registrar General in respect of the provision by the Registrar General to any persons of copies or other records of any information held by the Registrar General.

(2) The regulations may—

(a) specify the amount of any fee payable under the regulations, or

(b) set out how such a fee is to be determined.

(3) The regulations may provide for the reduction, waiver or refund of part or all of a fee whether by conferring a discretion or otherwise.

(4) Regulations under this section must be made by statutory instrument.

(5) Regulations under this section may—

(a) make different provision for different cases;

(b) provide for exemptions from any of the provisions of the regulations;

(c) contain such consequential, incidental, supplemental and transitional provision as the Minister considers appropriate.

(6) A statutory instrument containing regulations under this section is subject to annulment in pursuance of a resolution of either House of Parliament."

Civil Partnership Act 2004 (c. 33)

4 (1) Section 34 of the Civil Partnership Act 2004 (fees) is amended as follows.

(2) In subsection (1), omit ", of such amounts as may be specified in the order,".

(3) After subsection (1) insert—

"(1A) An order under this section may—

(a) specify the amount of any fee payable under the order, or

(b) set out how such a fee is to be determined.

(1B) Subsection (1C) applies where the order provides for a fee to be payable to a registration authority.

(1C) The order may provide for such part of the fee as may be specified by or determined in accordance with the order to be payable by the registration authority to the Registrar General in such circumstances as may be prescribed by the order."

(4) For subsection (2) substitute—

"(2) The order may provide for the reduction, waiver or refund of part or all of a fee whether by conferring a discretion or otherwise."

Marriage (Same Sex Couples) Act 2013 (c. 30)

5 In section 9 of the Marriage (Same Sex Couples) Act 2013 (conversion of civil partnership into marriage) after subsection (5) insert—

"(5A) Subsection (5B) applies where regulations under this section provide for a fee to be payable to a superintendent registrar or registrar.

(5B) The regulations may provide for such part of the fee as may be specified in or determined in accordance with the regulations to be payable by the superintendent registrar or registrar to the Registrar General in such circumstances as may be set out in the regulations.

(5C) The regulations may provide for the reduction, waiver or refund of part or all of a fee whether by conferring a discretion or otherwise."

PART 2

CONSEQUENTIAL AND RELATED AMENDMENTS

Places of Worship Registration Act 1855 (c. 81)

6 For section 5 of the Places of Worship Registration Act 1855 (fee to superintendent registrar) substitute—

"5 Fees

"5 Fees

(1) The Secretary of State may by regulations provide for fees to be payable to such persons as may be prescribed in the regulations in respect of the certification to the Registrar General under this Act of a place of meeting for religious worship.

(2) Regulations under this section may—

(a) specify the amount of any fee payable under the regulations, or

(b) set out how such a fee is to be determined.

(3) Subsection (4) applies where the regulations provide for a fee to be payable to a superintendent registrar.

(4) The regulations may provide for such part of the fee as may be specified by or determined in accordance with the regulations to be payable by the superintendent registrar to the Registrar General in such circumstances as may be set out in the regulations.

(5) The regulations may provide for the reduction, waiver or refund of part or all of a fee whether by conferring a discretion or otherwise.

(6) Regulations under this section must be made by statutory instrument.

(7) Regulations under this section may—

(a) make different provision for different cases;

(b) provide for exemptions from any of the provisions of the regulations;

(c) contain such consequential, incidental, supplemental and transitional provision as the Secretary of State considers appropriate.

(8) A statutory instrument containing regulations under this section is subject to annulment in pursuance of a resolution of either House of Parliament."

Savings Banks Act 1887 (c. 40)

7 In section 10 of the Savings Banks Act 1887 (price of certificate of birth, death or marriage)—

(a) the existing text becomes subsection (1),

(b) in that subsection (1), after "entered for" insert ", where the birth, death or marriage is registered in England and Wales, the appropriate fee or in any other case for", and

(c) after that subsection insert—

"(2) In subsection (1), "the appropriate fee" means the fee payable to the registrar or other person having care of the register concerned for a certified copy of an entry in the register by virtue of section 38A of the Births and Deaths Registration Act 1953 or section 71A of the Marriage Act 1949."

Marriage Act 1949 (c. 76)

8 The Marriage Act 1949 is amended as follows.

9 In section 27 (notice of marriage) omit subsections (6) and (7).

10 In section 31 (marriage under certificate without licence)—

(a) omit subsections (5F) and (5G),

(b) in subsection (5H), omit "or an order under subsection (5F)", and

(c) omit subsection (5I).

11 In section 41 (registration of buildings: marriage of a man and a woman) omit subsection (6).

12 In section 43D (regulations about registration of buildings) in subsection (1), omit "and the fees payable".

13 In section 51 (fees of registrars for attending marriages)—

(a) for the heading substitute "Fees of superintendent registrars for attending marriages in approved premises",

(b) omit subsection (1),

(c) in subsection (1A), omit paragraph (a) (and the "but" after it), and

(d) omit subsection (2).

14 In section 57 (quarterly returns to superintendent registrar) omit subsection (4).

15 In section 63 (searches in register books) in subsection (1), omit from ", on payment" to the end.

16 In section 64 (searches of indexes kept by superintendent registrars) in subsection (2), omit from ", on payment" to the end.

17 In section 65 (searches of indexes kept by Registrar General) in subsection (2), omit from ", on payment" to the end.

18 In section 65A (searches and records of information: additional provision) omit subsection (2).

19 In section 74 (regulations) in subsection (1)(b), after "this Act" insert "(other than section 71A)".

20 In section 78 (interpretation) in subsection (1), in the definition of "prescribed" after """"prescribed"""" insert "(other than in section 71A)".

Births and Deaths Registration Act 1953 (c. 20)

21 The Births and Deaths Registration Act 1953 is amended as follows.

22 In section 13 (registration of name of child or of alteration of name) in subsection (2), omit "on payment of a fee not exceeding £1.00".

23 In section 30 (searches of indexes kept by Registrar General)—

(a) in subsection (2), omit from ", on payment" to the end, and

(b) in subsection (3), omit "and on payment as aforesaid of the appropriate fee aforesaid".

24 In section 31 (searches of indexes kept by superintendent registrars) in subsection (2), omit from ", on payment" to the end.

25 In section 32 (searches in registers kept by registrars) omit from ", on payment" to the end of paragraph (c).

26 In section 33 (short certificate of birth) in subsection (1), omit from "on payment" to "and".

27 In section 33A (short certificate of death)—

(a) in subsection (1), for paragraphs (a) and (b) substitute ", on furnishing the prescribed particulars,", and

(b) omit subsection (3).

28 In section 34A (searches and records of information: additional provision) omit subsection (2).

29 In section 39 (regulations made by the Registrar General) in paragraph (a), for "and 34A" substitute ", 34A and 38A".

30 In section 39A (regulations made by the Minister: further provisions)—

(a) in subsection (1)(c), after "such" insert "consequential,",

(b) in subsection (2), after "provisions" insert "other than section 38A", and

(c) in subsection (5), for "and 34A" substitute ", 34A and 38A".

31 In section 41 (interpretation) in subsection (1), in the definition of "prescribed", for "and 10C" substitute ", 10C and 38A".

Registration Service Act 1953 (c. 37)

32 Omit section 16 of the Registration Service Act 1953 (general provision as to fees).

Factories Act 1961 (c. 34)

33 In section 178 of the Factories Act 1961 (certificates of birth)—

(a) in subsection (1), after "payment of" insert "the appropriate fee in England and Wales or",

(b) also in subsection (1), before ", be entitled" insert "in Scotland", and

(c) after subsection (2) insert—

"(3) In subsection (1), "the appropriate fee" means the fee payable to a registrar or superintendent registrar for a certified copy of an entry in the register concerned by virtue of section 38A of the Births and Deaths Registration Act 1953."

Public Expenditure and Receipts Act 1968 (c. 14)

34 In Schedule 3 to the Public Expenditure and Receipts Act 1968 (variation of fees)—

(a) omit the entry relating to the Education Act 1996,

(b) omit the entry relating to the Marriage Act 1949,

(c) omit the entry relating to the Births and Deaths Registration Act 1953,

(d) in the entry relating to the Savings Banks Act 1887, in the second column, omit "Secretary of State or, as regards Scotland, the",

(e) in the entry relating to the Factories Act 1961, in the second column, omit "Secretary of State or, as regards Scotland, the",

(f) in the entry relating to the Social Security Administration Act 1992, in the second column, omit "Secretary of State or, as regards Scotland, the", and

(g) omit the entry for the Places of Worship Registration Act 1855.

Marriage (Registrar General's Licence) Act 1970 (c. 34)

35 Omit section 17 of the Marriage (Registrar General's Licence) Act 1970 (fees).

Social Security Administration Act 1992 (c. 5)

36 (1) Section 124 of the Social Security Administration Act 1992 (provisions relating to age, death and marriage) is amended as follows.

(2) In subsection (3), for the words from "a fee" to "Wales and" substitute "the appropriate fee in England and Wales and a fee of".

(3) In subsection (3A), for paragraph (b) substitute—

"(b) on payment of the appropriate fee;".

(4) In subsection (5), in paragraph (a) after the opening words insert—

"""the appropriate fee" means the fee payable to the registrar or superintendent registrar for a certified copy of an entry in the register concerned by virtue of section 38A of the Births and Deaths Registration Act 1953, section 71A of the Marriage Act 1949 or section 9 of the Marriage (Same Sex Couples) Act 2013."

Education Act 1996 (c. 56)

37 (1) Section 564 of the Education Act 1996 (certificates of birth and registrars' returns) is amended as follows.

(2) In subsection (1), for paragraph (b) substitute—

"(b) on payment of the appropriate fee,".

(3) In subsection (4)—

(a) after the opening words insert—

"""the appropriate fee" means the fee payable to the registrar having custody of the register concerned for a certified copy of an entry in the register by virtue of section 38A of the Births and Deaths Registration Act 1953;", and

(b) in the definition of "register of births and deaths", for "the Births and Deaths Registration Act 1953" substitute "that Act".

Adapted and published by GRANGIS under the OGL Licence 3.0.

www.nationalarchives.gov.uk/doc/open government licence/version/3/

GRANGIS - UK PUBLISHING 2022.

Thank you for taking the time to leave us a review regarding this version

★★★★★

For further inquiries, contact us at:
www.grangis.com / contact@grangis.com

www.ingramcontent.com/pod-product-compliance
Lightning Source LLC
LaVergne TN
LVHW060211210926
848481LV00008B/2699